The Project Management Professional (PMP®) Exam Guide

Aligned with the PMBOK® Guide 3rd Edition

Sturgeon Publishing
Phoenix

Copyright Information
Copyright 2005 The Project Management Excellence Center, Inc.

No part of this publication may reproduced, stored in a retrieval system, or transmitted in any form or by any means, electronic, mechanical, photocopying, recording, scanning, or otherwise, except as permitted under Sections 107 or 108 of the 1976 United States Copyright Act, without either the prior permission of the Publisher or author.

The author and publisher have made their best efforts to prepare this book. The author and publisher make no representation or warranties of any kind with regards to the completeness or accuracy of the contents herein and accept no liability of any kind, including but not limited to performance, merchantability, fitness for any particular purpose, or any losses or damages of any kind caused or alleged to be caused directly or indirectly from this book.

Trademarks: www.pmptools.com, inc. has attempted throughout this book to distinguish proprietary trademarks from descriptive terms by following the capitalization style used by the manufacturer.

Published by: Sturgeon Publishing in association with The Project Management Excellence Center, Inc.

Email: publishing@pmptools.com

Library of Congress Control Number: 2003095560

ISBN 0-9726656-4-1 (paperback)

Manufactured in the United States of America
10 9 8 7 6 5 4 3 2 1

Table of Contents

Preface — 9
- What is PMP® Certification? — 9
- Requirements for Earning PMP® Certification? — 9
- Requirements for Maintaining PMP® Certification? — 9
- Structure and Content of the PMP® Certification Exam — 9
- How to Prepare for the PMP® Exam? — 10
- Tips for Taking the PMP® Exam — 11

Chapter 1 - Introduction — 13
- Guide to the Project Management Body of Knowledge — 14
- What is a Project? — 14
- Progressive Elaboration — 14
- What is Project Management? — 15
- Project Management Knowledge Areas — 15
- Programs — 16
- Sub-Projects — 16
- Project Phases and Project Life Cycle — 16
- Project Phases — 17
- Project Life Cycles — 17
- Project Stakeholders — 17
- Organizational Cultures and Style — 18
- Key General Management Skills — 18
- Four Functions of the Project Manager — 19
- Socioeconomic Influences — 19
- Standards and Regulations — 19
- Internationalization and Cultural Influences — 20

Chapter 2 – Project Life Cycle and Organization — 21
- Characteristics of a Project Life Cycle — 22
- Project Stakeholders — 23
- Organizational Influences — 23
- Organizational Systems — 23
- Organizational Cultures and Style — 23
- Forms of Organization — 24
- Project Management Office — 26
- Project Life Cycle — 26
- Conflict and the Project Life Cycle — 27

Chapter 3 – Project Management Processes for a Project — 29
- Project Management Life Cycle — 31
- Project Management is an Iterative Process — 31
- Initiating Process Group — 32
- Planning Process Group — 33
- Executing Process Group — 35
- Monitoring and Controlling Process Group — 36
- Closing Process Group — 38

Chapter 4 – Project Integration Management — 41
- Project Charter — 43
- Project Selection Methods — 46
- Project Planning Methodology — 46
- Project Management Information System (PMIS) — 47
- Develop Preliminary Project Scope Statement — 47
- Project Management Plan — 47
- Configuration Management System — 48

Change Control Systems	49
Direct and Manage Project Execution	49
Deliverable	50
Requested Changes	50
Administrative Closure Procedures	50
Monitor and Control Project Work	50
Corrective and Preventive Action	50
Earned Value Technique	51
Integrated Change Control	51
Change Control Board (CCB)	51
Configuration Management	52
Basic Steps in Configuration Management	52
Change Control in Configuration Management	52
Close Project	53
Administrative Closure	53
Lessons Learned	53
Contract Closure	54

Chapter 5- Project Scope Management — 59

Key Definitions	59
Scope Planning	62
Expert Judgment	62
Project Deliverables	62
Project Charter	62
Scope Definition	63
Product Analysis	63
Defining Project Scope	63
Project Scope Statement	64
Creating WBS - Work Breakdown Structure	65
Work Breakdown Structure Templates	67
Decomposition	67
WBS Dictionary	68
Scope Baseline	68
Scope Verification	68
Scope Control	69
Scope Creep	69
Change Control System	69

Chapter 6 – Project Time Management — 75

Activity Definition	78
Decomposition	79
Rolling Wave Planning	79
Planning Components	79
Activity List	79
Milestone List	79
Project Time Management – CPM & PDM	80
Arrow Diagramming Method (ADM)	80
Leads and Lags	80
Activity on Arrow (AOA)	81
Early Start / Forward Pass	81
Late Schedule / Backward Pass	81
The Critical Path	83
Activity-on-node Networks	84
Activity Relationships	85
Task Dependencies	85
Activity Duration Estimating	86
Critical Path Method (CPM)	87
Schedule Compression	87
Crashing and Fast-Tracking	88
Resource Leveling	88

Advantages of Scheduling Tools	91
Critical Chain Method	91
Project Schedule	93
Schedule Management Plan	93
Schedule Control	93
Variance Analysis	93
Schedule Updates	94
Corrective Action	94

Chapter 7 – Project Cost Management — 99

Life Cycle Cost	101
Fundamentals of Cost Estimating	102
Work Breakdown Structure	102
Chart of Accounts	102
Analogous Estimating / or Top-Down Estimating	102
Parametric Modeling	103
Bottom-up Estimating	103
Reserve Analysis	104
Triangular Distribution	104
Value Analysis	105
Cost Risk and Contract Type	105
Cost Budgeting	106
Cost Change Control System	107
Earned Value Management (EVM)	107
Cost Variance (CV)	107
Schedule Variance (SV)	108
Cost Performance Index (CPI)	108
Schedule Performance Index (SPI)	108
Estimate to Complete (ETC)	109
Estimate at Completion (EAC)	109
Variance at Completion (VAC)	109
The 50-50 Rule of Progress Reporting	110

Chapter 8 – Project Quality Management — 115

Pioneers of Quality Management	119
Awards for Quality Management Practices	120
Quality Planning	121
Quality Policy	121
Quality Management Plan	124
Quality Metrics	124
Quality Checklists	124
Types of Costs	125
Key Quality Planning Outputs	125
Standard Deviation	127
Process Control	128
Sampling	128
Prevention and Inspection	128
Special Causes and Random Causes	129
Tolerance and Control Limits	129
Statistical Quality Control	129
Quality Control Tools	129
Statistical Sampling	136
Corrective Action	136
Preventive Action	137
Continuous Improvement and Kaizen	137
Just-in-Time (JIT)	138
Impact of Motivation on Quality	138
Priority of Quality versus Cost and Schedule	138
Trend Analysis	139
Design and Quality	139

Chapter 9 – Project Human Resource Management — 143

- Forms of Organization — 145
- Project Interfaces — 147
- Organizational Planning Constraints — 147
- Key Human Resource Planning Outputs — 147
- Acquire Project Team — 148
- Virtual Teams — 148
- Functions of the Project Manager — 149
- Roles of the Project Manager — 149
- Qualifications of the Project Manager — 149
- Types of Power — 150
- Team Development — 150
- Team Building — 151
- Ground Rules — 153
- Co-location — 154
- Maslow's Hierarchy of Needs — 154
- Douglas McGregor — 155
- Theory X — 155
- Theory Y — 156
- Theory Z — 156
- Herzberg's Theory of Motivation — 156
- Expectancy Theory — 156
- Reward and Recognition Systems — 157
- Personnel Issues — 157
- Conflict Management — 157
- Conflict and the Project Life Cycle — 158
- One Party Conflict Management — 158
- Issue Log — 159
- Project Performance Appraisals — 159

Chapter 10 – Project Communications Management — 163

- Communication Skills — 165
- Communication Channels — 166
- Communications Planning — 167
- Communications Requirements — 167
- Communications Technology — 167
- Stakeholder Analysis — 168
- Communications Management Plan — 168
- Information Distribution — 169
- Communication Skills — 169
- Information Gathering and Retrieval Systems — 169
- Information Distribution Systems — 170
- Five Verbal Communication Skills — 170
- Barriers to Communication — 171
- Building Effective Team Communication — 171
- Management Styles — 172
- Management Skills — 173
- Performance Reporting — 173
- Status Review Meeting — 174
- Performance Reports — 174
- Documentation — 175
- Manage Stakeholders — 175
- Communications Management Plan — 175
- Importance of Communication — 176
- Interpersonal Communication — 176
- Methods of Interpersonal Communication — 176
- Written Communication — 177
- Types of Project Communications — 178
- Managing Meetings Effectively — 179
- Communication Channels and Links — 179

High Performance Communication	179
Guidelines for Active Listening (part of effective listening)	181
Communication Styles	181
How Project Managers Spend their Time	182

Chapter 11- Project Risk Management — 187

Types of Risk	190
Risk Factors	190
Risk Processes	191
Risk Management Planning	191
Risk Identification	192
Information Gathering Techniques	193
Other Risk Identification Tools and Techniques	193
Risk Identification Output	194
Qualitative Risk Analysis	194
Quantitative Risk Analysis	196
Statistical Independence	197
Expected Monetary Value (EMV)	197
Decision-Tree Analysis	197
Simulation	198
Monte Carlo Analysis	199
Utility Theory	199
Risk Response Planning	199
Contingency Planning	200

Chapter 12 – Project Procurement Management — 205

Plan Purchases and Acquisitions	207
Contract Categories and Risks	208
Contract Origination	209
Contract Incentives	210
Make-or-Buy Analysis	210
Expert Judgment	211
Plan Contracting	211
Procurement Management Plan	212
Contract Statement of Work	212
Bidder Conference	213
Qualified Seller List	213
Select Sellers	213
Evaluating Prospective Sellers	214
Contract Negotiation Stages and Tactics	215
Contract Administration	215
Changes and Change Control	217
Contract Closure	217
Force Majeure	218
Privity of Contract	219

Chapter 13 – Professional Responsibility — 223

Ensure Integrity and Professionalism	223
Contribute to Knowledge Base	225
Balance Stakeholders Interest	225
Interact with Team and Stakeholders	225
Defining Culture and Its Norms	225
Cultural Values	227
Verbal Communication	227
Nonverbal Communication	228
Negotiation Cross Cultures	229
Ethics and Legalities	229
Global Project Manager Compentcy	229

Preface

What is PMP® Certification?

The Project Management Institute (PMI®) offers certification as a Project Management Professional (PMP®). More detailed information is available from PMI® in a brochure called "Certification & Standards" and is available on the web at www.pmi.org.

PMI® conducts a certification program in project management. PMI's Project Management Professional (PMP®) certification is the project management profession's most globally recognized and respected certification credential. To obtain PMP® certification an individual must satisfy education and experience requirements, agree to and adhere to a Code of Professional Conduct, and pass the PMP® Certification Examination.

Worldwide there are more than 110,000 PMP®'s who provide project management services in 120 countries. Many corporations now require PMP® certification for individual advancement within the corporation or for employment.

Requirements for Earning PMP® Certification?

There are four main requirements for earning PMP® certification:
1. Having experience working in the field of project management—4,500 hours with a baccalaureate degree and 7,500 without a degree.
2. Signing a PMP® Candidate Agreement and Release form.
3. Completing the PMP® Certification Exam Application
4. Paying a fee of $555 for non-PMI® members and $405 for members.

Requirements for Maintaining PMP® Certification?

In order to maintain your PMP® certification, you must earn at least sixty Professional Development Units within a three-year cycle and adhere to PMI's PMP® Code of Professional Conduct. You may want to consult the PMI® Web site at http://www.pmi.org for more details.

Structure and Content of the PMP® Certification Exam

The PMP® exam consists of 200 multiple-choice questions that test your knowledge in the nine PMBOK® Guide knowledge areas of Integration, Scope, Time, Cost, Quality, Human Resource, Communications, Risk, and Procurement; the five PMBOK® process groups of Project Initiation, Project Planning, Project Execution, Project Control, and Project Closing; and the area of Professional Responsibility. The exam can be difficult, not because of the nature of the subject matter (which is actually quite basic), but because—
- Some questions are awkwardly worded and ambiguous; sometimes it is difficult to determine exactly what the test writer is asking.

- Some questions tend to test one's memory of specific language (that is, definition and terms) from the PMBOK® Guide, PMI® publications, and other reference materials. Many questions take an activity that could legitimately be done many different ways and ask you to choose the "best way", or "what is the first step" you would take given a particular situation.

The exam is mostly qualitative, not quantitative, and many of the quantitative questions are not that difficult. However, most exam takers seem to find the most problems with questions that address quality, cost, and risk topics. The quality questions are difficult for many people because they have learned a philosophy and practice of quality in their organizations that are somewhat different from that espoused by PMI® even though PMI's approach is consistent with many of the "gurus" in the field. The questions that address cost topics tend to cover a breadth of material much more diverse than the average test-taker has previously been exposed to. For example, in addition to having to know all the earned-value formulas, one needs to know a variety of information from benefit-cost ratio to understanding the two methods of capital depreciation.

How to Prepare for the PMP® Exam?

Like most people, you have probably developed your own study habits through the years, and you know what works best for you. I am not suggesting that I have identified the only way to study for this rigorous undertaking. In fact, there are several ways to approach this, which when combined with individual study can have powerful results. But I have identified some approaches over the years that seem to produce good results.

Do a little every day. Do not wait until the week before the exam to start studying. You are already too late.

Prepare for the exam with other test-takers. Studying with other people provides a powerful advantage enabling you to learn more information faster. Plan on lunch-hour sessions, if convenient, or before or-after-work sessions.

Within your group, you can create a division of labor where different persons are responsible for teaching the subject matter in specific sections of the PMBOK® Guide to others in the group.

Perhaps the most powerful of all approaches is to review in your group every practice test question you received. The process of discussing among yourselves how you selected your answer and what rationale you used for each answer is an extremely productive one. We guarantee that this group study method will, in all likelihood, result in your learning more about project management concepts and practice than any individual study method.

Ask people questions who have taken the exam. Get as much input as possible. Do not limit your questions to those who have passed the exam. If possible, ask those who have failed the exam what their experiences were.

One Month before the Exam
You do not have much time. You should be taking and retaking the practice test, studying the PMP®® Simulated Test Bank, and working with a study group (if possible). Keep track of the questions and definitions you are answering right and those you are getting wrong. Make sure you are studying a little every day.

Concentrate on those areas in which you are having problems. Spend a minimum of one hour each day in your three weakest areas. Implement the study strategies you know work best for you (should you answer all the easy questions first, the harder ones, or skip around, or some other approach?)

Write down your approaches and practice them. Using whatever format and approach you find helpful, go over at least ten new definitions every day.

One Week before the Exam
Continue to work through the practice questions (by Knowledge Area) and any practice test you may have. Also on a daily basis, start reviewing definitions.

Exam Day
Think confidently! Do not dwell on your weaknesses; concentrate on your strengths. You have been studying very hard, you are prepared, and you know what to expect.

Tips for Taking the PMP® Exam

- Make sure you have everything you need remember that pencils and calculators are usually provided. You will not be allowed to bring any additional items in with you.
- Listen carefully to the proctor's directions and comments as you do not want to make any procedural errors; it can result in lost time and possibly wrong answers.
- Review the exam, reading the directions carefully. Do not start answering the questions before you read the directions on the screen.
- Try and budget your time as you have a little more than a minute for each question. Realistically, you can answer some questions in a few seconds, and others will take several minutes to answer. Be mindful of the time you are spending in each section, but do not be obsessed with it. Very few people run out of time.
- Write down important formulas, facts, and statistics in the margin or on scratch paper as soon as you sit down. This can be done during the computer tutorial. This safeguard will ensure that you do not forget certain information if you become too nervous.
- Look for "qualifying" words in the stem of the question or in the answers. For example, words such as, rarely, often, seldom, many, always, and so on will determine the correct answer.
- Answer the easy questions first. A good way to reduce anxiety is to answer the easy questions first. This will build your confidence as you proceed through the rest of the exam section. If you attempt the more difficult questions initially, you will tend to feel uninformed, unprepared, and "unhappy."
- If you do not know the answer, mark (electronically or otherwise) the question and complete it later. There will be many questions for which the answer will not be immediately apparent. Rather than struggle with the question, move on to the next one. Return to those unanswered questions later. Chances are your memory will return, and you will be able to make a better educated guess the second or third time you read the question.
- Guess aggressively. Never leave a question blank. You are scored on the number of correct answers; points are not deducted for wrong answers.
- Use all the time allowed. If you finish early, check for errors. Review the directions once again to ensure that you have followed them correctly.
- Try not to think about your score while taking the exam. Thinking about your score will not raise it; thinking about the answers will!

Notes

Chapter 1

Introduction

Reference Material to Study
- A Guide to the Project Management Body of Knowledge (PMBOK® Guide 3rd Edition), Chapter 1
- Project Planning, Scheduling & Control, Chapters 1-4, Lewis, James P. 1995

What to Study
- Chapter 1 of the PMBOK® Guide – Introduction.
- Know what a Project Management is.
- Know what a Project is.
- Know the characteristics of a project.
- Know the difference between projects and operational work.
- Understand the concept of progressive elaboration.

Key Definitions
- **Generally Recognized** – A means that the knowledge and practices described are applicable to most projects most of the time, and that there is widespread consensus about their value and usefulness.
- **Good Practice** – A means that there is general agreement that the correct application of these skills, tools, and techniques can enhance the chances of success over a wide range of different projects.
- **Progressive Elaboration** – A means developing in steps, and continuing by increments.
- **Project Management** - Is the application of knowledge, skills, tools and techniques to project activities to meet project requirements.
- **Temporary** – A means that every project has a definite beginning and a definite end.

Guide to the Project Management Body of Knowledge

The Guide to the Project Management Body of Knowledge (PMBOK® Guide) is a term that describes the sum of knowledge within the profession of project management. The body of knowledge rests with the professionals and academics that apply and advance it.

The Guide to the Project Management Body of Knowledge (PMBOK® Guide) describes what is generally accepted, meaning that the knowledge and practices are applicable to most projects most of the time, and there is a widespread consensus about their value and usefulness. The text is published by the Project Management Institute, which is recognized as one of the authoritative association for project managers. Based on stringent requirements for project management experience, academic education, and a rigorous testing program, PMI® certifies individuals as Project Management Professionals (PMP®), the most recognized certification for project managers in the business world today.

What is a Project?

A project is a temporary sequence of tasks with a distinct beginning and an end that is undertaken to create a unique product or service. In addition, a project must have defined objectives in order to clearly indicate when the project has been completed. There are some necessary features that characterize all projects:
- Projects follow an organized process in order to meet specific goals.
- Project goals are based on specific quality standards.
- Projects use time, money, resources, and people that are allocated to the project.
- Projects have a distinct beginning and end.
- Projects generally have time and cost constraints.
- Projects are usually completed by a team of people.

There are several attributes that characterize a project:
- Projects are unique. The product or service being produced by the project is different and involves doing something that has not been done before.
- Projects have a purpose. Projects have a well-defined set of desired results. They can be divided into smaller tasks in order to achieve the overall project goal.
- Projects have a life cycle. Projects progress from an idea through the planning, executing, and controlling steps, and finally to a close. The project life cycle also indicates that projects are temporary, with a definite beginning and a definite end.
- Projects have interdependencies. The various tasks of a project interact with one another, while at the same time interacting with the parent organization.

Projects are temporary in nature, while operations are ongoing. Projects have definitive start dates and definitive end dates. Operations involve work that is continuous without an ending date and most often repeat the same process.

Progressive Elaboration

Progressive means "proceeding in steps; continuing steadily by increments". Elaboration means "worked out with care and detail; developed thoroughly".

What is Project Management?

Project management may be informally defined as "The art of directing and coordinating human and material resources to achieve stated objectives within limits of time, budget, and stakeholders' satisfaction." Or more formally defined as "The application of modern management techniques and systems to the execution of a project from start to finish, to achieve predetermined objectives of scope, quality, time and cost, to the equal satisfaction of those involved.

Project Management Knowledge Areas

Listed below are the nine project management knowledge areas:
1. **Project Integration Management** - Integration Management skills are used to integrate the work in other core areas. The primary focus of integration management is the creation of a cohesive, comprehensive, and well-designed project plan and the execution of that project plan. Another skill is the overseeing of the change control process, both as it is developed in the plan and as it is executed throughout the life of the project.
2. **Project Scope Management** - Scope Management is the skill project managers use to define the work that needs to be done on any given project. This entails making sure that all the work required is included and that no unneeded work is added. It includes formal project and phase initiations, developing the written scope statement (with scope exclusions), and listing major and intermediary project deliverables. It also includes the formal agreement by major players to the scope as defined and scope control (the ongoing process of evaluating project changes).
3. **Project Time Management** - Time Management is the skill that most people associate with project management because it is crucial for keeping on schedule. It includes creating or refining the project work breakdown structure, determining dependency relationships among the project tasks, estimating the effort and duration of the tasks, and creating a project schedule. It also includes the control component of monitoring and updating the project progress and making changes to estimates and schedules. A commonly misunderstood facet of project management is that, by the nature of projects, estimates and schedules will change. As long as the project manager stays on top of these changes, this should not affect the final target completion date.
4. **Project Cost Management** - Cost Management includes determining the project cost categories, estimating the use of each resource in each category, budgeting for that estimated cost and getting it approved, and then controlling the cost as the project progresses. Both fixed costs (such as equipment and software purchases) and variable costs (such as team member time) are included in the planning and estimating and are then monitored and controlled.
5. **Project Quality Management** - Quality Management has three subsets, generally referred to as Quality Planning, Quality Assurance, and Quality Control. In Quality Planning, a project manager defines what represents quality and how quality will be measured. In Quality Assurance, the project manager watches the overall quality of a project to see that standards will be met. In Quality Control, the project manager examines actual project outputs to evaluate their conformance to the standards set in the plan.
6. **Project Human Resource Management** - Human Resource Management addresses the people involved in a project. It includes the planning components of determining what skills are needed to perform the various project tasks, defining the participants' roles and responsibilities, and selecting potential candidates for those tasks. It also includes acquiring the appropriate resources (internally, from external departments, or even external companies or independent contractors) and any professional development that the team members may need to improve their project performance.
7. **Project Communications Management** - Communication Management is the often neglected, yet perhaps most important, component of project management. It includes deciding who needs what information, to what level of detail, and in what media and time

period. These needs are documented in the communication plan subsection of the project plan so that parties can review them and then follow them. The communication plan may also specify the format to be used for each communication, as well as turnaround times for each communication. Once the plan is approved, project managers then use their communication management skills to make sure the information is gathered and distributed according to the plan.
8. **Project Risk Management** - Risk Management starts with identifying the potential risks to a project and then determining the likelihood of each risk happening and how that risk would impact the project if it occurred. From this list and ranking, contingencies are developed for the highest risks. As the project is executed, one can use these contingencies to regain control of a project if a potential risk does occur.
9. **Project Procurement Management** - Procurement Management involves developing, executing, and monitoring contracts with service and product vendors. It also includes deciding what must be procured, soliciting bids for the products or services, selecting the appropriate vendor, and closing the contract once the project has been completed.

Relationship to Other Management Disciplines

Most of the knowledge and skills that a project manager needs are unique to the project management process. For example, general managers would not ordinarily need to complete a critical path analysis or understand how to put a project on the fast track.

However, there are some areas of overlap between general management and project management, such as planning the project, staffing a department, and executing a task.

Programs

The terms project and program are often used interchangeably. Although these terms are related, they are not the same thing. A program is a group of logically related projects. Likewise, projects are managed together in order to gain benefits that are not available from managing them separately, or because they include similar processes that will benefit from simultaneous management.

Sub-Projects

Very large projects may be divided into several sub-projects, each of which is a project in its own right. This division makes for better management control. For example, sub-projects can be defined at the department, division, or geographic level.

This artificial decomposition of a complex project into subprojects often simplifies the scheduling of resources and reduces the need for interdepartmental communications while a specific activity is worked on. The downside to dividing a project into sub-projects is that the projects are now interdependent.

Project Phases and Project Life Cycle

Projects are unique and subject to risk. Thus, dividing a project into to several parts called 'phases' allows better control and appropriate links to the ongoing operations. When grouped together, project phases are referred to as a "project life cycle."

Project Phases

Every project phase is associated with one or more deliverables upon completion. A deliverable is a tangible, verifiable work product and would generally follow sequentially in the development of a product of the project.

The end of a project phase should be linked with a review of key deliverables and project performance to:
- Decide if the project should move into the next phase.
- Recognize and rectify errors cost effectively.

These reviews are referred to phase exits, stage gates, or kill points.

Project Life Cycles

The project life cycle defines the beginning and end of a project and determines which transitional actions are included at the end of a project, linking the project to the ongoing operations.

Typically, a handoff will occur between project phases of the life cycle, and deliverables from the preceding phase should be approved before moving forward. However, in some cases, a subsequent phase will begin prior to completion of a preceding phase, a practice called fast tracking.

Some life cycles may be called a "project management methodology" where a disciplined, highly detailed approach is applied. Most life cycles share some common traits:

Project cost and initial staffing are low at the start, increase towards the middle and near the end of a project, and drop off rapidly at the end.

Risk and uncertainty are at their peak at the beginning of a project and gradually diminish as the project continues.

The ability of stakeholders to persuade or influence the final characteristics of the project product and final cost are highest at the start of a project and diminish as the project continues.

The cost of changes and error correction generally increases as the project continues.

Remember, a project life cycle is not the same as a product life cycle. A product life cycle will normally include the project life cycle as a subset of the overall product life cycle. The product life cycle will encompass the development, deployment, support, maintenance, upgrades (which may be a separate project), and eventual shutdown of the given product.

Project Stakeholders

A project stakeholder is an individual, group, or organization that is involved in a project, whose interests might be influenced as a result of project's achievement. It is important for the project manager or the project team to identify the stakeholders and their expectations. In addition, it is important to manage the stakeholders' expectations in order to reduce conflict. The key stakeholders in every project include:
- The project manager, because this individual is in charge of successful project completion.
- The project team, because these are the individuals most directly involved in completing the work of the project.
- The public is sometimes considered a stakeholder because they might be affected by the outcome of the project.

- The parent organization, because it provides the employees who work on the project.
- The customer, because this is the individual or organization that will use the product created by the project.

Organizational Influences

Most projects are a smaller part of a larger organization, and this organization will have significant influence on the conduct and success or failure of the project.

There are three primary organizational influences that can affect project management:

1. The organizational values, beliefs, and expectations can either be adopted or rejected by the project team, having a direct effect on the management of a project.
2. The structure of an organization can affect project management because it can dictate the availability of resources such as money and staff.
3. The organization's project philosophy can affect project management, since a project-based organization would reward different actions than a non-profit-based organization.

Organizational Systems

Project-based organizations operations are primarily projects. This would include organizations whose main source of revenue is projects (consultants, contractors) and organizations that manage by projects.

Non-project based organizations are more focused on operations, and seldom have management systems to facilitate project needs efficiently. This complicates the project management effort.

Organizational Cultures and Style

Obviously, each organization has developed its own culture and style, and the project teams must consider this. For example, a team suggesting a high—risk approach will more likely receive sponsorship in an entrepreneurial organization that may not have an established style. A project manager's approach should reflect the organization style, meaning a participative style will clash with a rigidly hierarchical organization, and an authoritative style will clash with a participative organization.

Key General Management Skills

General management deals with every aspect of managing an ongoing enterprise and includes finance and accounting, sales and marketing, research and development, manufacturing and distribution; strategic, tactical and operational planning; human resources issues and work relationships and personal time and stress management. Possession of these skills is also essential to a project manager. (It is practically impossible for a project manager to retain the full spectrum of technical skills necessary on a large project, but rather, they should focus on the project management skills required to effectively administer the project.)

There are five key abilities required for being an effective manager:
1. **Leading** - Leading is differentiated from managing in that managing is primarily concerned with consistently producing key results expected by stakeholders while leading involves establishing direction, aligning, motivating, and inspiring people.
2. **Communicating** - The successful transmission or exchange of information is essential so that the recipient understands what the sender intends. This includes verbal, nonverbal, and written communication. A key here is listening as well as communicating, and communications may be external or internal, formal or informal, vertical or horizontal.
3. **Negotiating** - This involves conferring with others to reach an agreement. It may involve scope, cost and schedule objectives, or changes to these; contract terms and conditions; assignments and resources.
4. **Problem Solving** - Problem solving involves a combination of problem definition (distinguishing between causes and symptoms) and decision-making (analyzing problems to determine viable solutions and then making a selection). Note that project decision-making is not limited to project managers. Customers, project team members, functional managers, or other project stakeholders may be involved in decision making.
5. **Influencing the Organization** - The ability to get things done is the mark of a great project manager. This requires the ability to identify political realities both inside and outside the organization, as well as having an understanding of the mechanics of power and politics. Power is the potential ability to influence behavior, change the course of events, and overcome resistance. It is the ability to get people to do something they wouldn't necessarily do. Politics involves getting a collective effort from a group of people with differing interests.

Four Functions of the Project Manager

It is widely held that a project manager has these four main functions:
1. **Planning** - The project manager determines the time, cost, and personnel resources needed to complete the work, which would include team assembly, development of work schedules, and human resource requirements.
2. **Organizing** - Assembling the personnel, financial, and physical resources to complete the project.
3. **Leadership** - This is necessary in order to combine resources and administer the project.
4. **Control** - Execution of the project plan, and continuous monitoring and measurement of progress as it relates to time, cost and quality.

Socioeconomic Influences

In addition to the influences that fall into the category of general management, PMBOK® Guide describes the socioeconomic influences that affect projects. The following categories are considered to be key influences with which you should be familiar.

Standards

A document that prescribes a specific consensus solution to a repetitive design, operating, or maintenance problem. Compliance is not mandatory

Regulation

A regulation is a document that defines product, process, or service characteristics, including the administrative provisions. Compliance is mandatory.

Internationalization and Cultural Influences

As organizations achieve global status, and as our world grows ever more interrelated, the project manager must consider the impact of internalization in terms of scope, time, cost, and quality. Time zones, distances, and travel requirements are major elements.

Culture involves the beliefs, behaviors, arts, institutions, and other aspects of a people. Cultural influences include political, economic, demographic, educational, ethical, and religious factors.

Chapter 2

Project Life Cycle and Organization

Reference Material to Study
- A Guide to the Project Management Body of Knowledge (PMBOK® Guide 3rd Edition), Chapter 2
- Project Planning, Scheduling & Control, Chapters 1-4, Lewis, James P. 1995

What to Study
- Chapter 2 of the PMBOK® Guide on Project Life Cycle and Organization
- Know what a Project Life Cycle is.
- Know the characteristics of the Project Life Cycle.
- Know the characteristics of Project Phases.
- Understand completely the concept of Project Stakeholders and who the major stakeholders are on a project.
- Know what is meant by Organizational Influences
- Know the different types of Organizational Structures

Key Definitions
- **Functional Matrix** - An organization type where the project has a team leader in each functional department and the products are passed from one team to the next.
- **Matrix Organization** - A combination of the advantages of the pure functional structure and the product organizational structure. The project manager has total responsibility and accountability for project success; functional managers provide technical and business assistance to the project manager from outside the project management office.
- **Project Life Cycle** - The sequence of phases through which the project will evolve. It is absolutely fundamental to the management of projects, and is the only thing that uniquely distinguishes projects from non-projects. It will significantly affect how the project is structured.
- **Project Management Office** (PMO) - The organizational entity with full time personnel to provide a focal point for the discipline of project management. Also known as project office, project management center of excellence, or directorate of project managers.
- **Project Management System** - The aggregation of the processes, tools, techniques, methodologies, resources, and procedures to manage a project.
- **Project Phase** - a group of related project activities that come together with the completion of a deliverable.
- **Stakeholder** - A person or group of people who have a vested interest in the success of an organization and the environment in which the organization operates.

Phases are defined by the project life cycle and connect the beginning of a project to its end. Phases are characterized by the completion and approval of one or more major deliverables and are distinct from Project Management Process Groups. The names and number of project life cycle phases for a project are dependent upon the type of project and/or product being developed and are determined by the organization or Project Team. Remember, the product life cycle is not the same as project life cycle – a product lifecycle can consist of multiple projects.

The project management processes that support the project phases are organized into five Project Management Process Groups. Each Process Group either interacts with the other Process Groups within a system development phase or across phases. These Process Groups are known as initiating, planning, executing, monitoring and controlling, and closing. These Process Groups may be repeated during any of the phases of the life cycle. For example, repeating the Planning Process Group during each phase helps to keep the project focused on the business need and cost, schedule, and performance objectives. The Project Management Process Groups are not discrete, one-time events; they are overlapping activities that occur at varying levels of intensity throughout each phase of the project.

Characteristics of a Project Life Cycle

Characteristics of a project life cycle initially define the beginning and the end of a project.
Although they vary based on the industry, organization, and/or application area, generally speaking, project life cycles define:
- The technical work to be done in each phase
- The skills involved in each phase

Most project life cycle descriptions share a number of common characteristics:
- Cost and staffing levels are low at the start; higher towards the end of implementation, and drop rapidly as the project nears conclusion.
- The probability of successfully completing the project is lowest at the start of the project. Hence, risk and uncertainty are highest at the start of the project. Generally speaking, the probability of a successful completion progressively increases as the project continues.
- The ability of the stakeholders to influence the final characteristics of the project product is highest at the start of the project and becomes progressively lower as the project continues. This can largely be contributed to the increased cost of changes and error correction as the project develops.

Each project phase is marked by completion of one or more deliverables. Each phase is concluded with a review of the key deliverables and the project performance to determine if the project should proceed to the next phase and to detect and correct costly errors. These phase-end reviews are often called phase exits, stage gates, or kill points. The practice of overlapping project phases when the risks are deemed acceptable is called fast tracking.

Subprojects within projects may also have distinct project life cycles.

Distinguish between project life cycle and product life cycle. For example, a project to deliver a new computer system to the market may be one phase or stage in the product cycle. The product life cycle could consist of several follow-on enhancements/releases (via unique projects) for this computer system before the product reaches the end-of-life phase (stage).

Project Stakeholders

Project stakeholders are individuals and organizations who are actively involved in the project. Project stakeholder's interests may be positively or negatively affected by the outcome of the project execution or completion. They also may exert influence over the project and its results.

The Project Team must identify the stakeholders, determine their requirements, and then manage as well as influence those requirements to ensure a successful project. Identifying project stakeholders is not an easy task. Key stakeholders on every project include:
- Project manager
- Customer
- Performing organization (the organization most involved in doing the work of the project)
- Project Team
- Sponsor

There are many different categories and names for stakeholders. Because stakeholders may have conflicting objectives, managing stakeholder expectations is often not easy.

Organizational Influences

Projects are influenced by the organization(s) that set it up. Projects can also be influenced by the maturity of the organization with respect to its:
- Project management systems (as related to organizational systems, below)
- Culture and style
- Organizational structure
- Project Management Office

Organizational Systems

Project-based organizations operations are primarily projects. This would include organizations whose main source of revenue is projects (consultants, contractors) and organizations that manage by projects.

Non-project based organizations are more focused on operations, and seldom have management systems to facilitate project needs efficiently. This complicates the project management effort.

Organizational Cultures and Style

Most organizations have developed unique and describable cultures. These cultures are reflected in their shared values, norms, beliefs, and expectations, policies/procedures, and view of authority relationships. Examples of organizational culture influencing projects:
- A team proposing an unusual or high-risk approach is more likely to secure approval within an aggressive or entrepreneurial organization.
- A project manager with a highly participative style is apt to encounter problems in a rigidly hierarchical organization while a project manager with an authoritarian style will be equally challenged within a participative organization.

Forms of Organization

PMI® recognizes the followings approaches to project organizational structure, and those are as follows:

- **Functional** - In a functional organizational structure, a project is assigned to the functional department that is best equipped to implement the project or that is most capable of ensuring the project's success.

    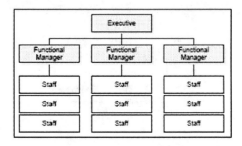
    Figure 1 - Functional Organization

    When using the functional organizational form to complete a project, the team comprises individuals from the functional department to which the project is assigned. This structure not only allows individuals to use their expertise and demonstrate special abilities, but also presents them opportunities for professional growth.

    A downside to this organizational structure is that no single person has full accountability for the project, which increases the likelihood that the project will fail. Since the project manager is not given much formal authority, the functional organizational structure placed the project manager in the weakest position of all the organizational structures.

- **Project Expediter** (PE) - The project expediter acts as a staff assistant to the executive who has ultimate responsibility for the project. The workers remain in their functional organizations and provide assistance as needed. The project expediter has little formal authority. The project expediter's primary responsibility is to communicate information between the executive and the workers. Most useful in the traditional functional organization where the project's worth and costs are relatively low.

    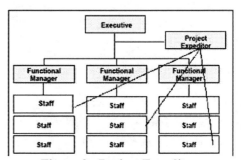
    Figure 2 - Project Expediter

- **Project Coordinator** (PC) - The project coordinator has more authority and responsibility than a project expediter. The project coordinator has the authority to assign work to individuals within the functional organization. The functional manager is forced to share resources and authority with the project coordinator. The size of projects in terms of dollars is relatively small compared to the rest of the organization.

    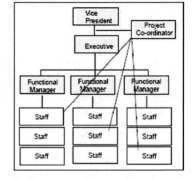
    Figure 3 - Project Coordinator

- **Matrix Organizations** - A matrix organizational structure is a combination of functional and purely project structures. Matrix organizations maintain the functional (vertical) lines of authority while establishing a relatively permanent horizontal structure to interact with all functional units supporting the projects. One result of the matrix is that workers frequently find themselves caught between the project manager and their functional manager.

    Advantages: Improved PM control over resources, rapid response to contingencies, improved coordination effort across functional lines, people have a "home" after the project is over, etc.

Disadvantages: Not cost effective due to excess administrative personnel, workers report to multiple bosses, more complex structure to monitor and control, higher potential for conflicts due to differing priorities, power struggles, and competition for resources, etc.

- **Weak Matrix** - In a weak matrix organizational structure, the project manager has a low level of authority. The project manager is in charge of making sure activities are completed but cannot do certain things such as reallocate resources or make changes to a project's schedule. Lack of authority to make project-related decisions puts the project manager at a disadvantage, so in order to ensure that project goals are met, the project manager must use technical and interpersonal skills to influence the direction of the project. In some instances, the project manager is given some authority, but must share that authority with a functional manager. Shared authority often results in power struggles that disrupt the project environment and can jeopardize the successful completion of a project.

- **Strong Matrix** - A strong matrix organizational structure is similar to a purely project structure in that the project manager has full decision-making authority. However, unlike a purely project organization, a strong matrix does not separate a project from the parent organization.

There is a general division of responsibility in the matrix organizational structure. For example, the project manager controls what the project team does and when they do it, while the functional manager controls who is assigned to the project and what technology is used.

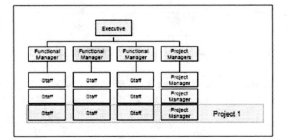

Figure 4 - Strong Matrix

Despite this division of responsibility, a strong matrix does not eliminate role ambiguity between project and functional managers. To avoid conflicts, the project and functional managers must communicate, negotiate, and be flexible when deciding who is responsible for what activities. The project manager has medium to high formal authority.

- **Balanced Matrix** - The balanced matrix is a structure that includes some weak matrix characteristics and some strong matrix characteristics. In this structure, the project manager's authority is considered to below to moderate given that only 15 to 60 percent of the organization's personnel are assigned to project work.

- **Projectized** - In a projectized organization, a separate, vertical structure is established for each project. Personnel are assigned to particular projects on a full-time basis. The project manager has total authority over the project, which is subject only to the time, cost, and performance constraints specified in the project targets. Departments either report directly to the project manager or provide services to the various projects. Team members are often collocated. Most of the organization's resources are involved in project work.

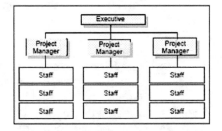

Figure 5 - Projectized Organization

Note that the term tight matrix refers to co-location of the project team in a single area such as a bull pen and is not an organizational structure. Also remember that all forms of organizations are described here, but you will want to know that there are functional organizations and project expeditors, which are little more than functionaries and help support the idea of project management, without really practicing the practice; the project coordinator is a step up from that. A weak matrix is where the project manager gets resources from functional organizations; a strong matrix is where the balance of power has shifted to the project manager.

The way to determine if the balance of power has shifted is to note where the money and the reporting flow from. If all money and reports are generated by the project and are respected as being from the project, then it is a strong matrix. If the functional organizations are seen as generating revenue for the organization rather than the project organizations, then it is a weak matrix. And if it is a mix? It is a balanced matrix. PMI's ideal organization is one that is projectized; it's a place where the project has its own little home within the organization.

Project Management Office (PMO)

Many organizations have a project office. Uses of the project office may vary from providing support to project managers to being responsible for the project results. In short a PMO is the organizational entity with full time personnel to provide a focal point for the discipline of project management.

Project Life Cycle

Numerous questions may appear on the test relating to the project life cycle. PMI® states that the project life cycle defines the beginning and end of the project, describes the technical work to be done in each phase, and identifies who should be involved. Life-cycle descriptions may be general or detailed with the more detailed approaches often called project management methodologies. Most life-cycle descriptions share these common characteristics:

- Cost and staffing levels are minimal at the start of the project, increase toward the end, and then drop off when the project comes to an end.
- The probability of successfully completing the project is low at the start because uncertainty is high. The probability of successful completion gets progressively higher as the project continues and work is completed. Therefore, there is always a higher degree of risk at the beginning of any project.
- The ability of stakeholders to influence the final characteristics of the project's product and final cost is highest at the start and then gets progressively lower as the project continues. This is because the cost of changes and error correction increases geometrically as the project nears completion. This fact underscores the importance of gathering accurate requirements at the beginning of a project.

Know the four phases of the life cycle and be able to identify activities associated with each life-cycle phase. The life cycle on the exam consists of the following four phases and associated activities:

Concept Phase
- Gather data
- Identify needs and alternatives
- Establish goals, feasibility, risk, and strategy
- Guesstimate resources
- Present proposal
- Develop project charter

What you need to take away from the concept phase is that this is the earliest stage of a project.

Development (Planning) Phase
- Appoint project manager and key team members
- Develop performance measurement baseline
- Establish master plan, budget, work breakdown structure, and policies/procedures
- Assess risks
- Confirm justification and obtain approval to proceed

The development phase is still early in the process. It is the phase where we draft the budget, the schedule, and the project plan. It is also when we make the first comprehensive draft of the work breakdown structure. We finalize the plan here and make the final commitment to do the work for the project.

Implementation (Execution) Phase
- Set up organization
- Establish detailed technical requirements
- Set up and execute work packages
- Direct, monitor, and control scope, quality, time, cost, and risks

In the implementation phase, we perform and do the work as prescribed in the WBS.

Termination/Closeout (Finishing) Phase
- Review and accept project
- Receive formal acceptance
- Transfer responsibility, document and evaluate results
- Release and redirect resources

We often overlook the termination phase. It is the most underrated of the phases. It is where we do both contract closeout and administrative closeout. A critical component here is lessons learned.

Conflict and the Project Life Cycle

The highest ranked sources of conflict evident in each phase of the life cycle are as follows:
- **Concept Phase** - project priorities and schedules
- **Development Phase** - project priorities, schedules and administrative procedures
- **Implementation Phase** - schedules, technical issues, and personnel resources
- **Termination Phase** - schedules, personality conflicts, and personnel resources

Notes

Chapter 3

Project Management Processes for a Project

Reference Material to Study
- A Guide to the Project Management Body of Knowledge (PMBOK® Guide 3rd Edition), Chapter 3
- Project Planning, Scheduling & Control, Chapters 1-4, Lewis, James P. 1995

What to Study
- Chapter 3 of the PMBOK® Guide on Project Management Processes for a Project
- Know what the definition of Project Management.
- Understand the concept of Process Interactions.
- Be familiar with the Project Management Process Map.
- Know the five Process Groups.

Key Definitions
- **Closing Process Group** - Formalizes acceptance of the product, service or result and brings the project or a project phase to an orderly end.
- **Executing Process Group** - Pulls together people and other resources to carry out the project management plan for the project.
- **Initiating Process Group** - Authorizes the project or a project phase.
- **Monitoring and Controlling Process** Group - Measures and monitors progress to identify variances from the project management plan so that corrective action can be taken when necessary to meet project objectives.
- **Planning Process Group** - Refines objectives, and plans the course of action required to attain the objectives and scope that the project was undertaken to address.
- **Project Management** - The process of directing and coordinating human and material resources throughout the project life cycle using modern management techniques to achieve established objectives of scope, quality, time, cost and stakeholder satisfaction.
- **Project Management Process** - Project cycle, phases, and activities that are managed by the techniques and tools of the ten project management elements to ensure that all project control gates are completed satisfactorily and that project objectives are accomplished. The formality of application is tailored to the type of project and value and risk of the project.

According to the PMBOK®:

A project is a temporary endeavor undertaken to create a unique product, service, or result.

A project exists only after a decision has been made to address a specific business need, either internal or external (customer need) to the organization, funding is available to support its execution, and measurable goals and objectives are well defined. Without knowing the expected results, quality level or capability of the end product, a project is difficult to plan, execute or conclude.

A project is unique and temporary in that there is a defined start (the decision to proceed) and a defined end (the achievement of the goals and objectives). Ongoing and repetitive business or maintenance operations are not projects. Process improvement efforts that result in better business processes or more efficient operations can be defined as projects.

The image below depicts the process flow of the Project Management Process Groups.

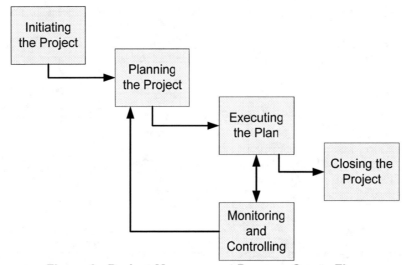

Figure 6 - Project Management Process Group Flow

In most organizations, there is a descending hierarchy of endeavors ranging from the strategic plan to programs, projects, and subprojects. According to the PMBOK®:

A program is a group of related projects managed in a coordinated way to obtain benefits and control not available from managing them individually.

A program should consist of several associated projects contributing to the achievement of the strategic plan. Programs may also contain elements of ongoing operations. Project Management Offices (PMOs) provide a variety of services to their respective organizations, which may include program/project management, project planning, guidance and mentoring, assessment and oversight, training, and standards development and dissemination. Many other benefits are derived from the PMOs, key of which are the ability to oversee and coordinate multiple related and/or unrelated projects (see the "big picture"), the ability to share and coordinate resources across all PMO projects, and the ability to develop and share common tools stored in a central repository to ensure consistency between PMO projects, and saving on development time.

Another means of grouping programs/projects for better management visibility and more effective decision-making is through Portfolio Management. This refers to the selection and support of projects from an enterprise perspective based on how they relate to the Strategic Plan. Those programs/ projects within a Portfolio usually receive increased visibility due to the fact that the Portfolio's success is usually the responsibility of Senior Managers or Senior Management Teams. Portfolio programs/projects are ranked based on their return on investment (ROI) and their contribution to the achievement of the Strategic Plan.

Project Management Life Cycle

Phases are defined by the project life cycle and connect the beginning of a project to its end. Phases are characterized by the completion and approval of one or more major deliverables and are distinct from Project Management Process Groups. The names and number of project life cycle phases for a project are dependent upon the type of project and/or product being developed and are determined by the organization or Project Team. Remember, the product life cycle is not the same as project life cycle – a product lifecycle can consist of multiple projects.

The project management processes that support the project phases are organized into five Project Management Process Groups. Each Process Group either interacts with the other Process Groups within a system development phase or across phases. These Process Groups are known as initiating, planning, executing, monitoring and controlling, and closing. Remember that these Process Groups may be repeated during any of the phases of the life cycle. For example, repeating the Planning Process Group during each phase helps to keep the project focused on the business need and cost, schedule, and performance objectives. The Project Management Process Groups are not discrete, one-time events; they are overlapping activities that occur at varying levels of intensity throughout each phase of the project.

These Process Groups and their relationship are depicted on the next page. Also identified are nine Project Management Knowledge Areas that can be applied to a given project.

Project Management is an Iterative Process

The application of project management is an iterative process. For example, within the Planning Process Group, several iterations of planning may occur as the team develops the optimal product solution for a customer. Identified solutions may require refinements to the schedule, the cost estimates, the quality requirements and/or the risk planning. As changes occur, the impact to other areas must be determined. Over time, the iterations should become smaller in magnitude and more defined as more detailed information is developed.

After the Planning Process Group has been completed for the initial project phase, feedback from the Executing Process Group (identified through the Monitoring and Controlling Process Group) may result in adjustments to the Project Management Plan. Adjustments due to feedback typify the project management process. Project Management is a dynamic effort and requires a continual process of evaluation. Evaluation activities, such as oversight, quality control, and executive review are ongoing activities and affect every phase of the project.

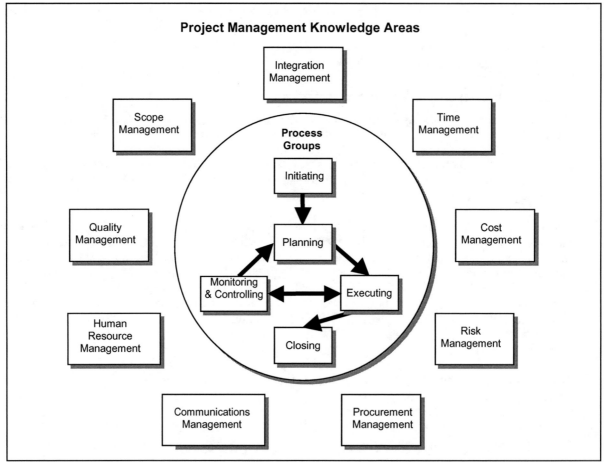

Figure 7 - Project Management Knowledge Areas

Initiating Process Group

The Initiating Process Group is the conceptual element of project management—the basic processes that should be performed to get the project started. This starting point is critical because those who will deliver the project, those who will use the project, and those who have a stake in the project need to reach an agreement on its initiation. Stakeholders may be able to exert influence that can positively or negatively affect the Project Team's ability to successfully complete the project, so it is very important to involve and manage, to the extent possible, all stakeholders in the Process Group activities. By garnering the buy-in and shared ownership of the project by the stakeholders, it generally improves the probability of satisfying customer requirements.

The basic processes for the Initiating Process Group are:
- Selecting the project
- Determining business needs
- Considering Enterprise Environmental Factors (e.g., historical data, marketplace conditions, organization structure, industry standards)
- Considering Organizational Process Assets (e.g., policies, procedures, plans, guidelines)
- Determining objectives
- Developing the Project Charter
- Developing the Preliminary Project Scope Statement
- Determining high level deliverables and estimates
- Developing a product description

- Identifying the qualifications of the Project Manager that would be best suited for the particular project
- Determining high level resource requirements
- Obtaining project initiation approval

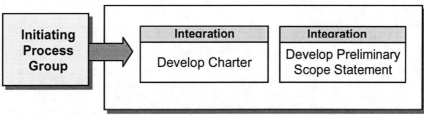

Figure 8 - Initiating Process Group Processes

For the project to get started "right," it is essential that all stakeholders participate in this critical Process Group. The success of the organization and the Project Team depends upon starting with complete and accurate information, management support, and the authorization necessary to manage the project. According to the PMBOK®, in order to have an effective project management team, the team needs to understand and use knowledge and skills from at least five areas of expertise. These areas are (1) The PMBOK®, (2) Application area knowledge, standards and regulations, (3) Understanding the project environment, (4) General management knowledge and skills and (5) Interpersonal skills.

The image above depicts the Initiating Process Group process flow.

The figure below illustrates the project Initiating Process Group stakeholder participation.

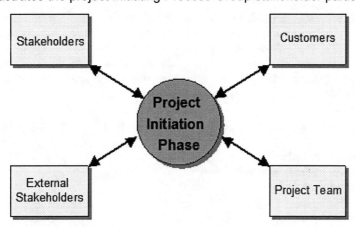

Figure 9 - Initiating Process Group Stakeholders

Planning Process Group

The Planning Process Group is considered the most important Process Group in project management. Time spent up front identifying the proper needs and structure for organizing and managing a project saves countless hours of confusion and rework during the

Project planning defines project activities that will be performed, the products that will be produced, and describes how these activities will be accomplished and managed. Project planning defines each major task, estimates the time, resources and cost required, and provides a framework for management review and control.

Planning involves identifying and documenting scope, tasks, schedules, cost, risk, quality, and staffing needs. This planning process:
- Identifies specific work to be performed and the goals that define the project
- Provides documented estimates regarding schedule, resources and cost for planning, tracking, and controlling the project
- Obtains organizational commitments that are planned, documented, and agreed upon
- Continues the development and documentation of project alternatives, assumptions, and constraints
- Establishes a baseline of the plan from which the project will be managed.

The result of the Planning Process Group, the Project Management Plan, will be an approved, comprehensive document that allows a Project Team to begin and complete the work necessary to achieve the project goals and objectives (product/process). The Project Management Plan will address how the Project Team will manage the project elements, including the Project Management System (i.e., set of tools, techniques, methodologies used to manage a project). The Plan will provide a high level of confidence in the organization's ability to meet the scope, timing, cost, and quality requirements by addressing all aspects of the project.

The Planning Process Group is comprised of a number of constituent project management processes that will estimate the project's size, technical scope, and the required resources. It will produce a schedule, Work Breakdown Schedule (WBS), WBS Dictionary, identify and assess risks, and negotiate commitments. Completing these processes is necessary to establish the entire, comprehensive Project Management Plan. Typically, several iterations of the planning processes are performed before the plan is completed and approved.

The image on the next page depicts the Planning Process Groups as a series of activities and steps to be completed that result in a complete Project Management Plan. These process activities will:
1. Produce a plan that will define how the project objectives will be achieved – scope, schedule, resources and cost.
2. Establish subsidiary management plans that will define how specific aspects of the project will be managed to make certain the objectives are met.

The Planning Process Group will result in the development of the subsidiary management plans which are:
- Cost management plan
- Human Resource management plan
- Scope management plan
- Schedule management plan
- Quality management plan
- Procurement management plan
- Communications management plan
- Risk management plan
- Integration management plan

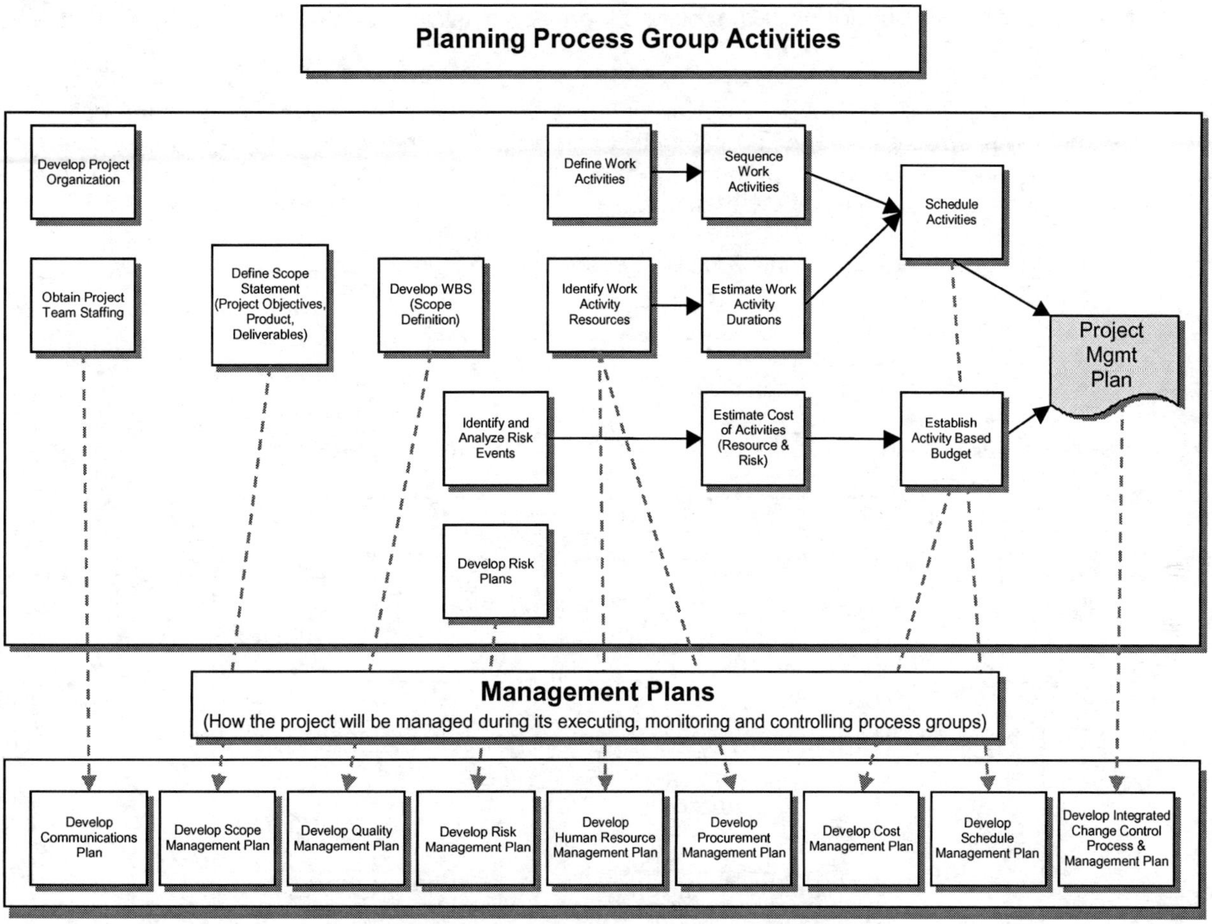

Figure 10 - Planning Process Group Activities

Executing Process Group

Once a project moves into the Executing Process Group, the Project Team and all necessary resources to carry out the project should be in place and ready to perform project activities. The Project Management Plan is completed and baselined by this time as well. The Project Team's and specifically the Project Manager's focus now shifts from planning the project efforts to participating in, observing, and analyzing the work being done.

The Executing Process Group is where the work activities of the Project Management Plan are executed, resulting in the completion of the project deliverables and achievement of the project objective(s). This Process Group brings together all of the project management disciplines, resulting in a product or service that will meet the project deliverable requirements and the customers need. In this Process Group, elements completed in the Planning Process Group are implemented, time is expended, and money is spent.

This Process Group requires the Project Manager and Project Team to:
- Conduct, coordinate and manage the ongoing work activities
- Perform quality assurance activities continuously to ensure project objectives are achieved
- Monitor identified risks for triggering events and implement containment or contingency strategies as necessary
- Distribute information to project stakeholders

In short, it means coordinating and managing the project resources while executing the Project Management Plan, performing the planned project activities, and ensuring they are completed efficiently.

The Executing Process Group allows the project's deliverables to be produced and the objectives to be met. This Process Group facilitates the completion of the work activities, the expenditure of resources, and the application of the quality assurance processes to ensure that the end product(s) is viable and meets customer requirements.

Several processes are part of this Process Group. They may include:
- Develop Team
- Select Sellers
- Perform Quality Assurance
- Information collection and distribution

The figure below shows how these processes fit into the Executing Process Group.

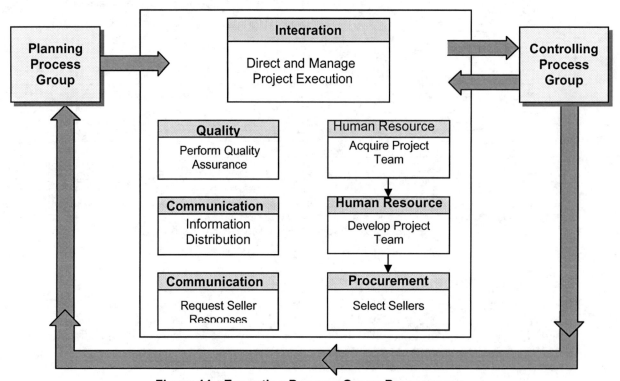

Figure 11 - Executing Process Group Processes

The Execution Process Group involves coordinating and managing project activities and the subsequent output. The focus of the Project Manager and the Project Team is on the day-to-day management of the overall effort. In addition to the processes and activities defined above, the subsidiary management plans are implemented and project performance is monitored and managed accordingly.

Monitoring and Controlling Process Group

Control is a formal process in project management. The PMBOK® defines Project Control as a project management function that involves comparing actual performance with planned performance and taking corrective action to yield the desired outcome when significant differences exists. By monitoring and measuring progress regularly, identifying variances from plan, and taking corrective action when necessary, project control ensures that project objectives are met.

Project control involves the regular review of metrics and report status to identify variances from the planned baseline. The variances are determined by comparing the actual performance metrics from the execution phase against the baseline metrics assigned during the planning phase. If significant variances are observed, adjustments to the plan are made by repeating and adjusting the appropriate Project Management Planning processes.

A significant variance from the plan does not explicitly require a change, but should be reviewed to determine whether preventive action is warranted. For example, a missed activity finish date may require adjustments to the current staffing plan, reliance on overtime, or trade-off between budget and schedule objectives. Controlling also includes taking preventive action in anticipation of possible problems.

While the Monitoring & Controlling Process Group relationship to other Process Groups is relatively concise and clear, control is often difficult to implement as a formalized system. Project control is still important however, because a project is unlikely to be considered successful by stakeholders if it is not monitored and controlled effectively. Success in this context translates to metrics (project, cost, completion dates, etc.) and customer's expectations (features, functionality, performance, etc.).

The control processes implemented during this Process Group are the Performance Reporting and Integrated Change Control, with several constituent processes interacting with these processes as depicted in the image on the following page.

Only by monitoring and controlling a project can project progress and stakeholder's expectations be achieved in unison. Projects rarely fail because of one issue. Rather, failure is usually a collection of minor items that individually have negative impact in a specific project area. However, when looked at over the life of a project, these minor items can cause significant impact to cost, schedule, risk, and functionality and can manifest themselves as deviations from the original Project Management Plan.

As discussed in the Planning Process Group section, the Project Management Plan will include the initially agreed upon baseline project schedule and budget. These become the primary tools for evaluating project performance.

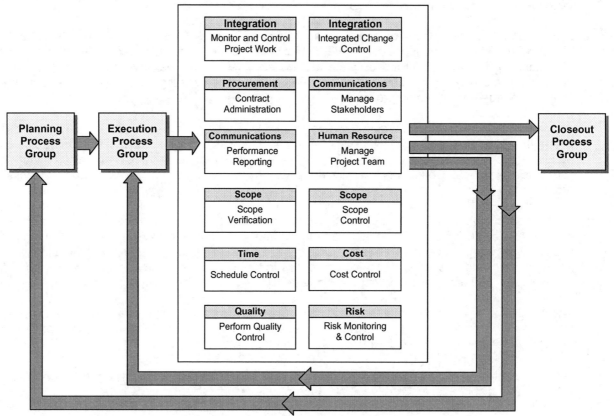

Figure 12 - Monitoring and Controlling Process Group Processes

Closing Process Group

The last major Process Group of a project's life cycle is the project Closing Process Group. Project closeout is performed after all defined project objectives have been met and the customer has formally accepted the project's deliverables and end product or, in some instances, when a project has been cancelled or terminated early. Project closeout is fairly routine, but it is an important process. By properly completing the project closeout, organizations can benefit from lessons learned and information compiled at closure.

The Closing Process Group is comprised of two processes: close project and contract closure. These are depicted in the figure below.

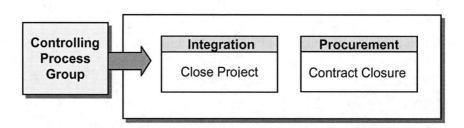

Figure 13 - Closing Process Group Processes

Some of the key elements to project closeout are:
- Completion and closeout of any contractual agreements with suppliers or providers
- Formalizing customer acceptance
- Closeout of any financial matters
- Preparation of the project's final performance report
- Conducting a project review
- Documenting lessons learned
- Completing, collecting and archiving project records
- Celebrating project success.

Notes

Chapter 4

Project Integration Management

Reference Material to Study
- A Guide to the Project Management Body of Knowledge (PMBOK® Guide 3rd Edition), Chapter 5
- Project Planning, Scheduling & Control, Chapters 1-4, Lewis, James P. 1995

What to Study
- Chapter 4 of the PMBOK® Guide on Project Integration Management processes: Develop Project Charter, Develop Preliminary Project Scope Statements, Develop Project Management, Direct and Manage Project Execution, Monitor and Control Project Work, Integrated Change Control and close project. Be familiar with the Inputs, Tools and Techniques, and Outputs of each process.
- Know what a Project Charter is and what it is used for.
- Know what a Project Management Plan is and what it is used for.
- Know how to label the levels of a WBS chart.
- Know how to close a project and what is involved.

Key Definitions
- **Administrative Closure** - Generating, gathering, and disseminating information to formalize phase or project completion.
- **Amount at Stake** - Is the extent, or impact, of adverse consequences which could occur to a project.
- **Assumptions** - Factors which for planning purposes can be considered to be true, real, or certain.
- **Benchmarking** - Is the process where an organization will compare its processes, products, performance against other organizations. These other organizations can be in the same or other industries.
- **Change Control** - Influences factors that create any change; including changes to project deliverables.
- **Configuration Management** - Defines and controls changes to project deliverables. Any documented procedure used to apply technical and administrative direction and surveillance to: define and document characteristics of a system; control changes; record and report changes; ensure conformance to requirements.
- **Constraints** - Factors which will limit the project management team's options.

- **Control Account Plan** (CAP) - A management control point where the integration of scope, budget and schedule occurs and the measurement of performance will happen. CAPs are placed at selected management points of the work breakdown structure.
- **Earned Value Management** - A method for integrating scope, schedule, and resources, and for measuring project performance. It compares the amount of work that was planned, versus actually earned, versus actually spent, to determine if cost and schedule performance are as planned.
- **Functional Manager** - A manager responsible for activities in a specialized department or function. (e.g., engineering, marketing, manufacturing)
- **Functional Organization** - An organizational structure in which staff are grouped hierarchically by specialty (e.g., production, marketing, engineering).
- **Integration** - Making trade-offs among competing objectives and alternatives.
- **Lessons Learned** - The learning gained from the process of performing the project. Lessons learned may be identified at any point. Also considered a project record.
- **Linear Responsibility Chart** - The same as an accountability matrix or responsibility assignment matrix.
- **Line Manager** - 1) The manager of any group that actually makes a product or performs a service. 2) A Functional Manager.
- **Management By Objectives** (MBO) - A system of managerial leadership that defines individual managerial responsibilities in terms of corporate objectives.
- **Project Charter -** A formal document providing authority to a project manager to conduct a project within scope, quality, time and cost and resource constraints as laid down in the document.
- **Responsibility Assignment Matrix** (RAM) - A structure which relates the project organization structure to the WBS to help ensure that each element of the project's scope of work is assigned to a responsible individual. Also called an Accountability Matrix, Responsibility Chart, or Responsibility Matrix.

The Project Integration Management section on the PMP® certification exam addresses critical project management functions that ensure coordination of the various elements of the project. As the PMBOK® Guide explains the processes in integration management are primarily integrative. Project integration management involves making trade-offs among competing objectives in order to meet or exceed stakeholder needs and expectations and addresses develop project charter, develop preliminary project scope statement, develop project management plan, direct and manage project execution, monitor and control project work, integrated change control and close project. These seven processes not only interact with each other but also interact with processes in the other eight knowledge areas. Noting PMI's view that integration occurs in other areas also is important. For example, project scope and product scope need to be integrated; project work needs to be integrated with the other work of the ongoing organization, and deliverables from various technical specialties need integration.

The Project Integration Management questions are straightforward. In the past, most people find them to be easy. Nevertheless, because they cover so much material, you do need to study them carefully to become familiar with PMI's terminology and perspectives. PMBOK® Guide Figure 4.1 provides an overview of the structure of Project Integration Management.

The Project Integration knowledge area is concerned with coordinating all aspects of the project and is highly interactive. Project planning, project execution, and change control occur throughout the project and are repeated continuously while working on the project. Project planning and execution involve weighing the objectives of the project against alternatives to bring the project to a successful completion. Change control impacts the project plan, which, in turn, impacts execution, so you can see that these three processes are very tightly linked. The processes in this area also interact with other processes in the remaining knowledge areas.

Project Charter

A Project Charter announces that a project has begun. The purpose of the charter is to demonstrate management support for the project and the project manager. It is a simple, powerful tool.

As an announcement it has classically taken on many forms--anything from a memorandum, to a letter, to an e-mail, to the template that is advocated at the end of this subsection. The charter is then sent to everyone who may be associated with the project to give notice of the new project and new project manager.

Because the Project Charter is created to formally communicate the existence of the project, it is issued at the end of the Project Initiation Phase and is looked upon as the beginning of the Planning Phase of a project. It is used as the basis to create the Project Plan.

Inputs to developing the Project Charter include contracts (when applicable), project statement of work, enterprise environmental factors (such as marketplace conditions, available resources and infrastructure), and finally organizational process assets such as risk control procedures, standardized templates or change control procedures. These documents identify a need and establish senior management commitment.

Note of caution - there are typically two ways that a project charter may be interpreted. One is the way that has been described in this subsection; as a formal recognition that a new project has begun. The other way refers to what many have come to know as the Statement of Work. Both uses will probably continue to be widespread, and this note is a reminder of that fact.

The Project Charter contains the following attributes:
- General Information
- Project Purpose / Objective
- Project Scope
- Project Authority
- Roles and Responsibilities
- Management Checkpoints
- Signatures

"Why are we doing this project?" is the question that the purpose statement attempts to answer. As part of the project charter, it is the first element that announces why this project is being undertaken. The purpose statement is of paramount importance, especially when significant amounts of time and money are involved. Knowing the answer to this question will allow the project team to make more informed decisions throughout the project.

And although there are many "whys" in the context of a project, the charter does not attempt to answer them all. Neither the purpose statement nor the project charter itself should be used as the venue on which to build a business case or a cost benefit analysis.

Consequently, project objectives are used to establish performance goals—planned levels of accomplishment stated as measurable objectives that can be compared to actual results. Performance measures should be derived for each goal. These measures can be quantified to see if the project is meeting the organization's objectives. Project performance can then be traced directly to the organization's goals, mission, and objectives, enabling participants to correct areas that are not meeting those objectives.

Project scope is documented at a high level in the Project Charter. The level documented must be sufficient to allow for further decomposition within the Project Plan. For example, the requirement for training may be identified within the Project Charter. Decomposition within the Project Plan will document the types of training to be delivered, procurement or development of course materials, and so on. Project objectives within the Project Charter projects are executed to meet the strategic goals of an organization. Objectives are communicated in the Project Charter to ensure that all stakeholders understand the organization's needs that the project addresses.

Because of a project's complexity, many difficult decisions must be made to keep it on track. For this reason the Project Charter defines the authority and mechanisms to resolve potential problems. Three areas must be addressed. First, the organization's senior management must issue the Project Charter. A level of management is required that can provide organizational resources to the project and have control over the elements that affect it. Second, the Project Charter must establish a project manager who is given authority to plan, execute, and control the project. Finally, the Project Charter must establish a relationship between the project and senior management to ensure that a support mechanism exists to resolve issues outside the authority of the project manager.

In this way, the Project Charter becomes a contract between senior management and the project manager; both have duties and obligations to the project. The Project Charter should have a signature page, which all appropriate parties should sign.

The roles and responsibilities for initiating, planning, executing, controlling, and closing out a project are divided among many individuals of the project team. These roles and responsibilities are a result of various contributing factors:
- The size and nature of the organization
- The size and nature of the project
- The number of projects already underway
- The capabilities of the project team members
- The maturity of the project management function within the organization

Allocating roles and responsibilities for various phases, tasks, and activities of a project is essential to ensuring that work is done on time. From this perspective then, it becomes necessary to unambiguously identify work required, to clearly identify dependencies, to accurately estimate durations, to clearly define quality standards, to succinctly describe deliverables, and to develop measurable performance criteria for tasks.

Another manner to detail roles and responsibilities on a project would be to develop a responsibility matrix. In essence, a responsibility matrix lays out the major activities in the project. This matrix can help avoid communication breakdowns between individuals, departments, and organizations because everyone involved can see clearly who to contact for each activity.

A responsibility matrix can be as simple as a spreadsheet, or as intricately drawn from a graphics software application. The matrix can be pasted to a text document for inclusion as part of the project documentation. The image below shows an example of a Responsibility Matrix.

To ensure that the project progresses satisfactorily, management checkpoints or milestones should be clearly defined with planned dates to measure progress. Checkpoints are high-level milestones. Senior management uses them to approve the completion of a phase or milestone and as go/no-go decision points to proceed with the project. The checkpoints ensure that the products and services delivered meet the project objectives in the time frame established by senior management in the Project Charter.

Matrix Table: P - Primary Responsibility E - Primary Responsibility Electronics M - Primary Responsibility Mechanical	Product Design Documentation									Process Design Documentation									Test & Quality						Management						
Responsibility	System Architecture	Product Specification	Component Drawings/CAD Models	Assembly Drawing	Schematic/Net List	PCB Layout	Product Bill of Material	Design FMEA	Design Checklist	Advance Quality Plan	Packaging Specification	Manufacturing Plan	DFA Checklist	Build Order	Build Report	Process Flow & Manning Diagram	Supplier Tooling Plan	Fixture & Equipment Plan	Tooling & Fixture Design	Process Visual Aids	Assy & Test Equip. Programs	Process FMEA	Component Progress Sheet	Specified Characteristics	Test Requests	Functional Perf. Measurements	Dsgn Verification Plan & Rpt.	Control Plan	Process Capability Study	Dimensional Layout	Prototype Part Final Inspection Rpt.	Project Brief	Project Plan	Product Cost Estimates	Request for Appropriation-Tooling	Open Issues List	Sales Quote	Project Summary Report	Lessons Learned
Sales Engineer																																P					P		
Project Engineer				M																						P							P		P	P			P
System Engineer	P																									P													
Mechanical Engineer		P	P			P	P																						P										
Electrical Engineer		E			P		E	E	E																E	E	E	E											
PCB Designer					P																																		
Manufacturing Engineer												P	P	P	P	P		P	P	P	M	P							P	P								P	
Quality Engineer																															P								
Supplier Engineer							P										P						P								P								
Cost Estimator																																		P					
In Circuit Test Engineer																								E															
AI Programmer																								E															
Packaging Engineer											P																												

Figure 14 - Responsibility Matrix

There are eight major sections of the Project Charter:
- General Information
- Project Purpose
- Project Objective
- Project Scope
- Project Authority
- Roles and Responsibilities
- Management

After establishing the Project Charter, the project team begins the process of devising and maintaining a workable scheme to accomplish the business needs that the project was undertaken to address.

Because the Project Charter is an announcement, and because its purpose is to formally announce the project, it is not meant to manage changes that occur. The charter is intended as a one-time document; therefore, if a change occurs that is significant enough to outdate the charter's original purpose and scope then a new charter should be issued.

Project Selection Methods

PMI® feels strongly that organizations should have a formal process for deciding projects to sponsor and for ensuring that projects are supportive of the organization's strategic objectives. In many organizations, some type of senior management steering committee or Program Management Office (PMO) performs this project-evaluation and -selection process. Project-selection methods are the techniques used to execute this process, and they are organized into two major categories: benefit measurement methods and constrained optimization methods.

The project-selection method(s) used by an organization should be relevant to the objectives of the company and its managers and should be consistent with the capabilities and resources of the organization. The two methods of project selection are benefit measurement (comparative approach) and constrained optimization (mathematical approach). Listed below are the key points of these two method types.
1. **Benefit Measurement** (comparative approach) - Scoring models, cost-benefit analysis, review board, economic models. Benefit measurement is the most common approach.
2. **Constrained Optimization** (mathematical approach) - Linear programming, nonlinear programming, integer programming, dynamic programming, multi-objective programming. Constrained optimization makes use of math models and complex criteria and is often managed as a distinct project phase.

Expert Judgment

Expert judgment is mentioned in this chapter because develop project charter is the first PMBOK® process that lists expert judgment as a primary tool or technique. In this case, as in most, expert judgment is used to evaluate the inputs into the process. Specifically, expert judgment is used to assess the product description, the project-selection criteria, and the validity of the historical information. In addition, expert judgment could be used to identify key assumptions and constraints. Anyone with specialized knowledge and/or experience relevant to the goals of the project can be used as a source of expert judgment.

Project Planning Methodology

Be familiar with the use and purpose of a project planning methodology, that is, any structured approach to help prepare the project plan. It may be simple, consisting of forms and templates. Or it may be complex, such as required simulations to perform schedule or cost risk analysis. PMI® makes the distinction between "hard" tools in a methodology, such as project management software, and "soft" tools, such as a facilitated kickoff meeting.

When it comes to project planning, the key issue you need to understand here is that organizations should have some kind of methodology that they follow as to project planning, something that lends a little consistency to the processes they are using internally. This process should be a good blend of hard and soft tools. Make sure you have that distinction down as well.

Project Management Information System (PMIS)

A Project Management Information System (PMIS) facilitates project information to flow within an organization. The software application is a core component of the overall PMIS and is considered to represent the tools and techniques used to gather, integrate, and distribute output of the other project management processes (e.g. project management outputs such as the overall Project Management Plan and subsidiary plans).

Note that the PMIS is a tool used by each of the project integration management processes used to gather, integrate, and distribute the outputs of other project management processes. It is simply an information system that stores all of the information related to your project. The PMIS is used from the beginning of the project through closeout. It may be software such as Microsoft Project, Microsoft Access or it may be a manual system.

Knowing what a project management information system is used for is key. There will be several questions about the project management information system on the exam. They are not just looking for software tools. Tools such as computer software may be used as part of the information system, but the system is not exclusively made up of those components. It is made up of software, forms, templates, memos, and the processes that go into funneling information through your project.

Develop Preliminary Project Scope Statement

The development of a written statement, known as the Project Scope Statement, provides the basis for future project decisions. This statement is of singular importance to the project, as was previously stated, because it sets the overall guidelines as to the size of the project. The content of this statement, at a minimum, will include the following:
- **Project Results/Completion Criteria**: What will be created in terms of deliverables (and their characteristics) and/or what constitutes a successful phase completion.
- **The Approach to be Used**: What type of process or technology will be used, whether the project will be done internally or externally, etc.
- **Content of the Project**: What is and is not included in the work to be done.

The following documents may be helpful in developing a preliminary project scope statement:
- Project Work Statement
- Project Objectives (including identified constraints and assumptions)
- Project Feasibility Document
- Project Concept Document
- Project Charter

Note that during subsequent process phases the development of the preliminary project scope statement process validates and refines, if required, the project scope defined for that phase.

Project Management Plan

The Project Management Plan is the controlling document to manage a project. The Project Management Plan will address how the Project Team will manage the project elements, including the Project Management System (i.e., set of tools, techniques, methodologies used to manage a project). The Plan will provide a high level of confidence in the organization's ability to meet the scope, timing, cost, and quality requirements by addressing all aspects of the project.

The Project Management Plan describes the:
- Purpose, scope, and interim and final deliverables of the project
- Schedule and budget for the project
- Project assumptions and constraints
- Managerial and technical processes necessary to develop the project deliverables
- Resources required to deliver the project deliverables
- Additional plans required to support the project

The project management plan is a key integrative document that uses the outputs of the other planning processes and strategic planning to create a consistent, coherent document that can be used to guide both project execution and project control. Be familiar with what the project management plan is used for and what items are often included in a project management plan. Also, you should realize that although the project manager is responsible for seeing that the project management plan is accomplished, the entire project team must make important contributions to the various pieces of the plan.

When it comes to project management plan, what you really need to know is, what, do we use a project management plan for? It is used to guide project execution, to document the planning assumption and to document planning decisions regarding some alternatives that have been chosen. We use it to simplify communication between the project team and stakeholders and define key management reviews as to content, expense, and time. It is a baseline for progress management and project control. Is the WBS the project management plan? NO. The Work Breakdown Structure is not the project management plan—it is a key component of the project management plan, but it is not the project management plan. Also realize the project schedule is not the project management plan. The schedule lists planned dates for performing activities and meeting milestones identified in the project management plan.

Although the project manager is responsible for seeing that the project management plan is accomplished, all stakeholders, including the entire project team, must make important contributions to the various pieces of the plan. Note also that the project management plan is not the performance measurement baseline. The project management plan is expected to change throughout the project as more information becomes available, whereas the performance measurement baselines for technical scope, schedule, and cost are expected to change only intermittently and then, generally, only in response to an approved scope of work or deliverable change. PMI® stresses planning as a key success factor in projects.

Configuration Management System

The configuration management system describes the change control procedures used with an organization. It identifies the process for changes, including the use of any change order forms and the people involved in review and approval. Define the criteria for changes. What are the triggers for the need for a change request? (e.g. If a particular project is a day late, is the whole project plan readjusted or is the day absorbed in another section?

In short a configuration management system:
- Describes the required change management approach. Change happens and documentation of the reason (need or benefit), impact (cost and/or schedule), must be maintained.
- Describes how a change request is made (after each incident or only when a threshold is reached). Outline how the change request should be disposed (approval or rejected), and outline the number of business days after submittal. This disposal needs to be in writing and is typically 3 or 5 business days and rarely more than two weeks.
- Describe criteria for change.
- Change is the request to adjust any portion of the SOW, approved deliverable or approved change request.

- Change can be (and should be) more than an adjustment to scope.
- Change may be "compliance" or "non-compliance." A compliance change request adjusts something agreed to. A non-compliance change request defines something that did not happen as planned. Examples include system not being available (lost time) or people not performing their duties per R&R and the project plan.
- Change may be an incident of a risk.
- Change can also be time extensions to the project.

Change Control Systems

A change control system is a collection of formal, documented procedures that defines the steps by which official project documents may be changed. It includes the paperwork, tracking systems, and approval levels necessary for authorizing changes. The change control system must also include procedures to handle changes, which may be approved without prior review (e.g., changes that occur as the result of an emergency). These changes must still be documented and captured so that they do not cause problems later in the project.

Note that in short change control is the following:
- Influencing the activities that create changes to ensure that those changes are beneficial
- Determining that a change has occurred
- Managing the actual changes when they occur

Change control is not the prevention of changes. It is concerned with identification and management of possible changes to the project.

Management of the changes includes the administrative management, tracking, review, and assessment of proposed changes; the organized and timely review and decision on change approval; and the administrative process to ensure that the project team is informed of changes when they are approved.

Direct and Manage Project Execution

Once a project moves into the Execution Phase, the project team and the necessary resources to carry out the project should be in place and ready to perform project activities. The Project Plan should have been completed and baselined by this time as well. The project team, and specifically the project manager's focus, now shifts from planning the project efforts to participating in, observing, and analyzing the work being done.

A project manager's responsibilities do not stop once the planning of the project is done. Because a project manager is responsible to internal and external stakeholders, the project team, vendors, executive management, and others, the visibility of the position is intensified because many of these people will now expect to see and discuss the resulting deliverables that were so meticulously detailed in the Planning Phase. As a project manager, keeping oneself from getting "down in the weeds," especially on large projects, will be important during project execution. This will allow the project manager to focus attention on enabling the project plans and processes and managing the expectations of customers and stakeholders.

Particular attention during project execution will need to be paid to keeping interested parties up to date with project status, dealing with procurement and contract administration issues, helping manage quality control, and monitoring project risk. While the processes to control many of these elements are discussed within the Project Control Phase, it is still important that the project manager be cognizant of the issues as the project is being performed. Daily interaction and feedback from team members will be vital to project success.

Deliverable

Any measurable, tangible, verifiable outcome, result, or item that must be produced to complete a project or part of a project. Often used more narrowly in reference to an external deliverable, which is a deliverable that is subject to approval by the project sponsor or customer.

Requested Changes

Requests to expand or reduce the project scope, modify the costs or budgets, or revise schedules.

Administrative Closure Procedures

Administrative closure procedures documents the process preparing closure documentation of the product or process deliverable to the customer as well as taking other administrative actions to ensure that the project and its assets are redistributed. Delivering closure documentation does not simply mean getting an approval or acceptance signature on the deliverable but involves a series of steps to ensure that the product meets the customer's expectations and conforms to the product requirements and specifications that were laid out.

Monitor and Control Project Work

Monitoring and controlling project work involves the regular review of metrics and report status in order to identify variances from the planned project baseline. The variances are determined by comparing the actual performance metrics from the Execution Phase against the baseline metrics assigned during the Planning Phase. These variances are fed into a control processes to evaluate their meaning. If significant variances are observed (i.e., variances that jeopardize the completion of the project objectives), adjustments to the plan are made by repeating and adjusting the appropriate project planning processes. A significant variance from the plan does not explicitly require a change, but should be reviewed to see if preventive action is warranted. For example, a missed activity finish date may require adjustments to the current staffing plan, reliance on overtime, or trade-off between budget and schedule objectives. Controlling also includes taking preventative action in anticipation of possible problems.

While the Project Control Phase's relationship to other project phases is relatively concise and clear, control is often difficult to implement as a formalized project control system in an organization. Project control is still important, however, because a project is unlikely to be considered successful by stakeholders if it is not controlled effectively. Success in this context translates to raw metrics (project cost, completion date, etc.) and customers' expectations (features, functionality, performance, etc.).

Only by controlling a project can project progress and stakeholder's expectations be satisfied in unison. Projects rarely fail because of one issue. Rather, failure is usually a collection of minor items that individually have negative impact in a specific project area. However, when looked at over the life span of a project, these minor items can cause significant impacts to cost, schedule, risk, and functionality and can manifest themselves as deviations from the original Project Plan.

Corrective and Preventive Action

Corrective action appears throughout the PMBOK® Guide. Corrective action is defined as anything done to bring expected future performance in line with the plan. In short, corrective action is the day-to-day responses to all the obstacles and problems a project may encounter. Preventive action is anything that reduces the probability of potential consequences of potential risk events.

The description of corrective action: it is what is important about it when it comes to integration management. Specifically, this is the one and only spot that it is an input into the process. Throughout the rest of the PMBOK® Guide, it is an output.

Earned Value Technique

Earned value is mentioned throughout the PMBOK® Guide but its first mention is as a tool and technique for Monitor and Control Project Work. Earned value is used to integrate the project's scope, schedule, and resources and to measure and report project performance, from initiation to closeout.

Integrated Change Control

The purpose of integrated change control is to influence factors that create change so that the change is beneficial, determine when a change has occurred, and manage actual changes if and when they do occur. This process is concerned with coordinating changes across the entire project.

The change control system is the principal tool used for integrated change control. As described in PMBOK® Guide, it consists of formal, documented procedures that define the steps used to change formal documents.

A well-developed and documented change control process is crucial to the project management process success. The basic objectives of a change control system are to:
- Continually identify changes, actual or proposed, as they occur.
- Reveal the consequences of the proposed changes in terms of cost and schedule impacts.
- Permit managerial analysis, investigation of alternatives, and an acceptance or rejection checkpoint.
- Communicate changes to all stakeholders.
- Insure that approved changes are implemented.
- Update the development process.

Some organizations assign the project manager a level of authority for accepting change requests. This does not mean that the project manager can arbitrarily make the changes. It means the he can make recommendations for changes to the customer without first consulting management, provided the request is for a change that does not affect the budget or schedule more than a preset amount. Otherwise, the change requests are passed through the project manager to a change control board (CCB) for review.

Change Control Board (CCB)

The CCB may be part of a change control system and be responsible for approving or rejecting change requests. Although some projects may have multiple CCBs, there are circumstances under which the project manager may be able to handle certain types of changes without the need for a formal CCB review.

A change control system consists of a formal, documented procedure for handling change. However, you do need to be aware that a change control board, or a CCB, is what is responsible for authorizing the change that goes through this system.

Configuration Management

The purpose of the configuration management approach is to establish a contractual orientation. Make sure you do exactly what you said you would do and comply with the end user's stated desires. Configuration management protects the end user from unauthorized changes by project staff and protects the project staff from shifts in the end user's desires.

The basic thrust of configuration management is to do the following:
1. Carefully define a system deliverable.
2. Rigorously control changes to the deliverable.
3. Ensure that the ultimate deliverable is consistent with the defined system as modified by approved changes.

Basic Steps in Configuration Management

1. Develop the specifications - Develop the specifications for a complete program configuration item (CPCI). Have the end user sign off on these specifications.
2. Develop a general design - Develop the general design of a CPCI directly from the specifications describing the deliverable and nothing else. Thus the specifications serve as the baseline for the general design. There should be a one-to-one relationship between specification items and items in the general design. Inspect the specifications and general design to ensure that they are compatible.
3. Develop a detailed design - Repeat the process above, except this time use the general design as the baseline for the detailed design. Inspect the detailed design for compatibility with the general design.
4. Implement and test the system - Use the detailed design as the guide to carrying out the project. Rigorously control changes to the design. In testing the system, compare system performance against the original specifications (as modified through a controlled approval process). Remember that the original specification is the only document in which the user agreed upon a description of what the system is supposed to do.
5. Audit the items and system to verify conformance to requirements - An audit should be conducted to ensure that what has been designed conforms to the specific requirements. These audits may be called functional configuration audits or physical configuration audits.

Change Control in Configuration Management

The three basic objectives of a change control are:
1. Screen the user requests. Use a request for change form. Assess the consequences of the requested changes. If the request has no effect on the project it objectives, it can be accepted by the project manager. Otherwise, it should be approved by a higher level of management.
2. Keep track of accepted changes. Keep a file of accepted changes and always update specifications based on changes.
3. Update the development process. Update all baselines and inform project staff of changes.

The basic steps are outlines here, and what you need to understand is that these steps lead you to a notion called traceability. You can trace the general design, to the detailed design, back to the general design, and back to the specifications. Also understand that in configuration management change control, there is ardent screening going on. All changes must be screened, tracked, accepted, approved, and the development process updated.

Close Project

The last major phase of a project's life cycle is project closeout. Project closeout is performed once all defined project objectives have been met and the customer has accepted the project's product. Closing a project is a fairly routine process. Project closeout includes the following key elements:
- Redistributing resources – staff, facilities, equipment, and automated systems
- Closing out any financial issues such as labor charge codes and contract closure
- Completing, collecting, and archiving project records
- Documenting the successes and issues of the project
- Conducting a lessons learned session
- Celebrating project success

These activities are particularly important on large projects with extensive records and resources.

Administrative Closure

Administrative closure is the process of preparing closure documentation of the product or process deliverable to the customer as well as taking other administrative actions to ensure that the project and its assets are redistributed. Delivering closure documentation does not simply mean getting an approval or acceptance signature on the deliverable but involves a series of steps to ensure that the product meets the customer's expectations and conforms to the product requirements and specifications that were laid out.

The fact that project closure appears at the end of the project does not mean that all project closure activities need to be delayed until then. As project phases come to an end it is important to conduct milestone reviews to ensure that phase activities have been successfully completed to the satisfaction of all involved. This relieves the project manager and project team of potentially having to deal with old and obscure open action items and outdated information.

Lessons Learned

In addition to communicating the closure of a project in writing, it is also advisable to have a mechanism for group review. A "lessons learned" session is a valuable closure and release mechanism for team members, regardless of the project's success. Some typical questions to answer in such a session include the following:
- Did the delivered product meet the specified requirements and goals of the project?
- Was the customer satisfied with the end product?
- Were cost budgets met?
- Was the schedule met?
- Were risks identified and mitigated?
- Did the project management methodology work?

The lessons learned session is typically a large meeting that includes the following:
- Project team
- Stakeholder representation—including external project oversight
- Executive management
- Maintenance and operation staff. Such a session provides official closure to a project.

It also provides a forum for public praise and recognition and offers an opportunity to discuss ways to improve future processes and procedures. This means that problems encountered by the project team are openly presented. Problem identification on completed projects provides a method to discuss project issues encountered in hopes of eliminating their occurrence in future endeavors. It is important, however, that the problem discussions do not merely point a finger at some target other than the project team; responsibility and ownership for problem areas are critical to developing useful recommendations for future processes.

The individual problems that occurred throughout the course of the project should have been presented and documented when they occurred, then addressed and handled. The lessons learned documented in Project Closeout is more for upper management's review and action, as well as future project manager/team review, to prevent the same thing (bad) from happening again, or to make the same thing (good) happen again.

Problems encountered should be prioritized with focus on the top five to ten problems. It is not necessary to document every small event. However, all legitimate problems and issues should be discussed as requested by customers or management.

Because problems or sensitive issues may be discussed in the lessons learned document, it is helpful to have all organizations identified as contributors included in a review of the material prior to formally submitting the document. It is useful to have the reviews in an interactive forum where all parties can discuss their recommendations for improvement.

As stated earlier, the issue of primary importance with project closure is the acceptance of the product or project deliverable(s) by the customer for which they were created. The best way to resolve this is to convene a final meeting with all necessary stakeholders to review the product delivered against the baseline requirements and specifications. By this time any deviations from the established baseline will have been documented and approved, but it is still good policy to make all aware of the baseline deviations and justifications. Furthermore, any open action items or program level issues can be officially closed. By drawing all of the stakeholders together in a single meeting, the project manager avoids clearing up open issues on an individual basis.

The final deliverable of this meeting should be a statement created by the project manager describing the project's final deliverables in comparison with the authorized project baseline documents. Approval is verified via the signature of a project closure document by all of the stakeholders who signed the original project baseline documentation (e.g., the Project Plan). This document will be customized to the particular project to include pertinent deliverables, key features, and important information about final product delivery.

Contract Closure

Contract closure is the process of terminating contracts that outside organizations or businesses have with the organization as part of the project being performed. These contracts may be vehicles for providing technical support, consulting, or any number of services supplied during the project that the organization decided not to perform itself. Contracts can be brought to closure for variety of reasons, including contract completion, early termination, or failure to perform. Contract closure is a typical but important part of project management. It is a simple process, but close attention should be paid so that no room is left for liability of the organization.

Chapter Review

1. Integrated change control is concerned with:
   A. Influencing the factors which create changes to ensure that the changes are beneficial.
   B. Determining that a change has occurred.
   C. Managing actual changes when and as they occur.
   D. All of the above.

2. Assumptions are:
   A. Factors that influence the change control system.
   B. Factors that limit the project management team's options.
   C. Factors that are considered to be true, real, or certain.
   D. Factors that influence the scope of the project.

3. The primary function of a Change Control Board is to:
   A. Influence the factors which create changes.
   B. Approve or reject change requests.
   C. Managing actual changes when and as they occur.
   D. All of the above.

4. Which of the following is not a function of a Configuration Management System?
   A. To identify and document the functional and physical characteristics of an item or system and control any changes to those characteristics.
   B. To determine if a requested change is to be applied to management or project reserves.
   C. Recording and reporting the change and its implementation status.
   D. Auditing the items and system to verify conformance to requirements.

5. What is a key difference between the project management plan and the project performance baseline?
   A. The project plan is developed by the project manager and the project performance baseline is developed by the steering committee.
   B. The project plan is not a contractual deliverable while the project performance baseline is a contractual deliverable
   C. The project plan is expected to change over time while the project performance baseline will generally only change if new scope or deliverable changes are approved.
   D. The project plan is a formal, approved document while the project performance baseline is not a formal, approved document.

6. A project charter is:
   A. A formal, approved document used to guide both project execution and project control.
   B. A document issued by senior management that provides the project manager with the authority to apply organizational resources to project activities.
   C. A narrative description of products or services to be supplied.
   D. A document describing the organizational breakdown structure of the company.

7. The set of processes required to ensure that the various elements of the project are properly coordinated are called:
    A. Project Control Management
    B. Project Plan Execution
    C. Project Integration Management
    D. Project Communications Management

8. A formal procedure for sanctioning project work to ensure that work is done at the right time and in the proper sequence is called: (choose best answer)
    A. work package
    B. project plan
    C. project charter
    D. work authorization system

9. A project management plan is:
    A. A formal, approved document used to guide both project execution and project control.
    B. A document issued by senior management that provides the project manager with the authority to apply organizational resources to project activities.
    C. A narrative description of products or services to be supplied.
    D. A document describing the organizational breakdown structure of the company.

10. What is a Project Management Information System (PMIS)?
    A. A system that consists of the tools and techniques used to gather, integrate, and disseminate the outputs of project management processes.
    B. A system that supports all aspects of the project from initiating through closing and generally includes both manual and automated systems.
    C. A tool used during the development of the Project Plan.
    D. all the above

Answers

1. D, PMBOK® Guide 3rd Edition, page 96
2. C, PMBOK® Guide 3rd Edition, page 352
3. B, PMBOK® Guide 3rd Edition, page 98
4. B, PMBOK® Guide 3rd Edition, page 90
5. C, PMBOK® Guide 3rd Edition, page 369
6. B, PMBOK® Guide 3rd Edition, page 81
7. C, PMBOK® Guide 3rd Edition, page 77
8. D, PMBOK® Guide 3rd Edition, page 379. The key word in the question is "procedure". The project plan and project charter are documents.
9. A, PMBOK® Guide 3rd Edition, page 369.
10. D, PMBOK® Guide 3rd Edition, page 95

Notes

Chapter 5

Project Scope Management

Reference Material to Study
- A Guide to the Project Management Body of Knowledge (PMBOK® Guide 3rd Edition), Chapter 5
- Project Planning, Scheduling & Control, Chapters 1-4, 16, Lewis, James P., 1995
- The New Project Management, Chapters 8, 12-13, Frame, J. Davidson, 1994

What to Study
- Chapter 5 of the PMBOK® on the Project Scope Management processes: Scope Planning, Scope Definition, Create Work Breakdown Structure, Scope Verification, and Scope Control. (Be familiar with Inputs, Tools and Techniques, and Outputs for each phase)
- Know the difference between project and product scope.
- Know the difference between a scope statement and a statement of work (SOW).
- Know key definitions (see list above or PMBOK® glossary).
- Know what a Work Breakdown Structure (WBS) is and what it is used for.
- Know what a work package is and how it relates to the WBS.
- Know how to label the levels of a WBS chart.
- Know what a project plan is and how it is used.

Key Definitions
- **Accountability Matrix** - A structure which relates the project organizational structure to the work breakdown structure to help ensure that each element of the project's scope is assigned to a responsible individual. Also referred to as a Responsibility Assignment Matrix (RAM).
- **Baseline** - The original plan plus or minus approved changes.
- **Change Control Board** (CCB) - A formally constituted group of stakeholders responsible for approving or rejecting changes to the project baselines.
- **Chart of Accounts** - Any numbering system used to monitor project costs by category (e.g., labor supplies, materials). The project chart of accounts is usually based on the primary performing organization's corporate chart of accounts.
- **Code of Accounts** - Any numbering system used to uniquely identify each element of the work breakdown structure.
- **Deliverable** - Any measurable, tangible, verifiable outcome, result, or item that must be produced to complete a project or subproject.
- **Delphi Technique** - A form of participative expert judgment, it is an anonymous, interactive forecasting technique used to derive consensus about future events on a project. The purpose of the Delphi technique is to elicit information and judgments from participants to facilitate problem-solving, planning, and decision-making.

- **Fast Tracking** - Compressing the project schedule by overlapping activities that would normally be done in sequence. Also used to imply overlapping of normally sequential phases in a project life cycle.
- **Product Scope** - The features and functions that characterize a product or service.
- **Project Scope** - The work that must be done in order to deliver a product with the specified features and functions.
- **Project** - A temporary endeavor undertaken to create a unique product or service.
- **Project Charter** - A formal document issued by senior management which explains the purpose of the project including the business need the project addresses and the resulting product. It provides the project manager with the authority to apply organizational resources to project activities.
- **Project Management Team** - The members of the project team who are directly involved in project management activities. On some smaller projects, the project management team may include virtually all of the project team members.
- **Project Plan** - A formal, approved document used to guide both project execution and project control. The primary uses of the project plan are to document planning assumptions and decisions, to facilitate communication among stakeholders, and to document approved scope, cost, and schedule baselines.
- **Project Scope** - The work that must be done to deliver a product with the specified features and functions.
- **Project Team Members** - The people who report either directly or indirectly to the project manager.
- **Scope Change** - Any change to the project scope.
- **Scope Control** - Controlling changes to project scope.
- **Scope Definition** - Decomposing the major deliverables into smaller, more manageable components to provide better control.
- **Scope Planning** - Developing a written scope statement that includes the project justification, the major deliverables, and the project objectives.
- **Scope Management Plan** - A plan which describes how project scope will be managed and how scope change will be integrated into the project. Includes an assessment of how likely and frequently the project scope may change.
- **Scope Statement** - A documented description of the project as to its output, approach, and content. (What is being produced?, How is it being produced?, and What is included?)
- **Scope Verification** - Process of verifying that that all identified project deliverables have been completed correctly and satisfactorily and obtaining formal acceptance of the project scope from the stakeholders.
- **Statement of Work** (SOW) - A narrative description of products or services to be supplied under contract.
- **Stakeholder** - Individuals and organizations that are involved in or may be affected by project activities.
- **Work Authorization** - Process of sanctioning all project work.
- **Work Authorization/Release** - In cases where work is to be performed in segments due to technical or funding limitations, work authorization/release authorizes specified work to be performed during a specified period.
- **Work Breakdown Structure** (WBS) - A deliverable-oriented grouping of project elements which organizes and defines the total scope of the project.
- **Work Package** - A deliverable at the lowest level of the work breakdown structure. A work package may be divided into activities.

Chapter 5 - Project Scope Management

Scope management focuses on identifying and controlling the work that is required to complete a project. This action results in a product with well-defined features and functions. In order to manage the scope of a project successfully, you must understand the following components of scope management:

- **Scope Planning** – is the process of developing a written scope statement as the basis of future project decisions, in particular, the criteria used to determine if the project has been completed successfully.
- **Scope Definition** - consists of developing a detailed project scope statement for future project decisions.
- **Create WBS** - breaking down a deliverable in to smaller manageable parts to ensure better control.
- **Scope Verification** - ensuring all identified project deliverables have been completed satisfactorily.
- **Scope Control** - controlling, identifying and managing changes to the project scope.

The Project Scope Management questions on the PMP® exam cover a diverse, yet functional set of project management topics: project planning, work breakdown structures, project charter, scope statement, scope verification, scope management plan, and the scope changes are among the topics covered.

PMI® views project scope management as a five-step process that consists of scope planning, scope definition, create WBS, scope verification, and scope control. In the PMBOK® Guide figure 5.1 provides an overview of the structure.

The project scope management questions on the exam are straightforward. In the past most people have found them to be easy; do not be lulled into a full sense of security by past results. These questions cover a wide range of material, and you must be familiar with the terminology and perspectives adopted by PMI®.

Project Scope Management is concerned with the work of the project. All of the processes involved with the work of the project, and only the work that is required to complete the project are found in this knowledge area. All of the scope management processes involve detailing the requirements of the project and the activities that will eventually comprise the project plan, verifying those details using measurements techniques, and controlling changes to these processes.

Project initiation occurs when an individual or group recognizes that a project should begin. Although project initiation is not always a clearly defined process, it frequently includes determining what the project should accomplish, defining the goal of project, and developing a project charter. These actions might vary depending on the organization for which the project is done.

PMI® defines initiation as the process that formally recognizes the beginning of a new project or the continuation of an existing project into its next phase. Note that projects are authorized in different ways in different organizations. PMBOK® Guide section 5.1 lists typical reasons to authorize projects, including market demand, business needs, customer request, technological advance, or social need.

The PMBOK® Guide notes the importance of relating the product description to the business need or other stimuli that gave rise to the product. The PMBOK® Guide states that the product description will generally have fewer details in early phases and more details in later phases as the product characteristics are progressively elaborated. The PMBOK® Guide also notes the need for projects to support an organization's strategic plan. In the initiation process, the PMBOK® Guide identifies the identification and assignment of the project manager as a key output and suggests that the project manager be assigned as early as possible in the project but always before project plan execution begins.

Initiation is where we get our work. This is a concept that is important, since it is where the project manager is assigned and where he/she can point to the beginning of the project. This is challenging, since many projects might be born out of thin air and do not often have a clear beginning point.

Scope Planning

Scope planning is the process during which the scope statement is prepared. The scope statement is important because it serves as the basis for future project decisions and includes the criteria to determine whether the entire project or a particular phase of the project has been completed successfully. Furthermore, the scope statement forms the basis for an agreement between the project team and the customer by identifying the project objectives and deliverables.

It is important to realize that there are both intermediate and end deliverables. An end deliverable is the final product of the project. For example, a document that identified the technical specifications for a new software program is an intermediate deliverable, while the actual software program is considered the end deliverable. In order to clearly show how the work of the project will actually be completed, all deliverables should be defined in terms of a tangible, verifiable product or service.

Expert Judgment

Expert judgment is mentioned throughout the PMBOK® Guide but in scope management as a tool and technique in the scope planning process. Any group or individual with specialized knowledge applicable to the specific project may provide expertise—people in other units within the performing organization, outside consultants, stakeholders (including customers), professional and technical associations, and industry groups.

Project Deliverables

Project deliverables identify what the project is supposed to produce. For example, the purpose of a project might be to create a new service or to fix a current product defect. The term deliverables is used too frequently in project management because the focus is on the outputs. Focusing on outputs helps define the boundaries of the project and keeps the team focused on the project goal.

Project Charter

You should know what a project charter is and what it does for the project manager. The project charter officially does the following:
- Establishes the project
- Authorizes the project manager to use organizational resources to accomplish project activities
- Provides a general description of project objectives

You should also know that the charter should be created during the concept phase of a project, and it is normally created by upper management. The project manager may or may not be personally involved in creating the project charter (this practice varies among companies). It is a key output of in project integration management and normally is issued by a manager external to the project at a level in the organization appropriate to the needs of the project. Without a charter, it is difficult for the project manager to operate with the level of authority required, especially in a matrix environment.

This is a document that has gained much importance over the last few years; thus, you can expect to see at least a couple questions about it. It does establish the project and is only valid if it is signed.

There needs to be a signature on a project charter. Know that it also establishes the authority for the project manager.

Tools and techniques for scope planning include expert judgment and templates, forms and standards.

The PMBOK® Guide strongly recommends a written scope statement even if its elements have been included in other documents, such as the project charter. Elements that comprise the scope statement (project justification, project product, project deliverables, and project objectives) are discussed in the PMBOK® Guide.

The PMBOK® Guide also recommends that a scope management plan be prepared. The scope management plan should include a clear description of how scope changes will be identified and classified. This is particularly difficult, but it is absolutely essential when the product characteristics are still being elaborated. This may be a stand-alone document, or it may be part of the project plan.

If we have a good statement of work, do we need a scope statement? The answer is yes. We have a detailed project requirements document; do we need a scope statement? The answer is yes.

When don't we need a scope statement? The short answer is virtually never. PMI® is very big on the scope statement. It is a foundation document. It is a major component of the way business is done. It clarifies and guides; it is fundamental.

Scope Definition

Scope definition is taking the project deliverables and the work required to create those deliverables and breaking all of the major project deliverables into smaller elements. This process should be completed for each of the project deliverables listed in the scope statement. It is important to understand that scope definition is a component of the project scope variable and that it is also part of the second step in the project management process–planning.

Product Analysis

Product analysis is used to develop a better understanding of the project's product. You should be familiar with some of the product analysis techniques:
- **Product Breakdown** - Involves developing a better understanding of the product by breaking it down into constituent parts.
- **Value Engineering** - Examines each element of a product or system to determine whether there is a more effective and less expensive way to achieve the same function.
- **Value Analysis** - Focuses on optimizing cost performance. Systematic use of techniques to identify the required functions of an item, establish values for those functions, and provide the functions at the lowest overall cost without loss of performance.
- **Functional Analysis** - Examines the project's high-level requirements statements, identifying specific functions and estimating total costs based on the number of functions to be performed.

Defining Project Scope

There is often confusion in project teams regarding the difference between project objectives and project scope. The term "project scope" refers to the magnitude of the effort to complete a project. Conversely, the term "project objectives" refers to a description of the desired outcome of the project.

For example, the objective could be to build a new five-story building on the location of the back parking lot by next December. The scope could be to build the building with a prefabricated metal frame with a cement floor. Consequently, it is imperative that the project objectives and the project scope be clear to everyone to ensure project success.

Project Scope Statement

The development of a written statement, known as the Project Scope Statement, provides the basis for future project decisions. This statement is of singular importance to the project, as was previously stated, because it sets the overall guidelines as to the size of the project. The content of this statement, at a minimum, will include the following:

- Project Results/Completion Criteria: What will be created in terms of deliverables (and their characteristics) and/or what constitutes a successful phase completion.
- The Approach to be Used: What type of process or technology will be used, whether the project will be done internally or externally, etc.
- Content of the Project: What is and is not included in the work to be done.

To ensure that the project scope is completed correctly and in its entirety, it is imperative that a Project Scope Statement be completed and signed by the key stakeholders. Some of the major items included in the project scope statement include:

- **Project Objectives** - Project objectives, as described earlier, are those criteria within the project that will determine whether the project is a success or a failure. If the product or process designed does not meet the objectives as laid out by the project stakeholders, then customer satisfaction will be jeopardized. Remember that objectives should be set at an acceptable level with the intent of delivering product or process that meets the objectives. The objectives should be documented and agreed upon in order to deliver a suitable product. In short, project objectives planning is about defining the acceptable limits and looking for ways to meet them. Objectives can be described in two different ways:
- **Hard Objectives** - These relate to the time, cost, and operational objectives (scope) of the product or process.
- **Soft Objectives** - These relate more to how the objectives are achieved, and which may include attitude, behavior, expectations, and communications.
- **Project Scope Description** - See previous page.
- **Project Requirements** - Describes the conditions or capabilities that must be met or possessed by the deliverables of the project to satisfy a contract, standard, specification, or other formally imposed documents.
- **Project Boundaries** - Identifies generally what is included within the project. It states explicitly what is excluded from the project, if a stakeholder might assume that a particular product, service, or result could be a component of the project.
- **Project Deliverables** - Project deliverables include both the outputs that comprise the project, as well as project management reports and documentation. Depending on the project scope statement, the deliverables may be described at a summary level or in great detail.
- **Project Acceptance Criteria** - Acceptance criteria define what must exist in order to secure customer approval. This may include creating (and securing approval) of a template or a pilot. This should reduce or eliminate judgmental approval or rejection. It is not necessary to delay completion of the SOW while determining acceptance criteria for every deliverable. Those acceptance criteria not readily determined should be defined through another deliverable. However, the key is to have acceptance criteria approved before creation of the deliverable.
- **Project Constraints** - All projects have constraints, and these need to be defined from the outset. Projects have resource limits in terms of people, money, time, and equipment. While these may be adjusted up or down, they are considered fixed resources by the project manager.
- **Project Assumptions** - Similarly, certain criteria relevant to a project are assumed to be essential. For instance, it is assumed that an organization will have the foresight to make the necessary budget appropriations to fund internal projects. Project assumptions need to be

defined before any project activities take place so that time is not indiscreetly utilized on conceptualizing and initiating a project that has no basis for funding.
- **Schedule Milestones** - A summary-level schedule, which easily identifies the major milestones for the customer or project team.
- **Fund Limitations** - Any restrictions that may be placed upon funds for the project, whether in total value or over specified over a certain time frame, such as monthly or quarterly.
- **Cost Estimates** - Estimating the cost of the resources needed to complete project activities.

Creating WBS - Work Breakdown Structure

If you were to take a car trip to a town less than 100 miles away, you may not need to do a lot of planning. Just hop in the car and go. However, if you were driving from New York City to Miami and then Los Angeles, you would most likely spend some time looking at maps and researching your route. Somehow, you would break the big trip down into smaller pieces, like miles per day or geographic borders such as states. Nevertheless, whatever approach you use, the only way to accurately plan a trip of this size is to break it down into smaller parts.

The same is true for projects. You may understand a project well enough to balance its cost-schedule-quality equilibrium, but you also need to be able to break it down—to understand the whole project by understanding it parts. The work breakdown structure (WBS) is the tool for breaking down a project into component parts. It is the foundation of project planning and one of the most important techniques used in project management. If done well, it can become the secret to successful project management.

The work breakdown structure identifies all the tasks in a project; in fact, a WBS is sometimes referred to simply as a task list. It turns one large, unique project, into many small manageable tasks. The WBS uses outputs from project definition and risk management and identifies the tasks that are the foundation for all subsequent planning.

A WBS is a technique for breaking down a project into its component elements. It is a graphic picture of the hierarchy of the project, broken down level by level into subprojects and finally into tasks. It organizes the project by defining all the tasks that must be performed in the conception, design, development, fabrication, and test of the project hardware, software, or service. As the levels become lower, the scope, complexity, and cost of each subproject become smaller, until the tasks that are completely capable of accomplishment are reached. These smallest tasks, called work packages, must be identified as manageable units that can be planned, budgeted, scheduled, and controlled. Work component descriptions often are collected in a WBS dictionary that will include work package descriptions as well as planning information, such as schedule dates, cost budgets, and staff assignments. The WBS indicates the relationship of the organizational structure to the project objectives and tasks, and so provides a firm basis for planning and controlling the project.

The WBS is first and foremost a technical data gathering structure, deployed so that the achievement in technical progress can be measured and analyzed against a formal baseline plan. The WBS aids the customer in understanding the status of the project as time elapses. The WBS aids the customer's customer in understanding the status of the project. All managers, internal and external need to use the planning and status information within the WBS structure to aide in the adjustment to the current program paths and for maximizing the attainment of short-term and long-term goals.

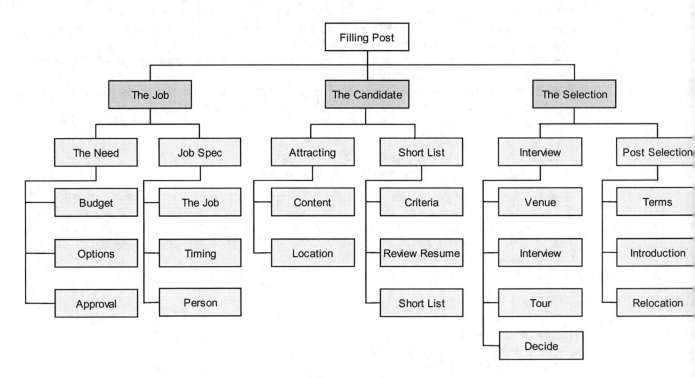

Figure 15 - Sample Work Breakdown Structure

There are no hard-and-fast rules for preparing a WBS; good judgment is the only criterion. However, the size of these work packages is very important because they must be small enough in terms of cost and labor to permit realistic estimates to be made, and to simplify control. Many believe that the "80-hour rule" can be of tremendous help in formulating the WBS and keeping it under control. This rule states that each task should be broken down into work packages that require no more than 80 hours of work for completion. At the end of each 80-hour-or-less period, the work package is reported simply as either completed or not completed. "By means of such periodic check-ins, drifting of a project can be controlled early" (Stuckenbruck, The Implementation of Project Management). Other writers have mentioned the use of other "rules" for work package durations. However, PMI® has used the 80-hour rule in its exam for many years. So be on the lookout for it.

Benefits of Using a WBS
- Builds the project team
- Provides a framework to identify projects separately from organizations, accounting systems, and funding sources
- Clarifies responsibilities
- Focuses attention on project objectives
- Forces detailed planning and documentation
- Identifies specific work packages for estimating and assigning work

Uses of the WBS
- Planning and budgeting
- Funding
- Estimating
- Scheduling
- Performance measurement
- Configuration management
- Integrated logistic support
- Test and performance evaluation

Development of the WBS
- Use Work Breakdown Structure templates
- Decomposition - This requires subdividing the major project deliverables into smaller, more manageable components until the deliverables are defined in sufficient detail to support development of project.
- Identifying the major deliverables of the project, including project management
- Deciding whether adequate cost and duration estimates can be developed in sufficient detail for each deliverable. If not, then identify constituent components of the deliverable in terms of tangible, verifiable results. When adequate detail exists, the last step is to verify the correctness of the breakdown. To do this, you need to determine whether: (1) the lower-level items are both necessary and sufficient for the broken down item; (2) each item is clearly and completely defined; and (3) each item can be appropriately scheduled, budgeted, and assigned to an organizational unit.

You need to understand the Work Breakdown Structure for this exam. PMI® currently emphasizes the product orientation to the work breakdown structure—the deliverable as orientation. Most important, you should know the Work Breakdown Structure is a decomposition of the project work that has to be done. Know how they are numbered and be able to read the numbering system and how it contributes to understanding the project. Also, be aware of the 80-hour rule. Know all of the uses, benefits, and be familiar with the fact that the Work Breakdown Structure contributes to customer communication.

Work Breakdown Structure Templates

All projects are unique; however, many projects are similar at a high level. Organizations that implement similar projects should develop templates to assist in the planning process. A WBS template, a generic definition of project scope, provides an excellent starting point to tailor the specifics of a unique project. Templates should be at a relatively high level and in an automated format to allow for ease of use. Because of the many types of projects that may exist in a single organization, different templates should be created. If tailoring a template requires extensive work, create your own WBS. It may be useful as a template for a later project.

Work breakdown structure templates provide the following:
- A generic structure for elements understood throughout the organization, allowing for consistent communication.
- The ability to ensure that the entire scope for a project is defined by starting with a template that breaks down WBS elements typically found in similar projects.
- A reduction in the amount of time spent developing a WBS.

Decomposition

In order to define the scope of a project, you must decompose the project deliverables. Decomposition is the process of breaking a project into manageable chunks of work, resulting in smaller deliverables that make up the final product. When decomposing a project, you begin with large chunks of work and break them down into smaller chunks so they are easy to plan, manage, and schedule. The lowest level of decomposed item is considered a work package. The following are some advantages to decomposition:
- Estimates for cost, time, and resources are much more accurate.
- The smaller deliverables are more manageable, resulting in fewer changes being made once the project begins.
- Each project deliverable can be clearly assigned to a team member, resulting in a greater level of accountability.

- The project manager can measure team members' performance against completion of these smaller deliverables.
- Control of the project is easier, since you are dealing with smaller pieces of the overall project.

The WBS is decomposed into discrete products and services to be delivered during the project. Higher level elements represent groupings of products and services to be delivered. Decomposition identifies discrete products and services. Elements are decomposed in the following way:
- A discrete product or service is identified
- Responsibility to deliver the product or service is assigned to one individual or functional area
- Scope is clearly understood
- Cost is reasonably estimated
- The element is manageable
- Higher risk or more critical elements are decomposed to a lower level

After the WBS is decomposed to the lowest level, responsibility is assigned to all elements. Assignment at the higher level ensures that management is responsible for the entire project scope. Individuals assigned to the lower level elements are responsible for planning, controlling, and delivering the product.

WBS Dictionary

Once defined, an element's scope is described. This description is often referred to as a "Work Breakdown Structure Dictionary". The purpose of the work breakdown structure dictionary is to clearly describe what scope is to be delivered within each element so that the functional area responsible for delivery can accept it, plan it, and manage the delivery. The work breakdown structure dictionary also provides boundaries and hand-offs between functional areas responsible for delivery. The WBS Dictionary is often a separate document that the WBS references. Senior management within the project reviews and approves the WBS and its supporting dictionary. Those personnel who are assigned responsibility should accept the responsibility to deliver the scope of each element. This step is essential in assuring management commitment to the project.

Scope Baseline

Once the deliverables are confirmed in the scope statement, they need to be developed into a work breakdown structure (WBS) of all the deliverables in the project. The scope baseline includes all the deliverables produced on the project, and therefore identifies all the work to be done. These deliverables should be inclusive. Building an office building, for example, would include a variety of deliverables related to the building itself, as well as such things as impact studies, recommendations, landscaping plans, etc.

Scope Verification

Scope verification is the project management responsibility that focuses on ensuring that the products created during the Project Execution Phase are correct and meet agreed upon requirements. This may sound similar to quality control, but according to the Project Management Body of Knowledge, "Scope verification differs from quality control in that it is primarily concerned with the acceptance of the work results while quality control is primarily concerned with the correctness of the work."

How Is Scope Verified?
The baseline for the creation of any deliverable is the baseline scope plus or minus any agreed upon changes (see the Project Scope Control subsection). Falling short of or going beyond the agreed upon scope will jeopardize the acceptability of the deliverable. Scope verification is achieved through

inspection or formal reviews of the deliverables. Once a project deliverable is accepted by the customer, a formal acceptance document should be drafted and signed stating such.
It is important to understand that scope verification is a component of the project scope variable and that it is also part of the third step in the project management process–executing.

Inspection is the tool and technique used for scope verification and involves activities, such as measuring, examining, and testing that are undertaken to determine whether results conform to requirements. You should be familiar with terms that could be used for inspections, including reviews, product reviews, audits, and walkthroughs.

Accepted deliverables is the output from scope verification. It is documentation that the client or the sponsor has accepted the product of the project, phase, or major deliverable. Recognize that this acceptance may be conditional, especially at the end of a phase.

PMI® wants you to know who verifies the scope and the answer is all the critical stakeholders should verify the scope. All the key stakeholders need to have a voice in determining what the scope is, and what is going to be delivered by the project team.

Scope Control

Scope control is a straightforward concept. The intent of implementing a scope control process is to identify and manage all elements (e.g., people and requirements) inside and outside of the project that increase or decrease the project scope beyond the required or defined need of the original, agreed upon Project Scope Statement. Attributes of Scope Control include:
- Influencing the factors that create scope changes to ensure that the changes are beneficial
- Determining that a scope change has occurred
- Managing the actual changes when and if they occur. Scope changes will come from the perceived need for a change in a project deliverable that may affect its functionality and in most cases the amount of work needed to perform the project. A scope control change is a very crucial occurrence.

Scope Creep

Scope creep is a common project affliction that results from slowly adding more work over the life of the project. These changes are a problem if scope creep is so great that all of the original cost and schedule estimates become unachievable. A clear scope statement enables the project team to realize immediately that extra work is being added. Therefore, a clear scope statement is a beneficial tool to control scope creep.

When combating scope creep, it is important to realize that changes will occur during all projects. The project manager must be aware of these scope changes and compensate for them so they do not have a negative effect on the project's objectives.

Change Control System

A scope change most likely will require additional project funds, resources, and time. Therefore, a committee that consists of stakeholders from all areas of the project should be willing to convene and discuss the potential change and its anticipated impact on the project and the organization. This group of stakeholders should be a predefined cross section of people that will have the ability to commit their interests at a strategic management level. Once a decision is made to increase or reduce scope, the change must be authorized by all members of the committee. Any changes that are agreed upon must be documented and signed as a matter of formal scope control.

In addition, the impact of the scope change will be felt throughout the Planning Phase processes and documents. Documents such as the WBS and Project Schedule will have to be re-evaluated and updated to include the scope change impacts. Scope changes need to be communicated clearly and effectively to the project team by the project manager. Team members will want, and need, to understand how the scope change affects their roles in the project.

The inputs to baseline project scope include documenting the requirements and objective of the project. Sources of this documentation are customer requirements, business case materials, and other documents developed in the planning processes and utilized during Project Execution. They include the following:
- Work breakdown structure
- Performance reports
- Change requests
- Project Scope Statement

A work breakdown structure, as described in the Planning Phase, will organize and help clearly define the total scope of the project. With the successive decomposition of deliverables into smaller work packages, it should serve to develop and clarify a common understanding of the project goals and objectives between stakeholders.

Performance reports, created as part of the Execution Phase, will provide information on scope performance measured against the plan. The resulting variances are reviewed and interpreted to determine if there is a need for corrective action. These reports will also provide information on the progress of interim products and deliverable completion.

Change requests may occur in many forms—oral or written, clear or subtle, internally or externally driven, operation or regulatory requirements, or driven by technology limitations. The problem, as stated earlier, is not that changes occur, but that changes go unmanaged. Changes in scope may be an expansion or reduction in scope of the project. Most change requests in scope are the result of the following:
- An external event
- An error or omission in the original definition of scope of the product (e.g., failure to include electronic funds transfer as a payment option)
- An error or omission in the defining of the scope of the project (e.g., failure to include training in the project implementation)
- A value-adding change (e.g., use of Internet access versus dial-up telecommunications)

The Project Scope Statement includes a section that describes how changes in project scope are to be handled. The Project Scope Statement is normally included as part of the Project Plan. While agencies may have general guidelines, the basic needs of the "Approach" section of the Project Scope Statement should address the following:
- How scope changes will be identified and documented
- How scope changes will be approved and by whom
- How often scope changes will be made and accepted
- The point at which the approval of scope changes must be approved at higher levels

Chapter Review

1. A technique used to validate that the project can meet the required performance and business objectives is:
    A. Cost/Benefit Analysis
    B. Statistical Regression Analysis
    C. Pareto Analysis
    D. Decomposition

2. A high-technology project has been initiated. This project will require the coordination of several different high technology functional areas. What kind of organizational structure would be appropriate for this project?
    A. Functional
    B. Matrix
    C. Strong Matrix
    D. Balanced Matrix

3. Which of the following statements is not true about the WBS?
    A. The WBS indicates when certain activities are to be done.
    B. The WBS is a hierarchical breakdown of the project deliverables.
    C. The WBS represents the entire scope of the project.
    D. The WBS shows both products and services.

4. A work package is:
    A. The code of accounts
    B. The definition of the scope statement
    C. Items at the lowest level of the WBS
    D. Activity that can be assigned to more then one person

5. The baseline may be modified for what reasons? (choose the best answer)
    A. The project manager decides to expand the scope of the project.
    B. A change in a government regulation has occurred which impacts the project.
    C. A change request for enhanced function has been received and approved through the Scope Change Control Process.
    D. b and c.

6. Decomposition involves:
    A. Identifying the major elements of the project.
    B. Deciding if adequate cost and duration estimates can be developed at this level of detail for each element.
    C. Identifying the constituent elements of the deliverable.
    D. All of the above.

7. What is the purpose of the WBS?
    A. To show which work elements have been assigned to organizational units.
    B. To ensure that all work within a project is identified and defined within a common framework.
    C. To show the organizational structure of a program.
    D. To indicate which individuals have responsibility for which work packages.

8. The unique identifiers assigned to each item of a WBS are often known collectively as:
    A. The work package codes
    B. The project identifiers
    C. The code of accounts
    D. The element accounts

9. Change requests can occur due to:
    A. An external event such as a change in government regulation.
    B. An error or omission in defining the scope of the product.
    C. A value-adding change.
    D. all of the above

10. What is the difference between scope verification and quality control?
    A. There is no difference.
    B. Scope verification is primarily concerned with the correctness of work results while quality control is primarily concerned with the acceptance of work results.
    C. Scope verification is concerned with ensuring that changes are beneficial while quality control is concerned that the overall work results are correct.
    D. Scope verification is primarily concerned with the acceptance of work results while quality control is primarily concerned with the correctness of work results.

Answers

1. A, PMBOK® Guide 3rd Edition, page 185
2. C, Multiple, specialized functions will require strong guidance and control from the Project Manager
3. A, PMBOK® Guide 3rd Edition, page 31
4. C, PMBOK® Guide 3rd Edition, page 112
5. D, PMBOK® Guide 3rd Edition, page 121-123
6. D, PMBOK® Guide 3rd Edition, page 114
7. B, PMBOK® Guide 3rd Edition, page 117
8. C, PMBOK® Guide 3rd Edition, page 117
9. D, PMBOK® Guide 3rd Edition, page 109
10. D, PMBOK® Guide 3rd Edition, page 105

Notes

Chapter 6

Project Time Management

Reference Material to Study
- A Guide to the Project Management Body of Knowledge (PMBOK® Guide 3rd Edition), Chapter 6
- Project Planning, Scheduling & Control, Chapters 5-7, Lewis, James P., 1995
- Project Management, A Managerial Approach, Chapters 8-9, Meridith & Mantel
- The New Project Management, Chapter 9, Frame, J. Davidson, 1994

What to Study
- The PMBOK® Guide processes for Project Time Management: Activity Definition, Activity Sequencing, Activity Duration Estimating, Schedule Development, Schedule Control (Be familiar with Inputs, Tools and Techniques, and Outputs for each process)
- Be familiar with the different types of scheduling charts (Gantt, Milestone, Networking)
- Be familiar with the different techniques of networking (ADM and PDM)
- Understand the concept of critical path and how to determine critical path.
- Know how to facilitate recovery through techniques such as crashing, fast tracking, managing slack and overtime.
- Be familiar with the different schedule development tools and techniques in particular: critical path method, schedule compression, what-if scenario analysis, resource leveling and critical chain method.
- Know the concept of the Schedule Performance Index (SPI) and how to calculate it.
- Understand the logical relationships between tasks. (FS, FF, SS, SF, lead, and lag)
- Know what float and total float is and how to determine it.
- Know how to calculate Early Start, Early Finish, Late Start, and Late Finish.

Key Definitions
- **Activity** - An element of work performed during the course of a project. (Normally has duration, expected cost, and expected resource requirements.) Also called a work item.
- **Arrow Diagram Method** (ADM) - A network diagramming technique in which activities are represented by arrows. The tail of the arrow represents the start, and the head of the arrow represents the end of the activity. Activities are connected at points called nodes to illustrate the sequence in which activities are expected to be performed.
- **Backward Pass** - The calculation of late finish and start dates for the uncompleted portions of all network activities. Determined by working backwards through the network logic from the project's end date. The end date may be calculated by a forward pass or set by the customer or sponsor.

- **Bar Chart** - A graphic display of schedule related information. Typically, activities or project elements are listed on the left side of the chart, dates are displayed across the top, and activity durations are shown as date-placed horizontal bars. Also called a Gantt Chart.
- **Baseline** - The original plan plus or minus approved changes.
- **Calendar Unit** - The smallest unit of time used to schedule the project. The unit can be months, weeks, days, hours, minutes, or shifts. Primarily used in conjunction with project management software tools.
- **Concurrent Engineering** - Generally speaking, an approach to project staffing that calls for the implementers to be involved in the design phase. (Sometimes confused with fast tracking.)
- **Crashing** - Taking action to decrease the total project duration after analyzing a number of alternatives to determine how to get the maximum duration compression for the least cost.
- **Critical Activity** - Any activity on a critical path. Most commonly determined by using the critical path method.
- **Critical Path** - A sequence of activities which determines the earliest possible completion (duration) of the project. The critical path is usually defined as those activities with float less than or equal to a specified value (usually zero). It is the longest path through the project. A project may have multiple critical paths.
- **Critical Path Method** (CPM) - A network analysis technique used to predict project duration by analyzing which path (sequence of activities) has the least amount of scheduling flexibility (float or slack). Early dates are calculated using a forward pass; late dates are calculated using a backwards pass.
- **Dummy Activity** - An activity of zero duration used to show a logical relationship in the arrow diagramming method. Dummy activities are used when logical relationships cannot be completely or correctly described with regular activity arrows. Dummies are shown graphically as a dashed line headed by an arrow.
- **Duration** - The number of work periods (not including holidays and other non-working periods) required to complete an activity or other project element. Typically expressed as workdays or workweeks.
- **Duration Compression** - Shortening the project schedule with reducing the project scope. Compression is not always possible and often requires an increase in cost. (Crashing utilizes duration compression)
- **Early Finish Date** (EF) - In the critical path method, the earliest possible date in which the uncompleted portions of an activity or project can complete based on the network logic and any schedule constraints. Can change as the project progresses and changes are made to the project plan.
- **Early Start Date** (ES) - In the critical path method, the earliest possible date in which the uncompleted portions of an activity or project can start based on the network logic and any schedule constraints. Can change as the project progresses and changes are made to the project plan.
- **Event-on-Node** - A network diagramming technique in which events are represented by boxes (or nodes) connected by arrows to show the sequence in which the events are to occur.
- **Fast Tracking** - Compressing the project schedule by overlapping activities that would normally be done in sequence (such as design and construction).
- **Float** - The amount of time that an activity may be delayed from its early start without delaying the project finish date. Float is a mathematical calculation and can change as the project progresses and changes are made to the project plan. Calculated by subtracting LS - ES or LF - EF. Both results should be the same.
- **Forward Pass** - The calculation of the early start and early finish dates for the uncompleted portions of all network activities.
- **Free Float** (FF) - The amount of time an activity can be delayed without delaying the early start of any immediately succeeding activities.
- **Gantt Chart** - A graphic display of schedule-related information using bars. See Bar Chart.
- **Hammock** - An aggregate or summary activity. (A group of related activities is displayed at one and reported at a summary level.)

- **Hanger** - An unintended break in a network path. Hangers are usually caused by missing activities or missing logical relationships.
- **Lag** - A modification of a logical relationship that directs a delay in the successor task. For example, in a FS relationship with a 10 day lag, the successor can start until 10 days after the completion of the predecessor.
- **Late Finish Date** (LF) - In the critical path method, the latest possible date that an activity may be completed without delaying a specified milestone (usually the project finish date).
- **Late Start Date** (LS) - In the critical path method, the latest possible date that an activity may begin without delaying a specified milestone (usually the project finish date).
- **Lead** - A modification of a logical relationship which allows an acceleration of the successor task.
- **Milestone** - A significant event in the project, usually completion of a major deliverable.
- **Milestone Schedule** - A summary level schedule which identifies the major milestones.
- **Monte Carlo Analysis** - A technique that performs a project simulation many times to calculate a distribution of likely results.
- **Near Critical Activity** - An activity that has low total float.
- **Negative Float** - A condition noted in project management software which indicates less than zero float. This condition is usually caused by using imposed dates and is an indication to the project manager that the schedule must be adjusted.
- **Parametric Estimating** - An estimating technique that uses a statistical relationship between historical data and other variables.
- **Path Convergence** - The node in the schedule where parallel paths merge or join. At that node, delays or elongation or any converging path can delay the project. In quantitative risk analysis of the schedule, significant risk may occur at this point.
- **Percent Complete** - An estimate, expressed as a percent, of the amount of work that has been completed on an activity or group of activities.
- **Precedence Diagram Method** (PDM) - A network diagramming technique in which activities are represented by nodes. Activities are linked by precedence relationships to show the sequence in which the activities are to be performed. Also called Activity-On-Node (AON)
- **Resource Leveling** - Any form of network analysis in which start and finish dates are driven by resource management concerns.
- **Schedule Performance Index** (SPI) - The schedule efficiency ratio of earned value accomplished against the planned value. The SPI describes what portion of the planned schedule was actually accomplished. SPI = EV/PV.
- **Schedule Variance** (SV) - 1) Any difference between the scheduled completion of an activity and the actual completion of the activity. 2) In earned value, SV = EV - BCWS. (Budgeted Cost of Work Scheduled)
- **Scheduled Finish Date** (SF) - The point in time work was scheduled to finish on an activity. The scheduled finish date is normally within the range of dates delimited by the early finish date and the late finish date. It may reflect leveling or scarce resources.
- **Scheduled Start Date** (SS) - The point in time work was scheduled to start on an activity. The scheduled start date is normally within the range of dates delimited by the early start date and the late start date. It may reflect leveling or scarce resources.
- **Standard Deviation** (SD) - Calculated as: (P-O)/6 , where O = most optimistic time, P = most pessimistic time
- **Time-Scaled Network Diagram** - Any project network diagram drawn is such a way that the positioning and length of the activity represents its duration. Essentially, it is a bar chart that includes network logic.

The Project Time Management questions on the PMP® exam focus heavily on the Critical Path Method (CPM) and the Precedence Diagramming Method (PDM), and the differences between these techniques. The exam tests your knowledge of how these networks are constructed, how schedules are computed, what the critical path is, and how networks are used to analyze and solve project scheduling, and resource allocation and leveling issues.

The exam may also contain some scheduling exercises. There is a focus on fast tracking as a method to accelerate the project schedule. You must know the advantages offered by networks over bar charts and flow diagrams and understand the two ways in which networks can be represented (activity-on-arrow and activity-on-node). You should also understand the notion of float (or slack) and how it presents challenges and opportunities to project schedulers.

In the PMBOK® Guide, the functions of Project Time Management are separated into six phases: activity definition, activity sequencing, activity resource estimating, activity duration estimating, schedule development, and schedule control. Review PMBOK® Guide figure 6.1.

This knowledge area is concerned with estimating the duration of the project plan activities, devising a project schedule, and monitoring and controlling deviations from the schedule. Collectively, this knowledge area deals with completing the project in a timely manner.

In many cases, all of the activity processes described here along with schedule development are completed as one activity. Sometimes, only one person is needed to complete these six processes, and they're all worked on at the same time. Time management is an important aspect of project management as it concerns keeping the project activities on track and monitoring those activities against the project plan to assure the project is completed on time.

As you go through this section of the exam, you do not want to spend quite as much time as you might anticipate studying the calculations associated with the whole network. Instead, what you want to look at are some unusual relationships—start-start, finish-finish, and lag and lead times, and examining the issues associated with the classical representations of schedules. That includes CPM, PDM, AOA (activity-on-arrow), and AON (activity-on-node).

Activity Definition

The purpose of activity definition is to clarify the main project activities, which are outlined on the work breakdown structure. The purpose of activity sequencing is to arrange activities in a logical order for completion. As you define the project's main activities from the WBS, you should compile those activities into an activity list. The finished activity list then becomes a guide you can use during activity sequencing. Before starting activity definition, you should choose the duration estimating technique you'll use, so you know the detail level of activity definition needed for that technique.

Activity definition and sequencing are important because it ensures that no activity is omitted or left unfinished. It is also important because it includes specifying the order in which activities are to be executed. The primary input to this process is the WBS in which each work package is broken down into the activities that need to be completed to produce the deliverable.

PMI® points out that typically the WBS and the activity list are developed sequentially. The activity list should be organized as an extension to the WBS. Note that as the activity list is developed, the project team may identify missing deliverables or may decide that the deliverable descriptions need clarification. These updates are known as refinements.

Decomposition

Decomposition as it relates to activity definition, is the process of breaking a project into manageable chunks of work, resulting in smaller deliverables called schedule activities. This process (activity definition) defines the smaller deliverables (outputs) as schedule activities rather than deliverables which is done when creating the work breakdown structure.

Rolling Wave Planning

Rolling wave planning is a phased iterative approach to project development, applicable to new product development, information systems and other technical development environments. It is based on the premise that you should only plan in detail as far ahead as is sensible at the time. It is an excellent formal project development approach for inventive work. When done well, it balances structured process with flexibility. It is appropriate for project life cycle models/methods that allow incremental development (spiral, evolutionary prototyping, etc.).

Planning Components

Be aware of the following two planning components:
- **Control Account** – The focal point for planning, monitoring, and controlling tasks. The Control Account represents work within a single WBS element, and it is the responsibility of a single organizational unit.
- **Planning Package** – A future segment of work within a Control Account that is not yet broken down into work packages. A planning package has a firm budget, estimated start and complete dates, and Statement of Work.

Activity List

The activity list must include all activities which will be performed on the project. It should be organized as an extension to the WBS to help ensure that it is complete and that it does not include any activities which are not required as part of the project scope. As with the WBS, the activity list should include descriptions of each activity to ensure that the project team members will understand how the work is to be done.

Milestone List

The milestone list is used to provide a series of indicators regarding project progress to date and achievements or goals yet to be reached. It gives management a clear sense of specific levels of accomplishment (or consumption). The milestone list affords team members the same information, but more as a gauge of their own levels of achievement. The milestone list is generated after the planning process is sufficiently complete that critical process steps have been identified. It is used in management meetings as a simple checklist to clarify which accomplishments have been met and which have not.

Because milestones are binary (either met/complete or not), they present information to management or stakeholder's in a clear, comprehensible form. For team members, milestones provide both a history of accomplishment as well as a set of goals for the future. Every milestone checked brings the project one step closer to fruition.

Project Time Management – CPM & PDM

The exam tests your knowledge of the differences between CPM and PDM. The following notes highlight the individual characteristics of each of the network systems on which you will be tested.

Critical path method (CPM)
- Emphasis on controlling cost and keeping the schedule flexible
- One time estimate per activity
- Activity oriented (float)-activity-on-node

Precedence diagram method (PDM)
A method of constructing a project network diagram using nodes to represent the activities and connecting them with arrows that show the dependencies. This technique is also called activity-on-node (AON) and is the method used by most project management software packages.

PDM includes four types of dependencies or precedence relationships:
1. **Start-to-Start** - relationship in a precedence diagramming method network in which one activity must start before the successor activity can start.
2. **Start-to-Finish** - relationship in a precedence diagramming method network in which one activity must start before the successor activity can finish.
3. **Finish-to-Start** - relationship in a precedence diagramming method network in which one activity must end before the successor activity can start. This is the most commonly used relationship in the precedence diagramming method.
4. **Finish-to-Finish** - relationship in a precedence diagramming method network in which one activity must end before the successor activity can end.

You need to know what CPM and PDM are. Will regards to CPM, you will want to know a little shared of history here–that this came from the 1950s and was part of the Polaris Program was U.S. Navy based and under took the task of trying to launch missiles from submarines. The critical path method (also from the 1950s–remember that for the exam) works on a single data point, but it still works from the activity-on-arrow approach. Finally, the precedence diagramming method, the one you are most familiar with, comes from Stanford University in the 1960s. Know what the different relationships mean: start-to-start, start-to-finish, finish-to-start, and finish-to-finish.

Arrow Diagramming Method (ADM)

This is a method of constructing a project network diagram using arrows to represent the activities and connecting them at nodes to show the dependencies This technique is also called activity-on-arrow (AOA) and, although less prevalent than PDM, is still the technique of choice in some application areas. ADM uses only finish-to-start dependencies.

Leads and Lags

Leads and lags are delays that are imposed in the relationship between the independent and dependent activity. Leads and lags can help to shorten schedules as well as allow for delays between activities. Leads and lags are designated by adding a plus for lags and a minus for leads and the number of periods that the lead or lag adds to the schedule.
- **Leads** - In a network diagram, the minimum necessary lapse of time between the start of one activity and the start of an overlapping activity.
- **Lag** - The amount of time after one task is started or finished before the next task can be started or finished.

Activity on Arrow (AOA)

Activity sequencing concerns the order in which activities are performed and how many sets of activities can be under way at the same time (known as parallel paths). Sequencing is important because we often need to accomplish the project as quickly as possible, yet the schedule we develop must be realistic and achievable. Activity sequencing uses the following types of dependencies:

- **Mandatory Dependencies** (hard logic) - Mandatory dependencies are restrictions specific to an activity. Mandatory dependencies require that one activity be completed before another can begin. For example, when building a house, the foundation must be finished before raising the walls. Mandatory dependencies are static, which mean that they never change.
- **Discretionary Dependencies** (soft logic) - Discretionary dependencies, which are restrictions outlined by the project team, are based on two factors. First, if there are multiple methods of doing an activity, team members choose the best method. For example, if a team has an option to use one of two software programs, they can use the program they think best suits their needs for activity completion. Secondly, if there are many activity sequences, team members pick the one most desirable for achieving the project goals. It is important to use discretionary dependencies only after careful consideration, since they can affect the activity sequence throughout the entire project.
- **External Dependencies** - External dependencies that involve a relationship between project and non-project activities. Examples: testing activity in a software project may be dependent upon arrival of hardware; may need environmental hearings before site preparation can begin on a construction project.

Milestone events also need to be part of activity sequencing so that requirements for meeting the milestones are met. You need to realize that all activities in a network diagram have at least one predecessor and one successor activity, with the exception of the start and end activities. If this convention is followed, then the sequence is relatively straightforward to identify. When you establish a project schedule, you need to compute two schedules: the early schedule, which we calculate using the forward pass; and the late schedule, which we calculate using the backward pass.

Early Start / Forward Pass

The early schedule is simply the earliest time at which an activity can start and finish. These are calculated numbers that are derived from the dependencies between all the activities in the project.

Late Schedule / Backward Pass

The late schedule consists of the latest times at which an activity can start and finish without delaying the completion date of the project. These are also calculated numbers that are derived from the dependencies between all of the activities in the project.

By using these two types of schedules you will determine the window of time within which each activity must be started and finished for the project to complete on schedule; and the sequence of activities that determines the project completion date. The sequence of activities that determine the project completion date is called the critical path. The critical path can be defined in several ways: 1) the longest duration path in the network diagram; 2) the sequence of activities whose early schedule and late schedule are the same; and 3) the sequence of activities with zero slack or float. All of these definitions say the same thing: what sequence of activities must be completed on schedule in order for the project to be completed on schedule.

The activities that define the critical path are called critical path activities. Any delay in a critical path activity will delay the completion of the project by the amount of delay in that activity. This is a sequence of activities that will warrant the project manager's special attention.

The earliest start (ES) time for an activity is the earliest time at which all of its predecessor activities have been completed and the subject activity can begin. The ES time of an activity with no predecessor activities is set to 1, the first day on which the project can begin production. The ES time of activities with one predecessor activity is determined from the earliest finish (EF) time of the predecessor activity. The ES time of activities having two or more predecessor activities is determined from the latest of the EF times of the predecessor activities. The EF of an activity is calculated as [(ES + duration) - one time unit]. The reason for subtracting the one time unit is to account for the fact that an activity starts at the beginning of a time unit (hour, day, and so forth) and finishes at the end of a time unit. In other words, a one-day activity, starting at the beginning of a day, begins and ends on the same day. For example, take a look at the figure below titled Forward Pass Calculations. Note that activity E has only one predecessor, activity C. The EF for activity C is the end of day 3. Because it is the only predecessor of activity E, the ES of activity E is the beginning of day 4. On the other hand, activity D has two predecessors, activity B and activity C. When there are two or more predecessors, the ES of the successor, activity D in this case, is calculated based on the maximum of the EF dates of the predecessor activities. The EF dates of the predecessors are the end of day 4 and the end of day 3. The maximum of these is 4, and therefore the ES of activity D is the morning of day 5.

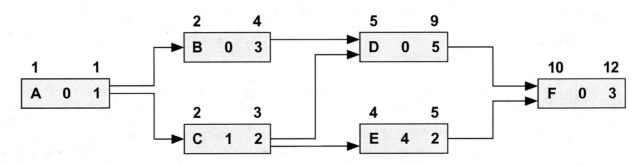

Figure 16 - Forward Pass Calculations

The latest start (LS) and latest finish (LF) times of an activity are the latest times at which the activity can start or finish without causing a delay in the completion of the project. Knowing these times is valuable for the project manager, who must make decisions on resource scheduling that can affect completion dates. The window of time between the ES and LF of an activity is the window within which the resource for the work must be scheduled or the project completion date will be delayed.

In order to calculate these times, you have to work backward in the network diagram. First set the LF time of the last activity on the network to its calculated EF time. Its LS is calculated as (LF - duration) + one time unit). Again, you add the one time unit to adjust for the start and finish of an activity within the same day. The LF time of all immediate predecessor activities is determined by the minimum of the LS, minus one time unit, times all of its successor activities.

Let's calculate the late schedule for activity E. (see image above) Its only successor, activity F, has an LS date of day 10. The LF date for its only predecessor, activity E, will then be the end of day 9. In other words, activity E must finish no later than the end of day 9 or it will delay the start of activity F and delay the completion date of the project. The LS date for activity E will be, using the formula, 9 - 2 + 1, or the beginning of day 8. On the other hand, consider activity C. It has two successor activities, activity D and activity E. The LS dates for them are day 5 and day 7, respectively. The minimum of those dates, day 5, is used to calculate the LF of activity C, the end of day 4. The complete calculation for the backwards pass is shown in the image on the next page.

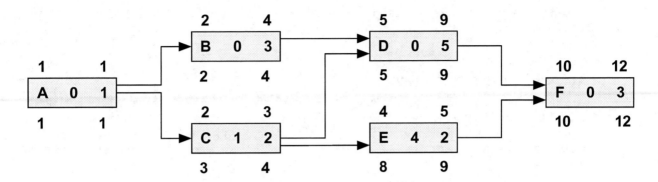

Figure 17 - Backward Pass Calculations

The Critical Path

The critical path is the longest path through the network. But it represents the shortest amount of time in which the project can be completed. Keep in mind that it is possible to have more than one critical path. The critical path drives the completion date of the project. Any delay in the completion of any one of the activities in the critical path sequence will delay the completion of the project. The easiest way to identify the critical path in a network diagram is to identify all possible paths through the network diagram and add up the durations of the activities.

Dummy activities are only required in activity-on-arrow networks and their purpose is to show multiple relationships or dependencies among project activities that otherwise are not in sequence. See the image below for an explanation on figuring the critical path. Dummy activities consume no time or resources; they are present only to show that a dependency exists between two activities. Relationships among activities are "finish-to-start."

Figuring the Critical Path
Using the image below and assuming all duration in days
Path 1:   A-D-H-J   Length = 1+4+6+3 = 14 days
Path 2:   B-E-H-J   Length = 2+5+6+3 = 16 days
Path 3:   E-F-J   Length = 2+4+3 = 9 days
Path 4:   C-G-I-J   Length = 3+6+2+3 = 14 days

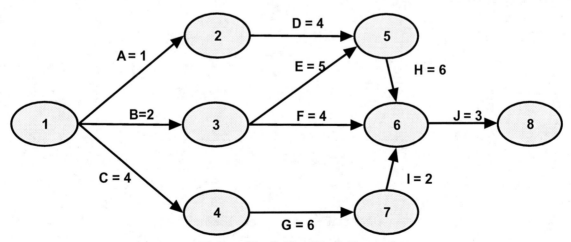

Figure 18 - Critical Path Example

Since the critical path is the longest path through the network diagram, Path 2, B-E-H-J, is the critical path for the project.

Activity-on-node Networks

No dummy activities are required. Activity-on-node networks incorporate lag-which is defined as waiting time between activities in a network; for example, we order something and must wait for it to arrive or we paint something and must wait for it to dry-and lead, which is defined as an acceleration of the successor task. For example, we can clean up after painting; we do not need to wait for the paint to dry.

Slack

Slack (also called float) is the amount of time that a particular activity can be delayed without delaying the project. Activities on the critical path usually have zero slack. Slack is a calculated number and it is the difference between the late finish and the early finish (LF - EF). If the result is greater than zero, then the activity has a range of time in which it can start and finish without delaying the project completion date. There are two types of slack:

- **Free Slack** - This is the span of dates in which an activity can finish without causing a delay in the early schedule of any activities that are its immediate successors. Free slack can be equal to but never greater than total slack. When you choose to delay the start of an activity, possibly for resource scheduling reasons, first consider activities that have free slack associated with them. Notice in the figure below that activity C has an early start (ES) of the beginning of day 2 and a late finish (LF) of the end of day 4. Its duration is two days and it has a 3-day window in which to be completed without affecting the early start (ES) of any of its successor activities. It therefore has free slack of only one day. If an activity's completion stays within the free slack range, it can never delay the early start date of any other activity in the project.
- **Total Slack** - This is the range of dates in which an activity can finish without delaying the project completion date. In reviewing the diagram below look at activity E and notice that it has a free float of four days as well as a total float of four days. If Activity E were completed more than three days later than its early finish (EF) date, it would delay completion of the project. All activities on the critical path must be done on their earliest schedule or the project completion date will suffer. If an activity with total slack greater than zero was delayed beyond its late finish (LF) date, it would become a critical path activity and cause the completion of the project to be delayed.

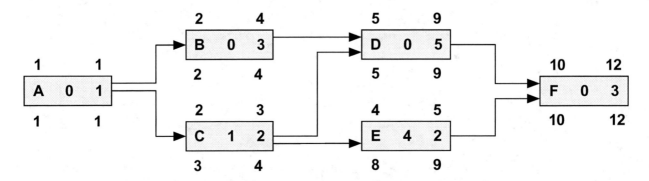

Figure 19 - Critical Path Diagram

Activity Relationships

You must know the definitions of these four terms:
1. **Finish-to-Start** - The finish to start (FS) dependency says that activity A must be completed before activity B can begin. This is the most commonly used relationship in the precedence diagramming method. For example, activity A can represent purchasing paint for a house and activity B can represent the painting of the house. To say that the dependency between A and B is finish-to-start means that once we have finished buying the paint we may start painting the house. The finish-to-start dependency is displayed with an arrow emanating from the right edge of the predecessor activity and leading to the left edge of the successor activity.
2. **Start-to-Start** - The start-to-start (SS) dependency says that activity B may begin once activity A has begun. Remember that there is a no-sooner than relationship between activity A and activity B. Activity B may begin no sooner than activity A begins. Altering the example used previously we could say that as soon as we begin buying the paint for the house (activity A) we may begin painting the house (activity B). We don't need all the paint for the house in order for activity B to commence. In this case there is a start-to-start (SS) dependency between activity A and B. As seen in the illustration below, the start-to-start dependency is displayed with an arrow emanating from the left edge of the predecessor (A) and leading to the left edge of the successor (B).
3. **Finish-to-Finish** - The finish-to-finish (FF) dependency states that activity B can't finish sooner than activity A. For example, painting the house (activity B) can't finish until purchasing all the paint for the house (activity A) is completed. In this case, activity A and B have a finish-to-finish dependency. The finish-to-finish dependency is displayed with an arrow emanating from the right edge of activity A to the right edge of activity B.
4. **Start-to-Finish** - The start-to-finish (SF) dependency is a little more complex than the finish-to-start and the start-to-start dependencies. Here activity B can not be finished sooner than activity A has started. For example, suppose your business organization has adopted a new computer network. You wouldn't want to eliminate the old system until the new system is operable. When the new network starts to work (activity A) the old system can be discontinued (activity B). The start-to-finish dependency is displayed with an arrow emanating from the left edge of activity A to the right edge of activity B as seen in the illustration on the next page.

Task Dependencies

Task dependencies is the nature of the relationship between two linked tasks. You link tasks by defining a dependency between their finish and start dates; For example, the "contact caterers" task must finish before the start of the "determine menus" tasks. There are four kinds of task dependencies.

This material is extremely important and most likely you will see at least six or seven questions relating to this information on the exam.

We will start with activity-on-arrow, which works with activity sequencing. It is always a finish-to-start relationship. Activity A must finish before Activity B can start. In activity-on-arrow diagrams, there are sometimes "dummy" activities.

The critical path is an important element here, and you will have a couple of questions on it. The critical path is the shortest time in which the project can possibly be accomplished. It is also referred to as the longest path through a network. It is the shortest period in which the project can be completed. Thus, it is the longest path through the network.

Activity-on-node networks also allow you the latitude of putting in lag. Know that slack is a synonym for float. However, float and slack are not the same thing as lag. Lag is something we assign when we want a delay. Slack or float describes what the function of a network is. **Memorize the relationships in the task dependency diagram.**

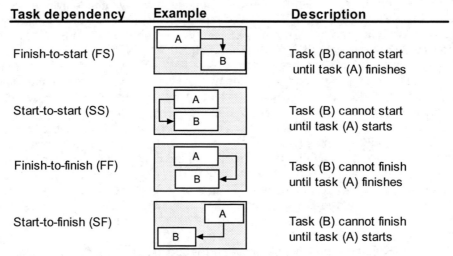

Figure 20 - Task Dependencies

Activity Duration Estimating

When developing a duration estimate for an activity, we are primarily concerned with identifying how many "work periods" the activity will take and its elapsed time. The estimate is based on the following:
- Number of resources assigned
- Capability of those resources to do the job
- Prior results

The person or group that is most familiar with the work should develop, or at least approve, the estimate.

During the estimating process, the project team also must consider information on identified risks. This involves the extent to which the effect of risks is included in the baseline duration estimate for each activity, including risks with high probabilities for impact.

You should be familiar with the tools and techniques used to estimate activity durations:
- Expert judgment
- Analogous or top-down estimating
- Quantitatively based durations: Quantities to be performed for each work category multiplied by the productivity unit rate
- Reserve time (contingency). Note that PMI® states that project teams may choose to incorporate an additional time frame, reserve contingency, or buffer that can be added to the activity duration or elsewhere in the schedule as recognition of the schedule risk. Later, when more information about the project is available, this reverse time can be reduced or eliminated.
- Parametric estimate – A mathematical model that uses parameters, or project characteristics, to forecast project costs.

PMI® recommends that duration estimates always include some indication of the range of possible results (for example, 2 weeks plus or minus 2 days or 85 percent probability that the activity will take less than 3 weeks). This is called range estimating.

Schedule Development

Schedule development is the process by which a project manager incorporates the project's main activities from a network diagram into a schedule. The purpose of project scheduling is to ensure that effective time management occurs during the project and that a project is completed within a reasonable amount of time. During schedule development, the project manager assigns a start and end date to each activity. It is critical to consider such things as activity relationships, activity duration, and resource availability when developing a project schedule.

Critical inputs are the project network diagram and the activity duration estimates. Project calendars (which affect all resources) and resource calendars (which affect only a specific resource or category of resources) must be considered when developing the schedule. Be familiar also with two categories of time constraints: imposed dates and key events or major milestones.

Imposed Dates

A project completion date might be imposed by an outside entity. For example, if a judge orders a landlord to make repairs at an apartment complex, the judge can dictate a date by which time all repairs must be made. If the repairs are not made by that date, the landlord might have to pay fines.

Key Events / Milestones

The second constraint to consider during development is the time frame expectations of project stakeholders. Since stakeholders expect to see progress, it is valuable to include milestones on project network diagrams and schedules. The milestones enable stakeholders to verify that progress has been made.

Other key inputs are the risk management plan and activity attributes, including responsibility and geographic area.

Critical Path Method (CPM)

Critical path method calculates a single, deterministic early start, late start, early finish, and late finish date for each activity (ES, LS, EF, and LF). The dates are calculated based on specified, sequential network logic and a single duration estimate. The focus is on calculating float to determine which activities have the least amount of scheduling flexibility.

Early start and early finish dates for all activities are calculated using a forwards pass. Late start and late finish dates for all activities are calculated using a backwards pass. Float, slack, total float, and path float all refer to the amount of time that an activity may be delayed from its early start without delaying the project finish date. Free float refers to the amount of time that an activity may be delayed from its early start without delaying the early start of any immediately succeeding activities.

Schedule Compression

Both crashing and fast-tracking are ways to speed things up when schedule pressures exist or when the project is falling behind schedule. The focus is always on critical path activities because it is those activities that determine the length of the project.

Crashing

Crashing involves adding more resources to activities on the critical path in order to accomplish the work faster. As you shorten the time, what happens to costs? Often, they go up. It is important to remember that, when you have to crash a project, you must take time to estimate the increased costs and get approval.

The following is the recommended approach to crashing a network:
- Compute the critical path.
- Establish an objective total duration.
- Identify the crash time and crash cost for each activity on the critical path.
- Prioritize the activities on the critical path that can be shortened at minimum cost.
- Shorten the highest priority activity by one time period and compare total duration with objective.
- Verify the critical path.
- Continue activity reduction until crash time is reached.
- Select next priority activity and continue reduction.

Fast-Tracking

Fast-tracking involves analyzing the critical path to see which activities could be done in parallel (as opposed to sequential execution). It also involves more aggressive use of such PDM activity relationships as start-to-start so that subsequent activities can begin before the prior activity has been completed. This overlapping also reduces the project schedule. It is similar to crashing in that it usually requires more resources to make it happen. Fast-tracking often results in rework. This approach usually increases risk, because of the greater coordination required to monitor and control multiple, concurrent activities.

When it comes to these two issues, you need to be able to differentiate between the two besides knowing the process. The difference between crashing and fast-tracking is that crashing compresses the time on given activities on the critical path. Fast-tracking looks at doing activities in parallel. Also, you need to know the difference between fast-tracking and concurrent engineering. Fast-tracking is when you do tasks in parallel. When you do concurrent engineering, you are doing whole phases and tasks in parallel.

Resource Leveling

The goal of resource leveling is to optimize the use of people and equipment assigned to the project. It begins with the assumption that, when possible, it is more productive to have consistent, continuous use of the fewest resources possible. In other words, it seeks to avoid repeatedly adding and removing resources throughout the project. Resource leveling is the last step in creating a realistic schedule. It confronts the reality of limited people and equipment, and adjusts the schedule to compensate.

Let us consider a few of the problems faced by project managers in the process of leveling resources. As you are aware, every project faces the reality of limited people and equipment. The idea is to avoid both over and under allocation.

Project managers need to remember that whether its people or equipment, there are rarely a bunch of spares sitting around waiting to be used. Those over-allocation problems can become especially acute if project managers imagine that they have a large supply of rare resources, such as unlimited time of the only subject matter expert.

The other side of the problem is under allocation. If the project team is not busy on your project, it will likely be reassigned to other projects and be unavailable when the next peak comes.

A further problem arises if people working on this project are also working on several others at the same time. If every project in the firm has wild swings in its resources, it is almost impossible to move people smoothly between projects. Instead, people are yanked off one project to help another catch up, only to be thrown at another that is even further behind.

Project managers must do their best to avoid resource peaks and valleys, and try to use a consistent set of people on the project at a consistent rate. This is not only more realistic, it is more efficient, because every upswing in resources has a cost, whether it comes from procuring additional equipment or transporting new team members to a site. The learning cost can be the steepest. On knowledge projects, the learning curve can be so long that adding additional developers for only a few weeks can actually result in negative productivity.

Resource leveling involves scheduling the project in a way that uses resources most effectively. By using positive float available on non-critical paths through the project, the project planner can arrange a schedule of work that accomplishes the same result in the same time while smoothing or leveling the peaks and valleys in the resources to be consumed. Float, then, is considered a "project resource." Resource leveling generally results in a schedule that is longer in duration than the preliminary schedule. The reason for this stems from the fact that when most people develop a preliminary schedule, they assume that each resource required to complete any activity is available at the early start date, and that the number of resources is also required. Thus, when a resource leveling exercise is undertaken, the actual number of resources, and their availability, is factored into the schedule, which generally results in a schedule that is longer in duration than the preliminary one.

Two types of constrained scheduling techniques are:
1. **Resource-Constrained Schedule** - The network schedule is allowed to change, based on the availability of identified resources.
2. **Time-Constrained Schedule** - The network schedule is fixed. The absence of required resources per activity is indicated by negative float.

Additionally, you should be familiar with the following approaches:
- **Resource-Based Method** - One in which resources are reallocated from non-critical to critical activities in order to bring the schedule back, or as close as possible, to its original intended overall duration.
- **Reverse Resource Allocation** - Used on projects that have a finite and critical project resource that must be scheduled in reverse from the project's end date.
- **Critical Chain** - A technique popularized by Eli Goldratt that is used to modify the project schedule to account for limited resources and to incorporate buffers to reduce schedule risk. Because random events occur that cause some project activities to be late, activity buffers are introduced. They do not solve the problem, so a project buffer is required. Then another problem occurs: paths that feed into the critical path may be late; and this in turn may cause the critical path to be delayed. Feeding buffers now must be used. However, still there may be a problem because a scarce resource may be used by the critical path and by feeding paths. The approach to follow, therefore, is to set up a schedule to allocate scarce resources by an equivalent to the minimum slack heuristic, except that the slack includes all the relevant buffers. The critical chain is the sequence in which the scarce resource activities are processed.

Be familiar with the intended use of each of the following four resource planning tools:
- **Responsibility Assignment Matrix** - Used to identify who does what. A matrix that lists what work must be done on one side and who is responsible for doing it on the other side.

- **Resource Spreadsheet** - Quantifies how much effort is needed from each resource on the project during each time period.
- **Resource Gantt Chart** - Borrows the Gantt chart concept to identify the precise periods of time when a particular resource is working on a particular task.
- **Resource Histogram** - A vertical bar chart that shows the total number of resources needed during each time period of the project. When compared to the number of resources that will actually be available, this planning tool is designed to identify any time periods for which insufficient resources are available. The idea is to work out these problems ahead of time so they do not cause problems or surprise the project manager during the course of the project. When it comes to resource leveling, remember that it is the reduction of the over-commitment of resources. That is what you are trying to do. You are trying to use resources most effectively. Resource smoothing involves roughly the same thing. Leveling involves, easing up on the commitment of resources, and smoothing involves trying to create some equilibrium among resources. In a resource-constrained schedule, leveling means that the network schedule is generally going to be extended. If you are cutting back on your resources' hours, generally it is going to take longer to complete the project. By contrast, in a time-constrained schedule, often leveling will result in a negative float. It will result in us moving out past the schedule due date, which means that we have a negative float. We have to make some kind of network correction to go back and resolve the conflict that is involved.

OBS units \ WBS activities	1.1.1	1.1.2	1.1.3	1.1.4	1.1.5	1.1.6	1.1.7	1.1.8
System Engineering	R	RP					R	
Software Development			RP					
Hardware Development				RP				
Test Engineering	P							
Quality Assurance					RP			
Config. Management						RP		
Integrated Support							P	
Training								RP

R = Responsible organizational unit
P = Performing organizational unit

Figure 21 - Resource Histogram

- **Monte Carlo Analysis** - Monte Carlo Analysis uses the power of a computer to simulate the project outcomes many times. It yields a range of possible outcomes (cost and schedule are usually of particular interest) and provides the probability for each outcome. This process gives a project manager much better information for planning a project. Note that PMI® considers the Monte Carlo Analysis the most popular form of what-if scenario analysis.
- **Heuristic Scheduling** (Rule of Thumb) - Heuristics are rules of thumb or guidelines that have been learned through experience and trial and error. An example of a heuristic is the PERT process, which has modified some statistical approaches to create a simpler but useful scheduling process; for example, the PERT formula for standard deviation is a heuristic (simple to use but yields good results). Heuristics, as defined by Webster's Dictionary, is learning by discovery. It is simple trial and error. We use heuristics in scheduling when we are trying to work from past experience. PERT is a good example of a heuristic, because it looks at the worst case, the best case, and the most likely, and works with those parameters to establish some standard deviation.

Advantages of Scheduling Tools

There are particular advantages to each tool. If you are working with networks, they are going to give you a sense of the relationships between activities–which ones comes first, how they interact, and how they are related. Networks also give you the critical path.

Bar Chart (Gantt Chart)
- Weak planning tool but effective progress reporting tool
- Easy to read
- No logical relationships between or among activities

Milestone Chart
- Shows significant events on the project
- Identifies only scheduled start or completion of major deliverables
- Good for communicating status with customers and upper management
- Milestones have zero duration

Networks (CPM, PDM)
- Show how project activities and events are related
- Identify critical path, project duration, and activity sequences

PMI® tends to think of the Gantt chart as this terrible useful tool, but for the exam you need to be aware that the bar chart or Gantt chart is considered an extremely weak planning tool. It is not a good planning tool, although you may use it every day. It is a fine progress-reporting tool. It works very well for reporting progress but not very well in terms of planning.

Milestone charts are good for the high-level perspective. They show significant events, and remember that a milestone is an activity of zero duration. It has no duration. They may try and trick you into believing that there is some reason you might want a milestone to have some duration.

The best way to know if it is a milestone - could it be expressed in the past tense in one way or another? If it can't–if it involves some activity or some time passing–it is not a true milestone.

Critical Chain Method

The Critical Chain Method (CCM) is an outgrowth of the Theory of Constraints (TOC) developed by Eliyahu Goldratt to scheduling and managing manufacturing. TOC focuses on identifying and fixing bottlenecks in order to improve the throughput of the overall system. Likewise, Critical Chain focuses on bottlenecks. For example, one pharmaceutical company was experiencing significant delays with drug approvals. After investigation, it found that the bottleneck was statisticians to analyze clinical trial data. The cost of hiring statisticians was more than offset by the revenue from getting products to market sooner.

Using the Critical Chain Method, projects can be completed more quickly and with greater scheduling reliability. The difference between traditional and Critical Chain scheduling is in how uncertainty is managed. In traditional project scheduling, uncertainty is managed by padding task durations, starting work as early as possible, multi-tasking, and focusing on meeting commitment dates. The following bullet points illustrate some of the problems associated with traditional project scheduling:
- Padding task durations (providing worst-case estimates) is done to ensure a high probability of task completion. The knowledge that there is so much safety time built into tasks results in various time wasting practices, e.g., waiting until the last moment to complete a task. As a result, all the safety time can be wasted at the start of the task so that, if problems are encountered, the task over-runs.

- Starting work as early as possible, even when not scheduled, is a response to worst-case estimates. When workers give worst-case estimates, they don't expect to stay busy with just one task – so they multi-task, working on several tasks at once by switching between them. The result is that everything takes a long time to complete and very little completes early.
- With the focus on meeting commitment dates (start and finish), output from a task completed early will rarely be accepted early by the next person needing this output. So, any effort spent in finishing early will be wasted. Early delivery of one task can't be used to offset lateness on another. Lateness, however, is always passed on and the lost time can't be made up without cutting the specifications or increasing resources allocated to subsequent tasks, if possible.

In Critical Chain scheduling, uncertainty is primarily managed by (a) using average task duration estimates; (b) scheduling backwards from the date a project is needed (to ensure work that needs to be done is done, and it is done only when needed); (c) placing aggregate buffers in the project plan to protect the entire project and the key tasks; and (d) using buffer management to control the plan. The key tasks are those on which the ultimate duration of the project depends, also known as the Critical Chain. The specific steps to identify and manage a Critical Chain schedule are as follows:

- Reduce activity duration estimates by 50%. Activity durations are normal estimates, which we know to be high probability and contain excessive safety time. We estimate the 50% probability by cutting these in half. (The protection that is cut from individual tasks is aggregated and strategically inserted as buffers in the project.
- Eliminate resource contentions by leveling the project plan. The Critical Chain can then be identified as the longest chain of path and resource dependencies after resolving resource contentions.
- Insert a Project Buffer at the end of the project to aggregate Critical Chain contingency time (initially 50% of the critical chain path length)
- Protect the Critical Chain from resource unavailability by Resource buffers. Resource buffers are correctly placed to ensure the arrival of Critical Chain resources.
- Size and place Feeding Buffers on all paths that feed the Critical Chain. Feeding buffers protect the Critical Chain from accumulation of negative variations, e.g. excessive or lost time, on the feeding chains. This subordinates the other project paths to the Critical Chain.
- Start gating tasks as late as possible. Gating tasks are tasks that have no predecessor. This helps prevent multitasking.
- Ensure that resources deliver Roadrunner performance. Resources should work as quickly as possible on their activities, and pass their work on as they complete.
- Provide resources with activity durations and estimated start times, not milestones. This encourages resources to pass on their work when done.
- Use buffer management to control the plan. Buffers provide information to the project manager, for example, when to plan for recovery and when to take recovery action.

Critical Chain approach is perhaps the most important new development in project scheduling in the last 30 years. Used properly, the Critical Chain approach is an extremely powerful means of gaining more predictability, productivity and speed from your project plans.

Project Schedule

The project schedule provides information regarding the overall project duration as well as each activity's duration. It reflects the project schedule baseline and is used to present that baseline information to team members, management, and the customer. The schedule may consist of a project-length timeline, as well as the specific activity information, including the activities:
- Working duration
- Effort hours
- Elapsed duration
- Earliest possible start date
- Earliest possible finish date
- Latest possible start date
- Latest possible finish date
- Available total float
- Available free float
- Relationships with other activities

As a complete set of project activities it can reflect all of the work in the project. As a subset of those activities, or fragnet (a self-contained subset of a project schedule), the project schedule can reflect a time-sensitive window of project activity.

Schedule Management Plan

Project managers cannot arbitrarily make changes to a schedule. A schedule management plan provides guidelines for project managers to follow when making changes to a project schedule. Schedule management plans are not necessarily formal or highly detailed, but should give enough detail to provide guidance when scheduling changes arise.

Schedule Control

From a time management point of view, time control or project control is about the schedule baseline and any changes that might occur. The schedule baseline is the original, approved project schedule and becomes the standard used to measure schedule performance. The baseline should never be changed without proper review and approval.

Change requests may occur in numerous ways but any approved change should be documented in writing. Changes may either extend or accelerate the schedule. Changes almost always increase the project cost!

Control is a big issue with PMI®, and when it comes to project schedule control, it is the same issue as with project cost control and project scope control. Control is governed by the baseline. You use a schedule baseline, you establish that baseline, and that is the original approved project schedule. Any variance to the schedule is going to be reflected against that schedule. Any change requests are going to be evaluated against that original baseline.

Variance Analysis

Variance analysis is a key tool and technique for schedule control. The general formula for any kind of variance is Plan-Actual. Therefore, if a task was planned to take four days and it actually takes five days, the schedule variance (SV) would be equal to -1 day. If the SV is a positive number, then more work was completed than originally planned up to that point. If the SV is a negative number, then less

work was completed than originally planned up to that point. The earned value formula for schedule variance follows:
- SV = EV-PV or
- SV = BCWP - BCWS
- Where EV is the earned value or the budgeted cost of work performed
- And PV is the planned value or budgeted cost of work scheduled

Comparing target dates with the actual and forecast start and finish dates provides useful information for the detection of deviations and for the implementation of corrective solutions in case of delays. Pay attention to the float variance and to critical and subcritical activities (for example, analyzing the ten subcritical paths in order of ascending float).

Schedule Updates

Sometimes schedules need to be changed or updated to reflect such things as changes in activity sequence or resource redistribution. It is important to keep a project's schedule up-to-date so team members can verify their activity completion times and resource constraints.

A revision is a type of schedule update. Revisions are alterations of a project's original start and completion dates. Most often, revisions are made based on changes to the project's scope. Rebaselining may be required if schedule delays are severe. Use rebaselining only as a last resort for schedule control; new target schedules should be the normal mode of schedule revision.

Corrective Action

Corrective action may be needed as a result of schedule control. This often involves expediting special actions to ensure completion of an activity on time or with the least possible delay. Root cause analysis may be needed to identify the causes of the variation.

Chapter Review

1. If you were crashing a project, you would focus your attention on:
   A. All non-critical tasks
   B. Only those task on the critical path without concern for cost
   C. Accelerating performance for minimum cost increase for all activities
   D. Accelerating performance for activities on the critical path for the least amount of incremental cost

2. Which of the following statements regarding reserve time (contingency) is false?
   A. Contingency may be added to the activity duration or elsewhere in the schedule as recognition of a schedule risk.
   B. Adding reserve time to the majority of the project activities is preferred and recommended.
   C. The reserve time may be reduced or eliminated once more precise information about the project becomes available.
   D. Reserve time should be documented along with other data and assumptions.

3. Schedule variance can be determined by:
   A. BCWP - ACWP
   B. ACWP - BCWP
   C. EAC - ACWP
   D. BCWP - BCWS

4. The project is behind schedule. Which of the following actions should the project manager most likely consider to bring the project back on schedule? (choose the best answer)
   A. Increase the number of daily status meetings and insist that the technical people attend
   B. Focus on all behind schedule activities, including those activities which have not exceeded slack
   C. Focus primarily on critical activities which are behind schedule. Consider alternatives for accelerating performance.
   D. Crash the schedule and fast track the majority of the activities. Worry about cost and risk, later.

5. Fast-tracking is:
   A. Obtaining the greatest amount of compression for the least incremental cost
   B. Doing activities in parallel that would normally be done in sequence to reduce project duration
   C. Completing multiple projects in parallel
   D. Reducing the duration of selected activities by vending out to another organization

6. In crashing the schedule, you would focus on:
   A. Accelerating as many tasks as possible
   B. Accelerating just the non-critical tasks
   C. Accelerating the performance of tasks on the critical path
   D. Accelerating the milestones

7. To calculate the early and late start and finish dates for a set of tasks, you must do:
   A. An analysis of the critical path
   B. A forwards pass
   C. A backwards pass
   D. all of the above

8. An activity that consumes no time or resources and shows only that a dependency exists between two activities is called:
    A. A milestone
    B. A hammock
    C. A dummy activity
    D. A hanger

9. A modification of a logical relationship that allows an acceleration of the successor task is represented by:
    A. Lead
    B. Lag
    C. Slack
    D. a or b

10. What are you likely to see as a project progresses in a schedule with must fix dates and little or no slack?
    A. Lots of free float
    B. Idle resources
    C. Negative float
    D. Positive float

Answers

1. D, PMBOK® Guide 3rd Edition, page 145. Since the intent of crashing is to reduce the total project duration (after analyzing several alternatives) for the least incremental cost, this can best be accomplished in the example by compressing the critical path.
2. B, PMBOK® Guide 3rd Edition, page 142. There's a definite purpose for reserve time; however, using it liberally will inflate the expected cost of the project.
3. D, PMBOK® Guide 3rd Edition, page 173
4. C, Option A seems to be a popular method for handling a schedule performance crisis. The danger (and complaint) is that technical people aren't getting the work done and are often distracted if they are statused to death. Option B is also commonly used especially among managers/project managers who micro-manage. The danger in over-focusing on all activities, not just the critical ones, is that non-critical activities may receive too much attention while critical activities are ignored. Crashing and fast tracking are not always the right answers and often result in increased costs, risks, and rework. These methods should be used after careful consideration.
5. B, PMBOK® Guide 3rd Edition, page 146
6. C, PMBOK® Guide 3rd Edition, page 145
7. D, PMBOK® Guide 3rd Edition, page 145
8. C, PMBOK® Guide 3rd Edition, page 359
9. A, PMBOK® Guide 3rd Edition, page 134
10. C, PMBOK® Guide 3rd Edition, page 145. Adding constrained dates like "must start" and "must finish" to a schedule with no float significantly increases the likelihood that negative float will appear.

Notes

Chapter 7
Project Cost Management

Reference Material to Study
- A Guide to the Project Management Body of Knowledge (PMBOK® Guide 3rd Edition), Chapter 7
- Project Planning, Scheduling & Control, Lewis, James P., 1995, Chapter 10
- Project Management, A Managerial Approach, Meridith, Jack R. 1995, Chapter 7, and Chapter 10, pgs. 457-459
- The New Project Management, Frame, J. Davidson, 1994, Chapters 8-9, 11

What to Study
- The PMBOK processes of Project Cost Management: Cost Estimating, Cost Budgeting, and Cost Control (Be familiar with Inputs, Tools and Techniques, and Outputs for each process)
- Cost Estimates and Ranges: Order of Magnitude, Budgetary, and Definitive
- Earned Value Analysis: EV (BCWP), PV (BCWS), ACWP, EAC, BAC, ETC, CV, SV, CPI, SPI
- Cost Estimating Techniques: analogous (also called top-down), parametric modeling, and bottom-up
- Present Value and Net Present Value
- Straight-Line, Double Declining Depreciation and Sum of Years Digits

Key Definitions
- **Actual Cost** (AC) / **Actual Cost of Work Performed** (ACWP) - Total actual costs incurred that must relate to whatever cost was budgeted within the planned value and earned value in accomplishing work during a given time period.
- **Baseline** - The original approved plan plus or minus approved scope changes.
- **Budget At Completion** (BAC) - The sum of the total budgets for a project.
- **Chart of Accounts** - Any numbering system used to monitor project costs by category (e.g., labor, supplies, and materials).
- **Code of Accounts** - Any numbering system used to uniquely identify each element of the WBS.
- **Contingency Planning** - The development of a management plan that identifies alternative strategies to be used to ensure project success if specified risk events occur.
- **Contingency Reserve** - The amount of money or time needed above the estimate to reduce the risk of overruns of project objectives to a level acceptable to the organization.
- **Control Account Plan** (CAP) - A management control point where the integration of scope, budget and schedule takes place, and where the measurement of performance will happen.
- **Cost Performance Index** (CPI) - The cost efficiency ratio of earned value to actual costs. CPI is often used to predict the magnitude of a cost overrun using the following formula: BAC/CPI = projected cost at completion, where CPI = EV/AC.

- **Cost Variance** (CV) - Any difference between the budgeted cost of an activity and the actual cost of that activity. In earned value, CV = EV-AC.
- **Earned Value** (EV) - 1) The physical work accomplished plus the authorized budget for this work. 2) The sum of the approved cost estimates (may include overhead allocation) for activities or portions of activities completed during a given period, usually from the beginning of the project until now.
- **Earned Value Management** (EVM) - A method for integrating scope, schedule, and resources and for measuring project performance. It compares the amount of work that was planned with what was actually earned with what was actually spent to determine if cost and schedule performance are as expected.
- **Estimate** - An assessment of the likely quantitative result. Usually applied to project costs and durations and should always include some indication of accuracy. (e.g. +/- percent) Usually used with a modifier (e.g., preliminary, conceptual, feasibility)
- **Estimate at Completion** (EAC) - The expected total cost of an activity, a group of activities, or of the project when the defined scope of work has been completed. Most techniques for forecasting EAC include some adjustment of the original cost estimate based on project performance to date. EAC = Actuals-to-date + ETC.
- **Estimate/Estimated To Complete** (ETC) - The expected additional cost needed to complete an activity, a group of activities, or the project. Most techniques for forecasting ETC include some adjustment to the original cost estimate based on project performance to date. ETC = EAC - AC.
- **Fixed Costs** - Costs that do not change based on the number of units. These costs are nonrecurring.
- **Indirect Costs** - Costs incurred by an organization irrespective of the project such as security, personnel and payroll. Costs not directly tied to the project.
- **Life Cycle Costing** - The concept of including acquisition, operating, and disposal costs when evaluating various alternatives. Also known as the total cost of ownership.
- Parametric Estimating - An estimating technique that uses a statistical relationship between historical data and other variables to calculate an estimate.
- **Payback Period** - The number of time periods up to the point at which cumulative revenues exceed cumulative costs and, therefore, the project has turned a profit.
- **Percent Complete** (PC) - An estimate, expressed as a percent, of the amount of work that has been completed on an activity or group of activities.
- **Planned Value** (PV) - The physical work scheduled plus the authorized budget to accomplish the scheduled work.
- **Project Cost Management** - A subset of project management that includes the processes required to ensure that the project is completed within the approved budget.
- **Reserve** - A provision in the project plan to mitigate cost and/or schedule risk. Often used with a modifier (e.g., management reserve, contingency reserve) to provide further detail on what types of risk are meant to be mitigated.
- **S-Curve** - A graphic display of cumulative costs, labor hours, percentage of work, plotted against time. The name derives from the S-like curve of a project that starts slowly, accelerates, and then tails off. Also a term for the cumulative likelihood distribution that is a result of simulation.
- **Schedule Performance Index** (SPI) - The schedule efficiency ratio of earned value accomplished against the planned value. The SPI describes what portion of the planned schedule was actually accomplished. The SPI = EV/PV.
- **Schedule Variance** (SV) - Any difference between the scheduled completion of an activity and the actual completion of that activity. In earned value, SV = EV - PV.
- **Value Engineering** (VE) - Value engineering is a creative approach used to optimize life cycle costs, save time, increase profits, improve quality, expand market share, solve problems, and/or use resources more effectively.

Project cost management includes the processes required to ensure that the project is completed within the approved budget. It is primarily concerned with the cost of the resources required to complete project activities.

A broader view of project cost management is often referred to as life-cycle costing. It involves including acquisition, operating, and disposal costs when evaluating various project alternatives. A creative approach used to optimize life cycle costs, save time, increase profits, improve quality, expand market share, use resources more effectively, and solve problems is called value engineering.

Life cycle costing and value engineering techniques are used together to reduce cost and time, improve quality and performance, and optimize the decision-making. In many application areas, predicting and analyzing the prospective financial performance of the project's product is done outside the project.

In some areas such as capital facilities projects, project cost management includes predicting and analyzing the prospective financial performance of the project's product. In these situations, project cost management will include general management techniques such as:
- Return on investment
- Discounted cash flow
- Payback analysis

Should consider the information needs of the project stakeholders and the different ways and times stakeholders measure project cost. For example, the cost of a procurement item may be measured when committed, ordered, delivered, incurred, or recorded for accounting purposes. When project costs are used as a component of a reward and recognition system, controllable and uncontrollable costs should be estimated and budgeted separately to ensure that rewards reflect actual performance.

The ability to influence cost is greatest at the early stages of the project. Early scope definition and requirements identification are critical to reducing costs in a project.

Life Cycle Cost

The life cycle cost of an item or a system is the total cost of acquiring (designing, producing, installing, testing, and so on), operating, and maintaining that item or system over its entire life, and disposing of the product at the end of its useful life. Some people refer to this idea as the total cost of ownership. Although some of the life cycle costs are normally incurred after the project is complete, PMI® has recently advocated that project teams consider taking any actions that may be necessary to reduce this overall cost of ownership. PMI® also states that life cycle costing and value engineering techniques are used to reduce cost and time, improve quality and performance, and optimize the decision—making process.

PMI® states that predicting and analyzing the prospective financial performance of the project's product often is done outside of the project. In some applications, though, this is part of project cost management. If these predictions and analyses are included, project cost management then includes additional processes and numerous general management techniques including return on investment, discounted cash flow analysis, and payback analysis.

For example, if the project product is a new kind of car, it is possible that the cost of the product life cycle would increase if a decision were made to decrease the number of tests run on the engine of the car. Since fewer tests would be run, customers would probably have to make engine repairs more frequently, resulting in higher costs to operate the product.

Fundamentals of Cost Estimating

Cost estimating is the process of developing an approximation (estimate) of the costs of the resources needed to complete project activities. In approximating cost, the estimator considers the causes of variation of the final estimate for purposes of better project management. Cost estimating includes identifying and considering various costing alternatives.

Where possible, estimates should be done prior to budget request rather than after budgetary approval is provided. Care must be taken to distinguish between cost estimating and pricing, especially for projects performed under contract.

Recognize that cost estimating is not pricing. Cost estimating involves developing an assessment of the likely quantitative result thus determining how much it will cost the performing organization to provide the product/service. Pricing is a business decision which determines how much the performing organization will charge for the product or service. The cost is taken into consideration along with other factors.

Work Breakdown Structure

The PMBOK® Guide indicates that the WBS identifies project activities that will need resources and will, therefore, require expenditures. The WBS also identifies all the work that must be scheduled and that will require expenditures. You will recall that the lowest level of project activity is known as the work package. A cost account or a control account is one level above the work package and is used for monitoring and controlling purposes. PMI® explains that a control account plan (CAP) is a management control point at which the integration of scope, budget, and schedule takes place, and at which performance is measured. CAPs are placed at selected points on the WBS. The chart of accounts is provided to describe the coding structure, used by the organization, to report financial information to its general ledger. Project cost estimates must be assigned to the correct accounting category. The project team should consider the extent to which the effect of risk is included in the cost estimates for each activity.

Chart of Accounts

Once all the cost approximations are complete for a project, these costs must be arranged correctly according to the organization's accounting department. A chart of accounts is a list of codes that are assigned to the various costs of a project. Each individual cost account generally represents a specific work package in the WBS, making it easy to monitor performance on a daily, weekly or monthly basis.

Expert Judgment and Estimating

The tools used in estimating are varied and are all likely to be used on the same project. Some activities can best be estimated using one method, some another. Expert judgment involves the use of people who have an expert understanding of the activity and are guided by historical information. In estimating a previous similar activity is used as a model for estimating future duration. It is a form of expert judgment and requires that the previous activity be truly similar to be accurate.

Analogous Estimating / or Top-Down Estimating

Analogous estimating is based on historical data and comparisons with similar projects within the group or company. Analogous estimating uses the actual cost of a previous similar project as the basis for estimating the cost of the current project. Is frequently used to estimate total project costs when there is a limited amount of detailed information about the project. (e.g., in the early project phases) Generally less costly than other estimating techniques, but it is also generally less accurate. Most reliable when 1) the previous projects are similar in fact and not just in appearance, 2) the individuals or groups preparing estimates have the needed expertise. Considered a form of expert judgment.

Parametric models are often used to extrapolate data from one project to fit another. It is most appropriate to use analogous estimating for top level planning and decision making. This type of estimate is accurate to within -10 percent and +25 percent. It should be noted that analogous estimating is good enough for planning, but not good enough for a final estimate.

Parametric Modeling

This type of estimating relies on knowledge of mathematical relationships between two or more characteristics of a project. Parametric modeling uses project characteristics (parameters) in a mathematical model to predict project costs. Models may be either simple or complex. Simple example of parametric modeling: Model the cost of constructing a residential home based on square footage of living space. A Complex example: Model software development costs using thirteen adjustment factors, each of which has five to seven points. Most reliable when 1) the historical information used to develop the model was accurate, 2) the parameters used in the model are readily quantifiable, and 3) the model is scaleable.

A commonly used statistical technique for modeling such relationships is known as regression analysis. The relationship is graphically represented on a scatter diagram. The regression line on the diagram estimates the average value for the dependent variable corresponding to each value of the independent variable.

A real-world example of a parametric model that sometimes relies on regression analysis is called the learning curve. The learning curve mathematically models the intuitive notion that the more times we do something; the faster we will be able to perform the task. Specifically, learning curve theory says that each time we double the number of times we have done something; the time it takes to perform the task will decrease in a regular pattern. The regression modeling process is able to determine the rate at which the decrease occurs.

Bottom-up Estimating

The bottom-up estimating method is the most accurate of the three methods. It is based on the work package level (lowest level) of the work breakdown structure and requires costing each package or task. Estimates are determined by the person who performs the task and the project manager should contact the person who will actually complete the task and ask him how long it will take to do the task and what the cost will be.

Accuracy of Estimates
PMI® offers the following guidelines for the accuracy of cost estimates:
- Order-of-magnitude estimates are approximations without detailed data, often done early in a project when a "ballpark guesstimate" is needed. Such estimates have an accuracy range of -25 percent to +75 percent.
- Budget estimates are based on slightly better data and are often used to establish initial funding and gain project approval. The range of accuracy is -10 percent to +25 percent.
- Definitive estimates are prepared from well-defined, detailed data. A bottom-up estimate would be an example of a definitive estimate, which is the most accurate (with a range of -5 percent to +10 percent).

Memorize these three types of estimating before taking the exam. When it comes to cost estimating, you can anticipate a number of questions specifically focusing on the idea that the WBS is still the best way to go, and the best tool you have when it comes to cost estimating. Why? Because the WBS supports bottom-up estimate. The WBS is critical to cost estimating because we estimate the activities, how much they are going to cost at the work package level, and then we roll them up to the cost accounts. PMI® also feels that this is the best method.

Analogous estimates are equally important. You will need to know what they are for the exam and that they are referred to as a type of top-down estimate. For the exam, think of analogous estimates as being top-down estimates.

Parametric estimating uses a variety of functions and tools that, in the end, come up with an estimate. Specifically, it is a formula used to express a mathematical relationship between the project and the dollars that are going to be invested in that project.

Accuracy of estimates will show up on the exam. You can anticipate a number of questions associated with the accuracy levels of the different types of estimates. Specifically, what you can expect is order of magnitude estimates to be described as +75/-25 percent.

Budget estimates have a greater accuracy rate: +25/-10 percent. Budget estimates, remember, are also known as top-down estimates.

Definitive estimates are bottom-up estimates. They are the WBS estimates. Definitive estimates have an accuracy range of +10/-5 percent.

Reserve Analysis

The word reserve is often used with a modifier (for example, contingency reserve or management reserve) in order to provide further detail on what types of risk are being mitigated. The PMBOK® Guide defines contingency reserve as the amount of money or time needed above the estimate that reduces the risk of overruns of project objectives to a level acceptable to the organization. For example, rework is certain; the amount of rework is not. Contingency reserves may involve cost, schedule, or both. Contingency reserves are intended to reduce the impact of missing cost or schedule objectives. They are normally included in the project's cost and schedule baselines. Management reserves are separately planned quantities used to allow for future situations that are impossible to predict (sometimes called "unknown unknowns"). Management reserves may involve costs or schedules. They are intended to reduce the risks of missing costs or schedule objectives. The use of a management reserve requires a change to the project's cost baseline. The purpose of a reserve is to reduce the chances of a cost-to-time overrun when risks turn into problems. Remember, in some application areas the definitions of management reserves and contingency reserves are exactly the opposite of those presented above. The important point for test-taking purposes is that you know what a reserve is and why one exists. The risk management plan often includes cost contingency, which can be determined on the basis of the expected accuracy of the estimate so the risk management plan serves as an input to cost budgeting.

Triangular Distribution

Triangular distribution is used only when we know the minimum, maximum and most likely values. It leads to a less conservative estimate of uncertainty. The triangular distribution is useful for stochastic modeling rather than statistical analysis because of its artificial nature. Distribution Formula: Probability (cost < most likely) = (most likely - min) ÷ (max - min)

Basics of Cost Management

The law of diminishing returns identifies a situation in which you are putting more and more of something (dollars, people, and so on) into your project, and then getting proportionately less and less out of it.

Variable versus fixed costs: Variable costs rise directly with the size of the project (for example, the costs associated with skilled labor or materials consumed directly by the project). Fixed costs do not change because you decide to produce fifty more units. Fixed costs are non-recurring expenses associated with putting a production line in place.

Direct versus indirect costs: Direct costs are incurred directly by a specific project and usually include such items as salaries of project staff (project manager and full-time functional experts), materials used directly on the project, subcontractor expenses, and so on. Indirect costs are part of the overall organization's cost of doing business and are shared (allocated to) among all the projects that are under way. These costs include such things as security guards, electricity, fringe benefits, insurance, tax, and in general, anything that would be considered part of overhead.

Depreciation of Capital

When money is spent to purchase capital equipment, there are several ways to write off these expenses from taxable income. The straight-line method takes an equal credit during each year of the useful life of the equipment. There are two methods of accelerated depreciation that are used for writing off the expense even faster than the straight-line approach: double declining balance and sum-of-the-year's digits. You do not need to know the formulas, just their names.

Value Analysis

Value analysis is a cost reduction tool that involves careful analysis of a design or item to identify all the functions as well as the cost of each function. The approach then considers whether the function is really necessary and whether it can be provided at a lower cost without degrading performance or quality. It is also a technique used in product analysis.

Cost Risk and Contract Type

This subject is covered more thoroughly in the section titled Project Risk Management. However, you might see several questions on the exam about which party to a contract bears the cost risk. The idea is simple and you can answer any question on this subject if you know the following:
- With a **fixed-price contract**, the seller is legally obligated to deliver the product or service described in the contract. This requirement holds true even if the contractor spends more money than expected in fulfilling the contract. Therefore, with a fixed-price contract, the seller bears the cost risk.
- Conversely, with a **cost-reimbursement contract**, the cost risk is borne by the customer. This is true because in such a contract the buyer agrees to cover the contractor's costs plus an agreed-upon amount of profit. Also, in such contractual arrangements, the contractor is legally required to provide only its "best effort" in fulfilling the contract deliverables.

For this section know that the seller has the biggest risk in a fixed-price contract. Likewise, in a cost-reimbursement or cost-plus contract, the big risk is going to be borne by the customer.

Cost Budgeting

Cost budgeting is the process of allocating cost to the individual work items in the project. Project performance will be determined based on the budget allocated to the various parts of the project. The result of the cost budgeting process is the cost baseline of the project. The cost baseline for the project is the expected actual cost of the project.

The cost baseline is the output of cost budgeting. It is a time-phased budget that is used to measure and monitor cost performance. Be aware that many projects may have multiple cost baselines that are used to measure different aspects of cost performance. An example is a spending plan or cash-flow forecast that can be used for measuring disbursements.

Cost Baseline

The cost baseline is the basis for the earned value reporting system. It is the budget for the estimated cost of the project spread over the time periods of the project. When managing a project we are concerned about three baselines: the schedule baseline, the cost baseline, and the scope baseline.

The cost baseline is the part of the project concerned with the amount of money that the project is predicted to cost and when that money will be used. The three baselines are closely related, and changes to one of them will result in changes to the others. If a change is made in the project scope baseline, either by adding or removing some of the work that is required, the schedule baseline and the cost baseline will probably have to be changed as well.

Cost Management Plan

A cost management plan is developed to provide guidelines for the project manager to follow when dealing with cost variances. The amount of detail included in a cost management plan is dependent on the needs of the project stakeholder. The plan should outline steps that need to be taken if the actual project costs are higher or lower than the approved project budget.

To make a cost management plan useful, the accumulated costs of the project must always be available by looking at the cost baseline, which is displayed as an S-curve. The project stakeholders can then compare the approved budget to the cost baseline to determine if the project costs are on target.

Cost Control

Cost control involves identifying when changes have been made to the cost baseline and managing those changes. In addition, cost control includes monitoring factors that cause changes to the cost baseline, as well as influencing those changes so that they are beneficial to the project.

Cost control is heavily related to other project variables and should be considered in conjunction with other control components, such as schedule control. For example, making changes based on cost variances can result in changes to the project schedule. Inappropriate responses to cost variances can cause quality or schedule problems or produce an unacceptable level of risk later in the project. An important part of cost control is to determine what is causing the variance and to decide whether the variance requires corrective action.

Cost Change Control System

Defines the procedures by which the cost baseline may be changed and is maintained in the cost management plan. It includes the forms and any necessary documentation necessary for authorizing changes.

Earned Value Management (EVM)

Comparing planned cash flow with actual cash flow has its uses, but it does not tell you whether the project will be over or under budget. To get the true picture of cost performance, the planned and actual costs for all completed tasks need to be compared. This is accomplished with a technique called earned value management. Earned value management uses cost data to give more accurate cost and schedule reports. It does this by combining cost and schedule status to provide a complete picture of the project. For example, projects can be ahead of schedule (good) but over budget (bad). Alternatively, they can be ahead of schedule (good) and under budget (good).

All EVM control account plans must continuously measure project performance by relating three independent values: the planned value, the earned value, and the actual costs incurred.

Planned Value (PV) = portion of approved cost estimate planned to be spent on the activity in a given period.

Question	Answer	Acronym
How much should be done?	Planned Value	PV
How much work is done? This is the actual earned value of the project, because it is the value of the work that has been completed.	Earned Value	EV
How much work did the "is done" work cost?	Actual Cost	AC
What was the total job supposed to cost?	Budget at Completion	BAC
What do we now expect the total job to cost? This is a re-estimate of the total project budget. It's a way of saying that if current cost performance trends continue, the final cost can be predicted.	Estimate at completion	EAC

Planned Value (PV) = portion of approved cost estimate planned to be spent on the activity in a given period.
Actual Cost (AC) = total of costs incurred in accomplishing work on the activity during a given period.
Earned Value (EV) = value of work actually completed. Interpretation of EV: "Task A, which I was supposed to complete today, is scheduled to cost $1,000. I have completed only 85 percent of this task. Thus, I have completed $850 worth of work, which is my earned value (EV)."

Cost Variance (CV)

Recalculating the estimated cost at completion using earned value implies that current trends will continue. Nevertheless, be careful not to assume that just because you are over budget now, you will be granted more money for your budget. Instead, the cost variance (CV) should be used as a warning flag to help you identify problems early, when there is still time to get back on track.

Interpretation of CV: "I have done $850 worth of work (EV), but it actually cost me $900 to do this (AC). It has cost me $50 more to do what I have done than I originally thought (CV)."
    Cost Variance (CV) = EV - AC
    CV = BCWP - ACWP

Schedule Variance (SV)

Is the project on schedule? This is a question that all stakeholders want answered. However, it can be difficult to measure the degree to which a project is ahead or behind schedule. What if the majority of tasks are on schedule, but a few are ahead of schedule and others are behind? What is the accurate description of this project's schedule status? In this kind of situation, earned calculations can help measure schedule variances (SV) just as they help measure cost variances (CV). Interpretation of SV: "As of today, I was supposed to have done $1,000 worth of work on Task A (PV). I have actually done $850 worth of work (EV). Thus, I am behind in my schedule by $150 worth of work (SV)."

Using the cost figures as the basis for schedule measurement is useful because it takes into account the number and size of tasks that are behind schedule. In other words, if ten concurrent tasks, each worth $25,000, are all one week behind schedule, the scheduled variances will be larger than if only one of those tasks is one week behind schedule.
Schedule variance (SV) = EV - PV

The formulas for cost variance (CV) and schedule variance (SV) will yield either a positive or negative numeric value. If the value is positive, then the project is under budget and ahead of schedule; if negative, then the project is over budget and behind schedule.

It is common to have a negative cost variance (i.e., to be over budget) and to have a positive schedule variance. This means that although you have overspent at that point, you are ahead of schedule. So the project is not necessarily in trouble. It may mean that you were able to begin some tasks sooner than planned.

Cost Performance Index (CPI)

CPI is the relationship between actual costs expended and the value of the physical work performed and is widely used as a forecasting tool because it is very accurate. Once a project is roughly 20 percent complete, the total CPI for a project generally does not change by more than 10 percent. Therefore, CPI gives the project team and stakeholders a quick and reliable estimate of final project costs.

Interpretation of CPI: "I have done $850 worth of work (EV). It has cost me $900 to do so (AC). Each dollar I actually spent generated 94.4 cents worth of work (cost performance factor)."
  CPI = EV ÷ AC / CPI = BCWP ÷ ACWP

Schedule Performance Index (SPI)

SPI is the relationship between the value of the initial planned schedule and the value of the physical work to be performed. Interpretation of SPI: "I have done $1,500 worth of work (EV). The value of work scheduled is $1,000. Each dollar of scheduled work generated $1.50 worth of work (schedule performance factor).
  SPI = EV ÷ PV / SPI = BCWP ÷ BCWS

To interpret CPI and SPI: if they are equal to 1, then the project is on budget and schedule; if the equation equals less than 1, then the project is over budget and behind schedule; if the equation is greater than 1, then the project is under budget and ahead of schedule.

CPI and SPI provide the same information as CV and SV whether the project is on budget and schedule – but in a decimal format. For instance a CPI of 0.85 means that for every dollar spent, you have generated 85 cents of worth or work. This is a much more meaningful measure and is very good for use in status reports.

Estimate to Complete (ETC)

The estimate to complete (ETC) is the amount of money needed to fund the project to completion. The estimate to complete (ETC) is a useful calculation because it tells the project manager how much money will be needed to complete the project. It is especially useful within small companies because it provides an estimate of cash-flow requirements for the project's remaining life.
 ETC = EAC – AC / ETC = EAC - ACWP

Estimate at Completion (EAC)

What do we now expect the total job to cost? The EAC is a forecast of most likely total project costs based on project performance and quantitative risk analysis.

The PMBOK® Guide provides three formulas for computing EAC:

Formula	When Used
EAC = AC + (Remaining PV ÷ CPI)	Use when current variances are seen as typical of future variances
EAC = AC + ETC	Use when past performance shows original estimates were fundamentally flawed or are no longer relevant because of a change in conditions
EAC = AC + Remaining AC	Use when current variances are seen as a typical

Another formula that may appear on the exam, and is not included in the PMBOK® Guide, is:
EAC = BAC ÷ CPI

Variance at Completion (VAC)

Compares what the total job is supposed to cost - Budget at Completion (BAC) to what the total job is expected to cost - Estimate at Completion (EAC). Variance at Completion (VAC) is calculated as:
BAC - EAC = VAC

BAC and VAC

Budget at completion, or BAC, is the estimated total cost of the project finished, which is generally calculated before a project begins. The BAC is calculated by assigning together all individual BCWS calculations for each portion of a project. Another name for BAC is the "baseline."

Variance at completion, or VAC, indicates a deviation from the budget at completion, which was projected before the project began. When finding the estimate at completion, or the total estimated cost for a project once the project is partially complete, you should determine the VAC using the following equation: VAC = BAC – EAC

Determining the VAC helps indicate any significant cost variances that should be reported to project stakeholders. If the variance is great enough, the project manager should consult the team's cost management plan in order to take the correct cost control measures.

The 50-50 Rule of Progress Reporting

The 50-50 rule was established to overcome the problem of making subjective estimates (for example, estimating how far along we are on a task).

When beginning a task, charge 50 percent of its PV to its account. When the task is finally completed, charge the remaining 50 percent to its account. Variations of the 50-50 Rule include:
- 20 - 80 rule: More conservative
- 0 - 100 rule: Most conservative. The assumption here is that a task does not have value until it is completed.

Revised Cost Estimates

These are adjustment and/or updates to the cost information portion of the project. They differ from budget updates, which are a special category of revised cost estimates. Budget updates are changes to an approved cost baseline and generally are revised only in response to scope changes. In some cases, cost variances may be so severe that re-baselining is required to provide a realistic measure of performance.

Specifically with this section you need to be comfortable with the following three components:
- Budget cost of work performed (BCWP): How much is the work that has been worth? How much money was planned to spend on the work that has been done so far?
- Budgeted cost of work scheduled (BCWS): What is the budget that was set aside as of today or up to this point in time – the budgeted cost for the work scheduled as of today?
- Actual cost of work performed (ACWP): What is the actual cost of the work performed? How much has been spent for the work that has been accomplished.

Chapter Review

1. If the schedule variance is negative, then:
   A. We have shortened the critical path.
   B. We are running the project in "fast track" mode.
   C. The cost has increased for critical path elements.
   D. We need more information to determine the cause of the variance.

2. You have calculated both the cost variance and schedule variance on your project and have found that they are exactly the same; -$200. This indicates that:
   A. The value of the work completed is equal to the value of the work scheduled.
   B. The actual cost of work completed is $200 less than the value of the work scheduled.
   C. The value of the work scheduled is equal to the actual cost of the work completed.
   D. The value of the work scheduled is equal to the value of the work completed.

3. Which of the following is not a key input to cost budgeting?
   A. Activity cost estimates
   B. Project scope statement
   C. Work breakdown structure
   D. Project management plan

4. The cost change control system:
   A. Should not be integrated with the integrated change control system.
   B. Compensates for inaccurate project cost estimates.
   C. Defines the procedures by which the cost baseline may be changed.
   D. Describes how cost variances will be managed.

5. The payback period of an investment is:
   A. The period of time required for the cash income to equal to the original investment plus the required investment margin.
   B. The period of time required for the cash income to equal the original investment.
   C. The period of time required for the original investment to return an amount equal to the cost of capital.
   D. The period of time required for the original investment to return an amount equal to the original investment less applicable taxes and depreciation.

6. When using Earned Value Management, the difference between what has been accomplished and what was scheduled is called the:
   A. Cost Variance
   B. Schedule Variance
   C. Projected Variance at completion
   D. Labor Variance

7. During the six month update on a 1 year, $50,000 project, the analysis shows that the PV is $25,000; the EV is $20,000 and the AC is $15,000. What can be determined from these figures?
   A. The project is behind schedule and over cost.
   B. The project is ahead of schedule and under cost.
   C. The project is ahead of schedule and over cost.
   D. The project is behind schedule and under cost.

8. For a project with original assumptions that are no longer relevant to a change in conditions, Estimated at Completion is most likely determined by which technique?
    A. ETC + AC
    B. AC + BAC - EV
    C. AC + (BAC - EV)/CPI
    D. ETC + EV

9. Which of the following statements concerning bottom-up estimating is true?
    A. The cost and accuracy of bottom-up estimating is driven by the size of the individual work items.
    B. Smaller work items increase both cost and accuracy of the estimating process.
    C. Larger work items increase both cost and accuracy of the estimating process.
    D. A and B

10. A Reserve is generally intended to be used for:
    A. Rework activities.
    B. Compensate for inaccurate project cost estimates.
    C. Reducing the risk of missing the cost or schedule objectives.
    D. Compensate for inaccurate project schedule estimates.

Answers

1. D, Schedule variance = EV - PV. If the variance is negative then PV > EV. This just tells us that the project is behind schedule, but not the reason for the delay.
2. C, SV = EV - PV and CV = EV - AC If SV = CV, then PV = AC since EV is the common variable in both equations.
3. D, PMBOK® Guide 3rd Edition, page 167
4. C, PMBOK® Guide 3rd Edition, page 167
5. B, This is the standard definition of Payback Period.
6. B, PMBOK® Guide 3rd Edition, page 173
7. D, PMBOK® Guide 3rd Edition, page 173
8. A, PMBOK® Guide 3rd Edition, page 173
9. D, PMBOK® Guide 3rd Edition, page 165
10. C, PMBOK® Guide 3rd Edition, page 166

Notes

Chapter 8

Project Quality Management

Reference Material to Study
- A Guide to the Project Management Body of Knowledge (PMBOK® Guide 3rd Edition), Chapter 8
- Quality Management for Projects and Programs, Ireland, Lewis R., 1991

What to Study
- The PMBOK® phases of Project Quality Management: Quality Planning, Perform Quality Assurance, and Perform Quality Control (be familiar with Inputs, Tools and Techniques, and Outputs for each phase)
- Know the difference between quality and grade
- Know the difference between Quality Control and Quality Assurance
- Project characteristics and attributes (Ireland, Chapter II)
- Cost of Quality (Ireland, Chapter IV)
- Statistical Concepts and Quality Tools (Ireland, Chapter V)
- Cost Trade-offs
- Know the difference between the ISO 9001 Certification and the Malcolm Baldrige Award.
- Know the difference between the Deming, Juran, and Crosby Management approaches
- Pareto and Fishbone diagrams

Key Definitions
- **Control** - The process of comparing actual performance with planned performance, analyzing variances, evaluating possible alternatives, and taking appropriate corrective action as needed.
- **Control Charts** - A graphic display of the results, over time and against established control limits, of a process. The charts are used to determine if the process is in control or in need of adjustment.
- **Corrective Action** - Changes made to bring expected future performance of the project in line with the plan.
- **Cost of Conformance** - The cost of conforming to Specifications, Planning, Training, Control, Validation, Test, and Audits.
- **Cost of Nonconformance** - The cost of not conforming is Scrap, Rework, Additional Work, Warranty, Complaint Handling, Product Recall, and Expediting.
- **Cost of Quality** - The cost incurred to ensure quality. Includes quality planning, quality control, quality assurance, and rework.

- **Grade** - A category or rank used to distinguish items that have the same functional use (e.g., "hammer"), but do not share the same requirements for quality (e.g., different hammers may be built to withstand varying degrees of force)
- **Monitoring** - The capture, analysis, and reporting of project performance, usually as compared to plan.
- **Monte Carlo Analysis** - A technique that performs a project simulation many times to calculate a distribution of likely results.
- **Pareto Diagram** - A histogram ordered by frequency of occurrence that shows how many results were generated by each identified cause.
- **Pareto's Law** - A supposition that states that a relatively small number of causes will typically produce a large majority of the problems or defects. Commonly referred to as the 80/20 principle in which 80% of the problems can be attributed to 20% of the causes.
- **Performance Reporting** - Collecting and disseminating information about project performance to help access project progress. Includes status reporting, progress measurement, and forecasting.
- **Project Quality Management** - The processes required to ensure that the project will satisfy the needs for which it was undertaken. Modern quality management complements modern project management in that both recognize the importance of customer satisfaction and prevention over inspection.
- **Quality** - The totality of characteristics of an entity that bear on its ability to satisfy stated or implied needs.
- **Quality Assurance** (QA) - 1) The process of evaluating overall project performance on a regular basis to provide confidence that the project will satisfy the relevant quality standards. 2) The organizational unit that is assigned responsibility for quality assurance.

The quality management process is the application of quality theory, methods, and tools to focus on customer requirements and to manage work processes with the objective of achieving continuous improvements or radical redesign.

Quality management includes "all activities of the overall management function that determine the quality policy, objectives, and responsibilities and implements them by means such as quality planning, quality assurance, quality control, and quality improvement, within the quality system." The image below depicts a high-level quality project management process.

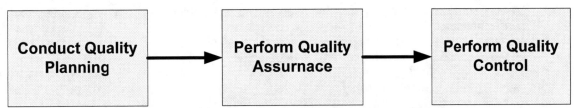

Figure 22 - The Quality Project Management Process

The purpose of using quality management is to improve products and services while achieving cost reductions throughout the project. Quality management requires broadening the scope of the quality concept to a systems approach. Many advocates of quality management will say that quality is an attitude or way of life that transforms the culture of an organization to one that emphasizes continuous quality improvement.

Because the three processes depicted in the figure above interact with each other, as well as other processes within project management, quality management must be regarded as a system.

"Quality Planning" involves identifying which quality standards are relevant to the project and determining how to satisfy them. The activities within the quality planning process basically translate existing quality policy and standards into a Quality Plan through a variety of tools and techniques.

"Quality Assurance" is the evaluation of overall project performance on a regular basis to provide confidence that the project will satisfy the relevant quality standards. It utilizes quality audits to ensure that quality standards ®and customer requirements are met.

Quality control involves monitoring specific project results to determine if they comply with relevant quality standards and identifying ways to eliminate causes of unsatisfactory performance.

Successful quality processes always strive to see quality through the eyes of the customer. Customers are the ultimate judge of the quality of the product they receive. They will typically judge a project by whether or not their requirements are met. To ensure delivery of a quality product, the project team should ensure that requirements are addressed at each phase of the project.

It is important to include a process that validates that the currently defined requirements will be satisfactory to the customer. It is counterproductive to develop a system that meets a documented requirement if you and the customer know that the requirement has changed. The change management process helps to control the number of such changes, but quality processes must be in place in order to make changes when they are necessary.

Every project member needs to buy in to the responsibility for producing a quality product. Through ownership of the organization's quality policy, the individual team members become the most effective way to implement quality into products efficiently and completely. A quality policy cannot rely on adding quality at the end of a process; quality must be built into the work of each individual on the team. It is far more cost-effective to have team members add quality into their day-to-day jobs than to have a quality analyst find a problem after a process has been completed.

Project quality management includes the processes required to ensure that the project will satisfy the needs for which it was undertaken. It also includes all activities of the overall management function that determine the quality policy, objectives, and responsibilities and implements these by means such as quality planning, perform quality assurance, perform quality control, and quality improvement within the quality system.

Project quality management must address both the management of the project and the product or service of the project. Failure to meet quality requirements in either dimension can have serious negative consequences for the project stakeholders. For example:
- Meeting customer requirements by overworking the project team may produce negative consequences in the form of increased employee attrition.
- Meeting project schedule objectives by rushing planned quality inspections may produce negative consequences when errors go undetected.

Modern quality management complements project management. For example, both disciplines recognize the importance of:
- Customer satisfaction understanding, managing, and influencing needs so that customer expectations are met. This requires a combination of conformance to requirements and fitness for use. (the product/service must satisfy real needs)
- Management responsibility - success requires the participation of all members of the team, but it remains the responsibility of management to provide the resources needed to succeed.
- Processes within phases - the repeated plan-do-check-act cycle described by Deming and others is highly similar to the Project Management Processes. (Described in Chapter 3 of the PMBOK® Guide.)

The Project Quality Management questions on the PMP® exam are straightforward. The exam reflects the current emphasis on customer satisfaction and continuous improvement through quality tools such as Pareto analysis and cause-and-effect diagrams. You must know the difference among quality planning, performing quality assurance, and performing quality control.

PMBOK® Guide includes all quality-related activities under the term Project Quality Management, which compromise the three quality processes mentioned above. Review PMBOK® Guide figure 8.1 for an overview of the Project Quality Management structure.

The Project Quality Management knowledge area assures that the project meets the requirements that the project was undertaken to produce. These processes measure overall performance, monitor the project's results, and compare them to the quality standards set out in the project planning process to assure that the customer will receive the product or service they thought they purchased.

Project Quality Management is composed of the following three processes:
- **Quality Planning** - involves defining quality standards and deciding how to achieve them.
- **Perform Quality Assurance** - consists of measuring project progress to ensure the product meets quality standards.
- **Perform Quality Control** - involves supervising project activity completion and correcting any errors.

The purpose of quality management during the project management process is to identify customers' needs, to develop goals based on those needs, and to identify factors that impede achievement of project goals. Another aim of quality management is to keep a project on schedule, which helps avoid sacrificing quality in the interest of time and cost.

Before beginning a project, it is important for you the project manager to have a solid understanding of quality management and how its components are integrated into the project management process.

The components of quality management fit into these steps of the project management process:
- Quality planning is part of the planning step of the project management process.
- Quality improvement is part of the executing step of the project management process.
- Quality control is part of the controlling step of the project management process.

The PMBOK® Guide defines quality as the totality of characteristics of an entity that bears on its ability to satisfy stated or implied needs.

Stated and implied needs are the inputs to developing project requirements. A critical aspect of quality management in the project context is turning implied needs into requirements through Project Scope Management.

It is important to recognize the difference between quality and grade. Grade is a category or rank given to entities having the same functional use but different technical characteristics. Low quality is always a problem; low grade may not be. For example:
- A software product may be of high quality (very few defects, a readable user's manual) but of low grade meaning it has a limited number of features.
- Or, a software product may be of low quality but of high grade meaning it has many defects but lots of customer features.

The project manager and team must determine and deliver the required levels of quality and grade.

One important area that is emphasized in the PMBOK® Guide is the growing attention to customer requirements as the basis for managing quality. Another concept that may appear on the test, which is not specifically mentioned in the PMBOK® Guide, is "gold-plating." Simply defined, gold-plating gives the customer more than what was required. Exceeding the specified requirements is a waste of time and money, with no value added to the project. The customer should expect and receive exactly what was specified. This is the underlying philosophy of project quality management espoused by PMI®; it is the process required to ensure that the project will satisfy the needs for which it was undertaken.

Quality Management

The PMBOK® Guide definition is similar to Philip Crosby's definition in Quality is Free (Mass Market Paperbacks, 1979). Quality management includes all activities of the overall management function that determine the quality policy, objectives, and responsibilities, and implements them by means such as quality planning, quality assurance, quality control, and quality improvement within the quality system. Quality management involves carrying out a project through its phases (for example, concept, development, implementation, and finish) with zero deviations from the project specifications. Policies, plans, procedures, specifications, and requirements are attained through the sub-functions of quality assurance and quality control.

Pioneers of Quality Management

Traditional quality performance standards were based on the assumption that defects and errors are inevitable. The following pioneers of quality management practices believed that defects and errors could be predicted and eliminated before taking root:

Dr. W. Edwards Deming

Dr. Deming theorized that when correcting problems, managers made changes to a project 85 percent of the time, and that 15 percent of the problems that occurred were errors that team members could fix or avoid. The Deming Cycle for Improvement calls for project planning, team member training, efficient activity execution, verification that activities meet project goals, and documentation of lessons learned. This is known as Deming's Four Step Cycle for Improvement: Plan, Do, Check, Act

Deming's Major Points for Implementing Quality
Participative approach   Adopt new philosophy
Cease mass inspection   End awards based on price
Improve production and service   Institute leadership
Eliminate numerical quotas   Education and training
Encourage craftsmanship

Dr. Joseph M. Juran

Dr. Juran developed what is called the Juran Trilogy, which emphasizes quality improvement, quality planning, and quality control. In addition to this trilogy, Dr. Juran is known for his Ten Steps to Quality Improvement. He recognized the importance of products being fit for customers' use and was concerned with the legal side of quality standards.

Phillip B. Crosby

Phillip Crosby assembled what he called the 14 Steps to Quality Improvement. He also developed Four Absolutes of Quality: a product must measure up to all requirements, error prevention is key to high quality, all projects should strive for "zero defects," and activities should be done correctly the first time.

Fourteen Steps to Improving Quality
1. Management commitment
2. Quality improvement team
3. Measurement
4. Cost of quality
5. Quality awareness
6. Corrective action
7. Zero defects planning
8. Employee education
9. Zero defects day
10. Goal setting
11. Error cause removal
12. Recognition
13. Quality councils
14. Do it over again

Four absolutes of quality management
1. Quality is conformance to requirements
2. The system of quality is prevention
3. The performance standard is zero defects
4. The measurement of quality is the price of nonconformance

Awards for Quality Management Practices

Awards for quality management are incentives for companies to excel at providing quality products and services. Awards, sometimes created by government agencies, encourage companies to implement strict quality standards. Two awards for exceptional quality management practices include:

The Malcolm Baldrige National Quality Award

The Malcolm Baldrige National Quality Award, which was established with the Malcolm Baldrige National Quality Improvement Act of 1987. This Act promotes company knowledge of quality management practices, and the award recognizes quality-related accomplishments. Covers the following seven categories: leadership, information and analysis, strategic quality planning, human resources, quality assurance, results and customer satisfaction.

The Deming Award

The Deming Award was established by the Union of Japanese Scientists and Engineers. The Union of Japanese Scientists and Engineers bestow the Deming Award based on such things as a company's quality and management policy, organization, policy implementation, and problem-solving capabilities.

Quality Planning

Quality planning involves defining the quality standards for a project and deciding how to achieve those standards. The scope statement is used as a point of reference during quality planning because it outlines not only the end results of a project, but also the project objectives, which should be in-line with the stakeholder expectations.

An important part of quality planning involves making sure quality is part of a product's design from the beginning of a project, since quality cannot be infused into a product through inspection. Remember that the result of the quality planning process is the quality plan. Also remember a fundamental principle from Deming is that "quality should be planned in, not inspected in."

Therefore, although inspection is certainly part of project quality management, increased inspection is not generally considered the best path to improved quality. So hiring more inspectors would not be the correct answer to the question, "What is the best way to improve quality?"

Quality Policy

PMI® stresses the importance of having a quality policy for the project. Quality policy is a company's statement of how it will produce quality products and what it will do if products are defective. Most often, upper management dictates a quality policy to be implemented by project managers and team members. Not all quality polices are formal documents. If a company does not have a formal quality policy, then the project managers and team members should draft one before starting a new project. It is important that a project's stakeholders know the terms of the quality policy before a project begins.

Quality Planning Tools and Techniques, PMI® discusses five quality planning tools and techniques.
1. **Cost Benefit Analysis** - Cost benefit analysis must be considered in the quality planning process. Cost benefit analysis weighs the benefits versus cost to make sure a project meets quality requirements without going over the project's budget. The project manager must consider cost benefit tradeoffs during quality planning. The primary benefit of meeting quality requirements is less rework which translates to higher productivity, lower costs, and increased stakeholder satisfaction. The primary cost of meeting quality requirements is the expense associated with project quality management activities. The benefits of the quality management discipline outweigh the costs.

2. **Benchmarking** - Involves comparing actual or planned project practices to those of other projects (either within the performing organization or external) to generate ideas for improvement and to provide a standard by which to measure performance.
3. **Design of Experiments** - Design of experiments is a statistical method that helps identify which factors might influence specific variables and is applied most often to the product of the project (for example, automotive designers may wish to determine which combination of suspension and tires will produce the most desirable ride characteristics at a reasonable cost.) It can also be applied to project management issues such as cost and schedule trade-offs. Example: senior engineers will cost more than junior engineers but will usually complete the assignment in less time. An appropriately designed experiment which computes project costs and duration for various combinations of senior and junior engineers will often yield an optimal solution from a relatively limited number of cases.
4. **Cost of Quality** (COQ) - One major area of emphasis on the exam is cost of quality. Cost of quality refers to the total amount of money and resources that are necessary to make sure a project's quality standards are met. It is defined as the cost of conformance (the cost of proactive quality processes) and the cost of nonconformance (the cost of a quality failure). In either form, cost of quality is a results-oriented approach to measuring and assessing the effectiveness or benefit of an organization's project quality management process. It is a useful means of bringing management's attention to the need for quality, but it provides little meaningful capability to manage quality proactively. Three types of incurred costs: prevention, appraisal, and failure. Failure costs are broken down into internal and external costs and may also be referred to as the cost of poor quality.

Additional quality planning tools - Other quality planning tools are also often used to help better define the situation and help plan effective quality management activities. These include:
Brainstorming - is simply listing all ideas put forth by a group in response to a given problem or question. Creativity is encouraged by not allowing ideas to be evaluated or discussed until everyone has run dry. Any and all ideas are considered legitimate and often the most far-fetched are the most fertile. Structured brainstorming produces numerous creative ideas about any given "central question". Done right, it taps the human brain's capacity for lateral thinking and free association.

Brainstorms help answer specific questions such as:
- What opportunities face us this year?
- What factors are constraining performance in Department X?
- What could be causing problem Y?
- What can we do to solve problem Z?

However, a brainstorm cannot help you positively identify causes of problems, rank ideas in a meaningful order, select important ideas, or check solutions. To conduct a successful brainstorm:
- Make sure everyone understands and is satisfied with the central question.
- You may want to give everyone a few seconds to jot down a few ideas before getting started.
- Begin by going around the table or room, giving everyone a chance to voice their ideas or pass. After a few rounds, open the floor.
- More ideas are better. Encourage radical ideas and piggybacking.
- Suspend judgment of all ideas.
- Record exactly what is said. Clarify only after everyone is out of ideas.
- Don't stop until ideas become sparse. Allow for late-coming ideas.
- Eliminate duplicates and ideas that aren't relevant to the topic.

A brainstorm starts with a clear question, and ends with a raw list of ideas.

Affinity Diagrams - the affinity diagram wasn't originally intended for quality management. Nonetheless, it has become one of the most widely used of the Japanese management and planning tools. The affinity diagram was developed to discovering meaningful groups of ideas within a raw list.

In doing so, it is important to let the groupings emerge naturally, using the right side of the brain, rather than according to preordained categories.

Usually, an affinity diagram is used to refine a brainstorm into something that makes sense and can be dealt with more easily. It is recommended using the affinity diagram when facts or thoughts are uncertain and need to be organized, when preexisting ideas or paradigms need to be overcome, when ideas need to be clarified, and when unity within a team needs to be created.

To create an affinity diagram, you sort the brainstormed list, moving ideas from the brainstorm into affinity sets, and creating groups of related ideas. As you sort ideas:
- Rapidly group ideas that seem to belong together.
- It isn't important to define why they belong together.
- Copy an idea into in more than one affinity set if appropriate.
- Look for small sets. Should they belong in a larger group?
- Do large sets need to be broken down more precisely?
- When most of the ideas have been sorted, you can start to enter titles for each affinity set.

Force Field Analysis - is a useful technique for looking at all the forces for and against a decision. In effect, it is a specialized method of weighing pros and cons. By carrying out the analysis you can plan to strengthen the forces supporting a decision, and reduce the impact of opposition to it. To carry out a force field analysis, follow these steps:
- List all forces for change in one column, and all forces against change in another column
- Assign a score to each force, from 1 (weak) to 5 (strong)
- Draw a diagram showing the forces for and against change. Show the size of each force as a number next to it

Once you have carried out an analysis, you can decide whether your project is viable. In the example above, you might initially question whether it is worth going ahead with the plan. Where you have already decided to carry out a project, Force Field Analysis can help you to work out how to improve its probability of success. Here you have two choices:
- To reduce the strength of the forces opposing a project, or
- To increase the forces pushing a project

Nominal Group Techniques - in the nominal group technique, participants are brought together for a discussion session led by a moderator. After the topic has been presented to session participants and they have had an opportunity to ask questions or briefly discuss the scope of the topic, they are asked to take a few minutes to think about and write down their responses. The session moderator will then ask each participant to read, and elaborate on, one of their responses. These are noted on a flipchart. Once everyone has given a response, participants will be asked for a second or third response, until all of their answers have been noted on flipcharts sheets posted around the room.

Once duplications are eliminated, each response is assigned a letter or number. Session participants are then asked to choose up to 10 responses that they feel are the most important and rank them according to their relative importance. These rankings are collected from all participants, and aggregated.

Sometimes these results are given back to the participants in order to stimulate further discussion, and perhaps a readjustment in the overall rankings assigned to the various responses. This is done only when group consensus regarding the prioritization of issues is important to the overall research or planning project.

The nominal group technique can be used as an alternative to both the focus group and the Delphi techniques. It presents more structure than the focus group, but still takes advantage of the synergy created by group participants. As its name suggests, the nominal group technique is only "nominally" a group, since the rankings are provided on an individual basis.

Matrix Diagrams - permit organization of knowledge so that relationships between factors, causes, objectives, (or any thing that one wants to show) can be shown. Matrices, of course, provide rows and columns with intersecting cells that can be filled with information that describes the relation between the items located in the rows and columns.

Flowcharts - are maps or graphical representations of a process. Steps in a process are shown with symbolic shapes, and the flow of the process is indicated with arrows connecting the symbols. Computer programmers popularized flowcharts in the 1960's, using them to map the logic of programs. In quality improvement work, flowcharts are particularly useful for displaying how a process currently functions or could ideally function. Flowcharts can help you see whether the steps of a process are logical, uncover problems or miscommunications, define the boundaries of a process, and develop a common base of knowledge about a process. Flowcharting a process often brings to light redundancies, delays, dead ends, and indirect paths that would otherwise remain unnoticed or ignored.

Prioritization Matrices - is a useful technique you can use with your team members or with your users to achieve consensus about an issue. The Matrix helps you rank problems or issues (usually generated through brainstorming) by a particular criterion that is important to your organization. Then you can more clearly see which problems are the most important to work on solving first. This tool should be used when:
- Key root causes have been identified and the most critical causes must be narrowed down
- When the issues are complex and they have strong interrelationships
- There are limited resources for improvement activities so you must concentrate on the critical few.

Quality Management Plan

The quality management plan describes how the project management team will implement its quality policy. The quality management plan should describe the project quality system: the organizational structure, responsibilities, procedures, processes, and resources needed to implement quality management. It also provides input to the overall project plan and must address quality control, quality assurance, and quality improvement for the project. The quality management plan may be formal or informal, highly detailed or broadly framed, depending on the requirements of the project.

Quality Metrics

A metric describes, in precise terms, what something is and how the quality control process measures it. A measurement is an actual value. Quality metrics should be used in all quality processes. Some examples of quality metrics would be system reliability, system availability and mean time to failure.

Quality Checklists

A quality checklist is a list of check-off items that permit data to be collected quickly and easily in a simple standardized format that lends itself to quantitative analysis. A quality checklist frequently contains a graphic representation of an object and is used to record such information as where specific damage was located. A quality checklist is intended to make data collection fast and easy and it should be carefully designed so that the data are useful and have a clear purpose. Checklists are frequently used to collect data on numbers of defective items, defect locations, and defect causes.

Types of Costs

There are two types of costs incurred in quality management. Be able to recognize examples of each: prevention costs and appraisal costs, which are the cost of conformance; and failure costs, which are the cost of nonconformance.

Cost of Conformance

Prevention costs: Up-front costs that are oriented toward the satisfaction of customer requirements:
- Design reviews
- Training and indoctrination
- Planning
- Vendor, supplier, and subcontractor surveys
- Process studies

Appraisal costs: Costs associated with the evaluation of the product or the process to see whether customer requirements were met:
- Product inspections
- Lab tests
- Vendor controls
- In-process testing
- Internal/external design reviews

Cost of Nonconformance (Failure Costs)

Internal failure costs: Costs associated with the failure of the processes to make the products acceptable to the customer before the products leave the control of the organization:
- Scrap / Rework
- Repair
- Downtime
- Defect evaluation
- Corrective actions

External failure costs: Costs associated with the determination by the customer that requirements have not been satisfied:
- Customer returns
- Customer complaints
- Customer inspections
- Customer visits to resolve quality complaints
- Corrective actions

Rework

Rework is the corrective action taken to make a defective product conform to a project's quality standards. Reworking a product takes more time and uses more resources than if the product is made correctly the first time. The use of additional time and resources increases the cost of quality, which is the total amount of money and work used to make quality products.

Key Quality Planning Outputs

The quality management plan describes the quality management system: the organizational structure, responsibilities, procedures, processes, and resources needed to implement quality management.

Operational definitions describe what something is and how the quality control process measures it. They may also be called metrics.

Checklists are outputs of quality planning that are used to verify that a set of required steps has been performed. Completed checklists (an output of quality control) should be part of the project's records.

Perform Quality Assurance

Perform quality assurance is a managerial function that addresses all the planned and systematic activities implemented within the quality system to provide confidence that the project will satisfy the relevant quality standards.

Quality assurance refers to project activities that are planned and executed to ensure quality products and services. The goal of quality assurance is the improved quality of a project's processes and improved quality of end products. Any problems encountered during the execution of quality assurance activities must be corrected. Correcting problems can lead to greater efficiency, decreased cost of production, and a higher-quality product.

Quality assurance is important not only because it leads to the correction of problems, but also because it gives customers and project stakeholder's confidence that the finished product will be free of defects.

The following issues and concepts fall under quality assurance:
- **Quality Audits** - This is a process of reviewing specific data at key points of the project's life cycle. The quality audit is a quality assurance tool and technique that serves as a structured review of quality management activities. Its objective is to identify lessons learned that can be used to improve performance on this project or on other projects in the organization.
- **Requested Changes** - Quality improvement includes taking actions to increase the effectiveness and efficiency of the project to provide an added benefit to the project stakeholders. This may require the use of change requests or corrective action.
- **Perform Quality Control** - Quality control is a technical function that involves establishing the technical baseline for the project and then collecting specific data by which to measure conformance to that baseline. Quality control measures are used throughout a project's life cycle to make sure work is done properly and that actual project results match the expectations outlined in the project's quality management plan. During quality control, both the processes used to complete the project, as well as the end product, are examined to make sure they meet quality standards.

The purpose of quality control is to ensure that a finished product has certain quality characteristics and that unacceptable product traits are corrected.

It is important to understand that quality control is not only a component of the quality management variable, but that it is also part of the fourth step of the project management process—project control.

The difference between quality control and quality assurance is that quality assurance focuses on developing and implementing quality-related activities, whereas quality control focuses on ensuring that the quality-related activities achieve their desired effect.

Quality control and quality assurance are similar in that both components use a project's quality management plan and operational definitions to evaluate whether or not a project and product are achieving the desired levels of quality. The quality control and quality assurance components are also similar in that both result in quality improvement.

Included below are some important terms and concepts associated with quality control:
- **Variable** - A quality characteristic that is measurable in increments. Examples are diameter measured in inches, cooking time measured in minutes, and weight measured in pounds.
- **Attribute** - A quality characteristic that is classified as either conforming or nonconforming to specifications or requirements. It results in a go or no-go decision. Attributes are easily segregated into a "yes-no" outcome. As an example in flipping a coin there is a 50-percent probability of getting "heads" on any single flip
- **Probability** - An important concept in quality control is that of probability. In its simplest form, probability refers to the chance that something will happen.

For variables, probability is a more complicated concept. We measure the occurrences of an event or characteristic, and distribute them over the entire range of the characteristic. Such a distribution is formally called a probability distribution. The most common probability distribution has a bell shape and is symmetric about its mean; it is known as a normal distribution or a bell curve.

A population is the entire group of items or occurrences that we might wish to measure. Because populations can be very large, however, we often sample the population, using a smaller group to get a picture of the larger group.

Standard Deviation

In measuring samples and comparing them to their overall population, one important concept is that of standard deviation. Simply defined, the standard deviation is the amount on either side of the mean of a normal distribution that will contain approximately 68.3 percent of the total population. The amount within two standard deviations will include 95.5 percent, and within three standard deviations will include 99.7 percent of the population.

Calculating standard deviation is complex. Most automated quality control packages include the provision to calculate standard deviation and other statistically important values. In fact, most pocket calculators available today can also provide this value for a series of discrete observations of a variable characteristic. The following is provided to show manually how to calculate standard deviation:

The "Standard Deviation" for data can be calculated in the following steps:
1. all the deviations (differences) from the mean of the set of numbers are squared
2. the mean of these squares is then calculated
3. the square root of the mean is the standard deviation

Given the set of numbers {20, 23, 25, 26}, the "Standard Deviation" can be calculated as follows:

Step 1:
The mean of these numbers is found to be 23.5 [eg. mean = (20+23+25+26)/4 = 23.5]. The deviations from the mean are respectively:
$$23.5 - 20 = 3.5$$
$$23.5 - 23 = 0.5$$
$$25 - 23.5 = 1.5$$
$$26 - 23.5 = 2.5$$

The squares of these deviations are:
$$3.5^2 = 12.25$$
$$0.5^2 = 0.25$$
$$1.5^2 = 2.25$$
$$2.5^2 = 6.25$$

Step 2:
The sum of these squares is 12.25 + 0.25 + 2.25 + 6.25 = 21. This is now divided by (n-1), which is 3, to get 7.

Step 3:
Finally, the square root of 7 is approximately 2.6457513

Answer:
In summary, the Standard Deviation of the set of numbers {20, 23, 25, 26} is 2.6457513

Process Control

Building on the statistical concepts we have just discussed, the PMBOK® Guide emphasizes process control as an important means of managing quality. Key to this concept is the idea of statistical process control (SPC) and its main tool—control charts—commonly called SPC charts.

A SPC chart will show you the current capability of the process—what is called voice of the process in some courses and recent publications. The important point to remember about SPC charts is that there are many different types you may use, depending on the characteristic you are measuring and its variability.

Sampling

Sampling is a useful means of assessing the value of a characteristic when examining an entire population is not feasible. There are two main types of sampling:
- **Attribute sampling** is the examination of one or more attributes in a lot. A limit of acceptability is established for the entire lot. For example, we may consider a "lot" of 10,000 parts. A random sample of 150 parts is selected for examination. For that sample, the acceptance number is 3, meaning that if more than 3 parts are found to be defective; the entire lot of 10,000 will be rejected. You can conduct single-attribute sampling, double-attribute sampling, multiple-attribute sampling, or sequential attribute sampling (single-attribute sampling performed sequentially on the same lot for different attributes).
- **Variable sampling** provides a more dynamic approach to sampling. This is the basis for creating control charts, where a process variable is measured and charted to determine process capability. Variable sampling may also be used to estimate the fraction of a lot that is nonconforming, and thus to make decisions about further inspection or use of the lot.

Both attribute sampling and variation sampling tell whether a product does or does not conform to quality standards. However, variation sampling also accounts for the degree to which a product does or does not conform.

Prevention and Inspection

Prevention and inspection have different purposes. Prevention requires careful planning to avoid errors before a project begins. Inspection occurs during project execution or after a project is completed. When defects are found during inspection, rework is required to correct the defects before products are distributed to customers.

Special Causes and Random Causes

Special causes of variation, which are often caused by human error, are generally unexpected or unanticipated. Random causes, also called common causes, of variation are normal difficulties associated with a certain process, such as equipment failure or faulty product design. Project team members who contribute to special causes of variation should be able to correct the causes on their own, whereas project managers are responsible for solving random causes of variation since the causes are part of the project's process.

Tolerance and Control Limits

Tolerance refers to the amount off acceptable variations from product quality standards. Control limits apply to a project's process rather than to a product. A project is considered "in control" if its processes are within specified control limits.

Statistical Quality Control

Statistical quality control is used to evaluate the extent of product variation and to identify what changes, if any, must be made to production processes in order to decrease product variation. Data points on a graph represent incidents of product variations, and a normal distribution curve indicates whether or not the variations are of a degree acceptable for quality standards.

Quality monitoring involves the use of statistics. Therefore, it is important to know the following basic statistical terms:
- **Population** – refers to the total number of product units produced during a project.
- **Sample size** – refers to the number of product units taken from the population for evaluation during a project's quality monitoring process. This number varies depending on the product, the time of the inspection, and a company's needs.
- **Mean** – this refers to the sum of the sample divided by the number of units in the sample. For example, in the sample {2, 4, 6, 8}, the mean is (2 + 4 + 6 + 8) ÷ 4. The mean is 5.
- **Median** – When an odd—numbered set of data is arranged sequentially, the middle number in the set is the median. For example, in the set {3, 6, 9}, the median is 6. When an even-numbered set of data is arranged sequentially, the median is the average of the middle two numbers. For example, in the set {2, 4, 8, 9}, the median is (4 + 8) ÷ 2, the median is 6.
- **Mode** – In a sample of data, the number that occurs most frequently represents the mode. For example, in the set {2, 3, 4, 3, 5, 3, 4}, the mode is 3.

Quality Control Tools

There are seven main quality control tools (often called the basic seven tools), which are illustrated and discussed below.

Flowcharts

Flowcharts permit you to examine and understand relationships in a process or project. They show how various elements of a system interrelate. They provide a step-by-step schematic, or picture, that serves to create a common language, ensure common understanding about sequence, and focus collective attention on shared concerns. Flowcharts are used in all three of the quality management processes. Several different types of flowcharts are particularly useful in the continuous improvement process. Three frequently used charts are known as the top-down flowchart, the detailed flowchart, and the work-flow diagram.

The top-down flowchart presents only the major or most fundamental steps in a process or project. It helps you or your team to easily visualize the process in a single, simple flow diagram. Key value-added actions associated with each major activity are listed below their respective flow diagram steps. You can construct a top-down flowchart fairly quickly and easily. You generally do so before attempting to produce detailed flowcharts for a process. By limiting the top-down flowchart to a value-added activity, the likelihood of becoming bogged down in detail is significantly reduced.

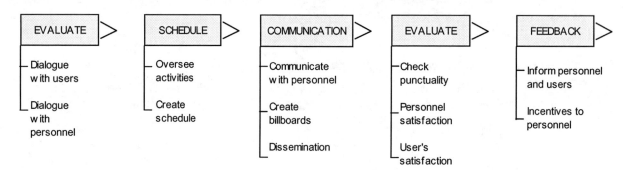

Figure 23 - Top-Down Flowchart

The detailed flowchart provides very specific information about process flow. At its most detailed level, every decision point, feedback loop, and process step is represented. Detailed flowcharts should be used only when the level of detail provided by the top-down or other simpler flowcharts is insufficient to support understanding, analysis, and improvement activity. The detailed flowchart may also be useful and appropriate for critical processes where precisely following a specific procedure is essential.

The work-flow diagram is a graphic representation of how work actually flows through a physical space or facility. It is very useful for analyzing flow processes, illustrating flow inefficiency, and planning process flow improvement.

Scatter Diagrams

Scatter diagrams are used to investigate the possible relationship between two variables that both relate to the same "event." A straight line of best fit (using the least squares method) is often included. Things to look for:
- If the points cluster in a band running from lower left to upper right, there is a positive correlation (if x increases, y increases).
- If the points cluster in a band from upper left to lower right, there is a negative correlation (if x increases, y decreases).
- Imagine drawing a straight line or curve through the data so that it "fits" as well as possible. The more the points cluster closely around the imaginary line of best fit, the stronger the relationship that exists between the two variables.
- If it is hard to see where you would draw a line, and if the points show no significant clustering, there is probably no correlation.

There is a maxim in statistics that says, "Correlation does not imply causality." In other words, your scatter plot may show that a relationship exists, but it does not and cannot prove that one variable is causing the other. There could be a third factor involved that is causing both, some other systemic cause, or the apparent relationship could just be a fluke. Nevertheless, the scatter plot can give you a clue that two things might be related, and if so, how they move together.

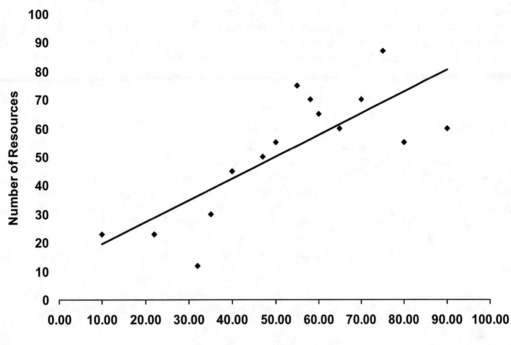

Figure 24 - Scatter Diagram

Histograms

A histogram is a specialized type of bar chart. Individual data points are grouped together in classes, so that you can get an idea of how frequently data in each class occur in the data set. High bars indicate more points in a class, and low bars indicate less points.

In the histogram shown below, the peak is in the 40-49 class, where there are four points. The strength of a histogram is that it provides an easy-to-read picture of the location and variation in a data set. There are, however, two weaknesses of histograms that you should bear in mind; the first is that histograms can be manipulated to show different pictures. If too few or too many bars are used, the histogram can be misleading. This is an area which requires some judgment, and perhaps some experimentation, based on the analyst's experience.

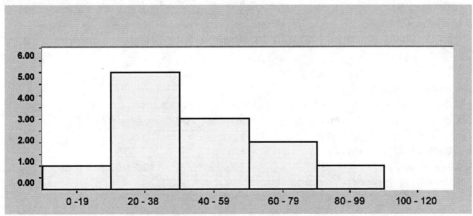

Figure 25 - Sample Histogram

Histograms can also obscure the time differences among data sets. For example, if you looked at data for number of births on a particular day in the United States in 2005, you would miss any seasonal variations, e.g. peaks around the times of full moons. Likewise, in quality control, a histogram of a process run tells only one part of a long story. There is a need to keep reviewing the histograms and control charts for consecutive process runs over an extended time to gain useful knowledge about a process.

Run Charts

Run charts (often known as line graphs outside the quality management field) display process performance over time. Upward and downward trends, cycles, and large aberrations may be spotted and investigated further. In a run chart, events, shown on the y axis, are graphed against a time period on the x axis. For example, a run chart in a hospital might plot the number of patient transfer delays against the time of day or day of the week. The results might show that there are more delays at noon than at 3 p.m. Investigating this phenomenon could unearth potential for improvement. Run charts can also be used to track improvements that have been put into place, checking to determine their success. Also, an average line can be added to a run chart to clarify movement of the data away from the average.

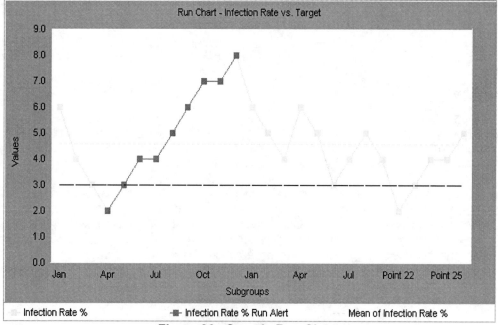

Figure 26 - Sample Run Chart

Questions to ask about a run chart:
1. Is the average line where it should be to meet customer requirements?
2. Is there a significant trend or pattern that should be investigated?

Two ways to misinterpret run charts:
1. You conclude that some trend or cycle exists, when in fact you are just seeing normal process variation (and every process will show some variation).
2. You do not recognize a trend or cycle when it does exist.

Both of these mistakes are common, but people are generally less aware that they are making the first type, and are tampering with a process which is really behaving normally. To avoid mistakes, use the following rules of thumb for run chart interpretation:
- Look at data for a long enough period of time, so that a "usual" range of variation is evident.
- Is the recent data within the usual range of variation?
- Is there a daily pattern? Weekly? Monthly? Yearly?

Pareto Charts

In the late 1800s, Vilfredo Pareto, an Italian economist, found that typically 80 percent of the wealth in a region was concentrated in less than 20 percent of the population. Later, Dr. Joseph Juran formulated what he called the Pareto Principle of Problems: only a "vital few" elements (20 percent) account for the majority (80 percent) of the problems. For example, in a manufacturing facility, 20 percent of the equipment problems account for 80 percent of the downtime. Because the Pareto Principle has proven to be valid in numerous situations, it is useful to examine data carefully to identify the vital few items that most deserve attention.

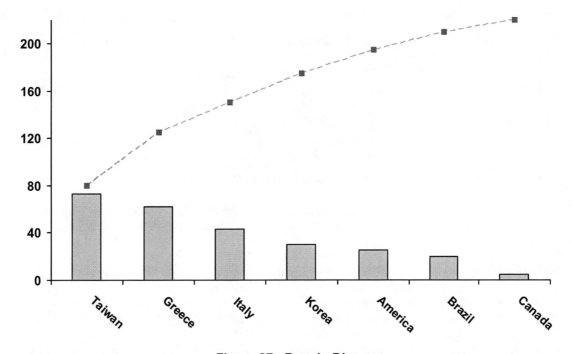

Figure 27 - Paredo Diagram

A Pareto Chart is a bar chart in which the data are arranged in descending order of their importance, generally by magnitude of frequency, cost, time, or a similar parameter. The chart presents the information being examined in its order of priority and focuses attention on the most critical issues. The chart aids the decision-making process because it puts issues into an easily understood framework in which relationships and relative contributions are clearly evident.

Cause and Effect Diagram

Cause and effect diagrams are the brainchild of Kaoru Ishikawa, who pioneered quality management processes in the Kawasaki shipyards, in Japan, and in the process became one of the founding fathers of modern management. The cause and effect diagram is used to explore all the potential or real causes (or inputs) that result in a single effect (or output). Causes are arranged according to their level of importance or detail, resulting in a depiction of relationships and hierarchy of events. This can help you search for root causes, identify areas where there may be problems, and compare the relative importance of different causes.

Cause and effect diagrams are frequently arranged into four major categories. While these categories can be anything, you will often see: manpower, methods, materials, and machinery (recommended for manufacturing) equipment, policies, procedures, and people (recommended for administration and service). These guidelines can be helpful but should not be used if they limit the diagram or are inappropriate. The categories you use should suit your needs.

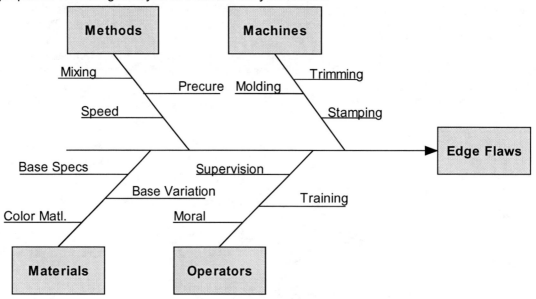

Figure 28 - Cause and Effect Diagram

The cause and effect diagram is also known as the fishbone diagram because it was drawn to resemble the skeleton of a fish, with the main causal categories drawn as "bones" attached to the spine of the fish, as shown above.

Cause and effect diagrams can also be drawn as tree diagrams, resembling a tree turned on its side. From a single outcome or trunk, branches extend that represent major categories of inputs or causes that create that single outcome. These large branches then lead to smaller and smaller branches of causes all the way down to twigs at the ends. The tree structure has an advantage over the fishbone-style diagram. As a fishbone diagram becomes more and more complex, it becomes difficult to find and compare items that are the same distance from the effect because they are dispersed over the diagram. With the tree structure, all items on the same causal level are aligned vertically.

Control Charts

A control chart is a graph that displays data taken over time and computed variations of those data. Control charts are used to show the variation on a variety of variables including average (X) and range (R) and also the number of defects (PN), percent defective (P), defects per variable unit (U), and defects per fixed unit (C). The control chart allows you to distinguish between measurements that are predictably within the inherent capability of the process (normal causes of variation that are to be expected) and measurements that are unpredictable and produced by special causes.

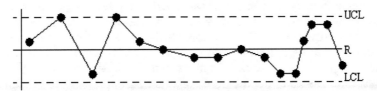

Figure 29 - Control Chart

The upper and lower control limits (UCL and LCL) must not be confused with specification limits. Control limits describe the natural variation of the process such that points within the limits are generally indicative of normal and expected variation. Points outside the limits signal that something has occurred that requires special attention because it is outside of the built-in systemic causes of variation in the process. Note that the circled point on the X-bar chart means that the process is out of control and should be investigated. These points outside the control limits are referred to as special events having either assignable causes or random causes.

The occurrence of assignable causes may be the result of unwanted, external effects such as the following:
- An equipment problem
- An employee problem (poor training, understaffed, and so on)
- Defective materials

There is another important guideline, known as the Rule of Seven, which should be observed whenever interpreting control charts. This rule of thumb (heuristic) states that if seven or more observations in a row occur on the same side of the mean (or if they trend in the same direction), even though they may be within the control limit, they should be investigated as if they had an assignable cause. It is extremely unlikely that seven observations in a row would be on the same side of the mean if the process is operating normally.

Why is this so? If a process is operating normally, the observations will follow a random pattern with some of the points falling above the line and some below the line. In fact, the probability that any single point will fall above or below the line is 50-50 (like a coin toss). Further, the probability that seven points in a row would be on the same side of the line would be calculated as 0.5 to the 7seventh power, which is equal to 0.0078 (or less than 1 percent). Again, this rule provides a guideline that alerts you that something unlikely is happening and you should check it out.

These charts will help you understand the following:
- The inherent capability of your processes
- Bring your processes under control by eliminating the special causes of variation
- Reduce tampering with processes that are under statistical control
- Monitor the effects of process changes aimed at improvement

Two additional concepts are important in the use of control charts. Both concepts involve the idea of standard deviation, often referred to as "sigma." For the exam, you need to understand only the concepts (no formulas or complex calculations are required).

The first concept involves the use by some companies of what is known as the Six Sigma Rule for setting control limits. You are already aware that three standard deviations (sigma) either side of the mean accounts for approximately 99.7 percent of the possible outcomes. Historically, many companies have used plus or minus three sigma's as their standard for setting control limits. In recent years, some companies have chosen to use plus or minus six sigmas as a guide for setting control limits. The use of this more stringent rule means that even fewer actual outcomes might fall outside the control limits.

The second concept involves the effect of sample size on the control limits. Again, you do not need to memorize any formulas, but it helps to know the following information about how the formula for setting control limits works. First, the standard deviation is part of the formula for establishing control limits. The larger the standard deviation, the wider the control limits will be. That much is fairly intuitive. In other words, the greater the natural variations in the process, the wider the control limits need to be. Now, how does sample size affect the control limits? Sample size affects control limits by its effect on the standard deviation. Sample size is in the denominator of the formula for variance from which standard deviation is computed; so whenever sample size is increased, the standard deviation will be smaller. Conversely, if the sample size is decreased, the standard deviation will be larger. Therefore, larger sample sizes will result in more narrow control limits, and smaller sample sizes will result in wider control limits.

Statistical Sampling

Statistical sampling involves choosing a population of interest for inspection. (e.g., selecting ten engineering drawings at random from a list of seventy-five). Appropriate sampling can often reduce the cost of quality control. In some application areas, the project management team must be familiar with a variety of sampling techniques.

Inspection

Quality cannot be infused into a project or a product by inspection. However, inspection is a useful tool for quality control. End products should always go through a final inspection to make sure that they conform to quality standards. Inspection includes activities such as measuring, examining, and testing undertaken to determine whether results conform to requirements. May be conducted at any level (e.g., the results of a single activity may be inspected or the final project product). May be called reviews, product reviews, audits, and walkthroughs. Note: in some application areas these terms have narrow and specific meanings.

Defect

Any type of undesired result is a defect. A defect is a failure to conform to requirements whether or not those requirements have been articulated or specified. This usually requires the product or service to be either repaired or replaced.

Defect Repair Review

Defect repair review is where the quality control department will explain how they plan to minimize defects for there project. A defect is any occurrence contrary to specifications within a deliverable which has already been quality assured. A plan for efficient removal of defects could include such items as standardized reporting mechanisms, effective and up-to-date system documentation, etc.

Corrective Action

Action to eliminate the cause of a detected nonconformity or other undesirable situation. Note: There can be more than on cause for a non-conformance. Corrective action is taken to prevent recurrence, whereas preventive action is taken to prevent occurrence.

Preventive Action
Action taken to eliminate the causes of a potential non-conformity, defect, or other undesirable situation in order to prevent occurrence.

Continuous Improvement and Kaizen
Kaizen was originally defined in the book Kaizen, the Key to Japan's Competitive Success, by Mr. Masaaki Imai. Kaizen means improvement. Moreover, Kaizen means continuing improvement in personal life, home life, social life, and working life. When applied to the workplace Kaizen means continuing improvement involving everyone—managers and workers alike.

Kaizen is a Japanese word meaning gradual and orderly, continuous improvement. The Kaizen business strategy involves everyone in an organization working together to make improvements "without large capital investments."

Kaizen is a culture of sustained continuous improvement focusing on eliminating waste in all systems and processes of an organization. The Kaizen strategy begins and ends with people. With Kaizen, an involved leadership guides people to continuously improve their ability to meet expectations of high quality, low cost, and on-time delivery. Kaizen transforms companies into "Superior Global Competitors."

There are two elements that construct Kaizen: improvement and change for the better and ongoing/continuity. Lacking one of those elements would not be considered Kaizen. For instance, the expression of "business as usual" contains the element of continuity without improvement. On the other hand, the expression of "breakthrough" contains the element of change or improvement without continuity. Kaizen should contain both elements.

Kaizen, as you could learn from the definition, is a common word and very natural to individual, continuous improvement in personal life, home life, social life, and work life. Everybody deserves to and should be willing to improve himself/herself for the better, continually. "If a man has not been seen for three days, his friends should take a good look at him to see what changes have befallen him," quoted from the old Japanese saying, describes how natural Kaizen is.

In our concepts, three functions should happen simultaneously within any organizations: maintenance, innovation, and Kaizen. By maintenance, we refer to maintaining the current status, the procedures are set, and the standards are implemented. This is generally the role of the people in the lower level of organizations—maintaining the company's standards.

Innovation refers to breakthrough activities initiated by top management: buying new machines, new equipment, developing new markets, directing research and design (R & D), change of strategy, etc....

In the middle, there is Kaizen: small steps, but continuing improvement. The lower/middle management and the workers, with the encouragement and direction of the top, should implement Kaizen. The top management responsibility is to cultivate a Kaizen working climate and culture in the organization.

For the PMP® exam know that Kaizen is small, tiny, incremental improvements—always looking for a way to make things better.

Just-in-Time (JIT)

Just-in-time is an inventory control approach process that continuously stresses waste reduction by optimizing the processes and procedures necessary to maintain an operation. Part of this process is JIT inventory where the materials needed appear just in time for use, thus eliminating costs associated with material handling and storage. The philosophy is that with no safety stock in the system, defective parts or processes will grind the system to a halt. A zero working-process inventory forces a company to find and fix quality problems, or it will constantly miss its schedule commitments.

The company benefits from JIT inventory/purchasing by developing long-term relationships with fewer suppliers, thus lowering subcontractor management costs. The contractor benefits by having long-term contracts.

Numerous companies in Japan have adopted JIT, because they believe JIT and high quality go together naturally, but in the United States it has only been marginally successful.

Just-in-time (JIT) is designed as a process that is going to keep flow coming to you, as a vendor, just in time to prepare it, process it, and get it to your customers. Vendors do not want to keep inventory on hand. They do not want to have material in a warehouse. Classic just-in-time management allows for the flow of materials effectively through an organization or process.

Impact of Motivation on Quality

It is generally believed that increased quality is likely to be associated with projects whose team members display pride, commitment, and an interest in workmanship. It is also believed that one way to harm this culture is by allowing frequent turnover of the people assigned to the project.

Priority of Quality versus Cost and Schedule

Quality use to receive lip service in many companies, but it was, in reality, less important than meeting schedules or containing costs. Such a situation was often tipped off by such signals as the quality manager reporting to the production manager (who often cared more about schedule pressures than quality). Although lip service has probably not been eliminated entirely, modern thinking emphasizes that quality should share equal priority with cost and schedule.

Philip Crosby titled his book Quality is Free on the premise that the cost of doing things twice is far greater than the cost of doing them right in the first time. When performance is cut, costs go up for many reasons, including these:
- Rework (performing the same tasks twice because they were not done right the first time) during the project will drive costs higher and delay completion.
- Rework after the project finishes is even more expensive than rework during the project. Any potential development cost savings are wiped out by the high cost of fixing the product.
- Failure due to poor product performance can also be expensive. Product recalls always bear the expense of contacting the consumers as well as fixing or replacing the product. Product failures such as collapsing bridges and malfunctioning medical equipment can even cost lives.
- Poor product performance causes damage to the reputation of the firm and ultimately reduces the demand for its products or services.

The above paragraphs are very important because they drive home the point that sometimes, in some quality practices, what you are doing in the real world may not really matter. This is one of them. The argument in most quality circles is that quality is of equal importance to cost and schedule. In some circles, it is even said that quality is more important than cost or schedule. Nevertheless, for the PMP® exam, you need to know that quality is of equal importance to cost and schedule. You need to know, if asked, what is more important, quality, cost, or schedule? The answer: they are equally important.

Impact of Poor Quality

The following effects on a project are possible results of poor quality:
- Increased project costs as a result of costs of nonconformance (for example, rework, scrap, product recalls, and so on)
- Decreased productivity
- Increased risk and uncertainty (less predictability in cost, schedule, and technical outcomes)
- Increased costs of monitoring (if conformance to specifications is low, increased monitoring will probably become necessary)

What happens when we do not have good quality? Look at the bullet points and memorize each and every one of them. They are listed as bullets in order to make it easier to remember. Poor quality results in higher costs, poor productivity, increased risk, and increased uncertainty.

Trend Analysis

Trend analysis uses scatter diagrams to monitor the performance of technical operations, project costs, and a project's schedule. During trend analysis, a project manager determines the mathematical equation that best fits the slope of the line on a scatter diagram. The equation is then used to predict how changing one project variable will affect another project variable.

Design and Quality

Quality should be designed into, not inspected into (worth repeating). More specifically, careful design of a product or service is believed to increase reliability and maintainability (two important measures of quality).

The primary responsibility for developing design and test specifications rests with the project engineers (they have the expertise needed to perform this vital task). Rework is any action taken to bring a defective or nonconforming item into compliance with requirements or specifications. The project team should make every effort to minimize rework.

Look at the first sentence. It says "Quality should be designed into, not inspected into." We do not inspect quality into something. You may be asked a few questions that lure you into the idea that going back and inspecting for quality is the right answer. IT IS NOT. We design quality so that it's built in. Remember, responsibility for quality rests with the person who owns that given activity. Quality on the project is the responsibility of the project manager. Quality on a task is the responsibility of the person doing that task.

Chapter Review

1. The rule of seven:
    A. States that a batch should be rejected if there are seven consecutive rejects
    B. States that seven consecutive observations on one side of the mean indicates a batch should be rejected
    C. Means that a minimum sample size of seven should be taken
    D. States that seven consecutive observations on one side of the mean is highly improbable

2. The continuous quality improvement process is a concept that states: (choose the best answer)
    A. The customer is the most important aspect of a quality product
    B. The work is continuously changing and that any procedure or process that is satisfactory today, will more than likely become unsatisfactory in the near future
    C. To succeed in business; it is important to retain customers and for them to have a willingness to repurchase
    D. The customer is driving the need to improve quality

3. Quality Planning is:
    A. Identifying which quality standards are relevant to the project and determining how to satisfy them
    B. Preparing the design to the customer's specifications
    C. Monitoring the project results to decide if the outputs fulfill the requirements
    D. Determining the necessary quality sampling techniques

4. A series of consecutive points on the same side of the average is called:
    A. A run
    B. A trend
    C. An outliner
    D. A cycle

5. Quality control charts are used for the:
    A. Monitoring and subsequent evaluation of process variations
    B. Determination of which projects to kill
    C. Activity known as curve fitting or least squares
    D. Lot rejection ratio

6. A Pareto diagram is most useful for:
    A. Identifying nonconformity types
    B. Providing an evaluation of data at a single point in time
    C. Determining where to focus corrective action
    D. Accepting or rejecting a production lot

7. A tool that analyzes the inputs of a process to identify the causes of errors is called:
    A. Cause and effect diagram or Ishikawa diagram
    B. Scatter diagram
    C. Trend diagram
    D. Pareto diagram

8. The concept of zero inventory is called:
   A. Six sigma
   B. Continuous improvement
   C. Just in Time
   D. Zero defects

9. Design of experiments is a statistical technique that helps:
   A. Determine how various elements of a system interrelate
   B. Anticipate what and where quality problems might occur
   C. Identify which factors might influence specific variables
   D. Establish a standard by which to measure performance

10. The philosophy that the majority of defects are caused by a small percentage of the identifiable problems can be contributed to:
    A. Edward Deming
    B. Philip Crosby
    C. Juran
    D. Pareto

Answers

1. D, Ireland pg. V-6. The probability of seven consecutive observations falling on one side of the mean is (0.5) ** 7 = .78%.
2. B, Ireland pg. I-6
3. A, PMBOK® Guide 3rd Edition, page 186
4. A, Ireland, pg. V-7
5. A, Ireland pg. V-3
6. C, PMBOK® Guide 3rd Edition, page 195
7. A, Ireland, pg. V-11
8. C, Ireland, pg. IV-7
9. C, PMBOK® Guide 3rd Edition, page 185
10. D, Ireland, pg. C-6

Chapter 9

Project Human Resource Management

Reference Material to Study
- A Guide to the Project Management Body of Knowledge (PMBOK® Guide 3rd Edition), Chapter 9
- Principles of Project Management, Adams, John, 1997
- Human Resource Skills for the Project Manager, Verma, Vijay K, 1996
- Organizing Projects for Success, Verma, Vijay K., 1995

What to Study
- The PMBOK® phases of Project Human Resources Management: Human Resources Planning, Acquire Project Team, Develop Project Team and Manage Project Team (Be familiar with Inputs, Tools and Techniques, and Outputs for each phase)
- Know the various organizational aspects which influence projects. These include: organizational cultures, styles, and organizational structures. (see PMBOK®, Chapter 2)
- Know the different types of organizational structures: functional, weak matrix, balanced matrix, strong matrix, and projectized are the main ones. Also be familiar with the differences between project expediter and project coordinator.
- Know the roles and responsibilities of the project manager. (see Principles of Project Management, pgs. 69-84)
- Know the primary sources of authority and control (power) for project managers: formal, coercive, reward, expert, and referent (see Human Resource Skills for the Project Manager, pgs. 232-233)
- Know the different leadership styles for project managers: autocratic, consultative autocrat, consensus manager, shareholder manager. (see Principles of Project Management, pg. 158)
- Know the various motivation theories of human behavior: Theory X, Y, and Z, Expectancy, Contingency, Goal-Setting, Reinforcement, and Equity. (see Human Resource Skills for the Project Manager, pgs. 70-75)
- Know the different methods of managing conflict: forcing, problem solving, compromising, smoothing, and withdrawal. (see Principles of Project Management, pgs. 178-179)
- Know the one party conflict management methods: win-lose, yield-lose, lose-leave, compromise, and integrative and understand the relation between this method and the above methods. For instance, forcing is considered a win-lose situation. (see Principles of Project Management, pgs. 179-180)

Key Definitions
- **Co-location** - Placement of project team members in the same physical location to enhance their ability to perform as a team.
- **Concurrent Engineering** - An approach to project staffing that, in its most general form, calls for implementers to be involved in the design phase. (Sometimes confused with fast tracking)
- **Functional Manager** - A manager responsible for activities in a specialized department or function. (e.g., engineering, manufacturing, marketing)

- **Functional Organization** - An organizational structure in which staff are grouped hierarchically by specialty (e.g., production, marketing, engineering, accounting) at the top level and then further divided within specialty.
- **Managing** - The action of producing the results expected by stakeholders.
- **Matrix Organization** - Any organizational structure in which the project manager shares responsibility with the functional managers for assigning priorities and for directing the work of individuals assigned to the project.
- **Organizational Breakdown Structure** (OBS) - A depiction of the project organization arranged so as to relate work packages to organizational units.
- **Project Coordinator** - Reports to a higher level manager than do the functional managers. Therefore, does have some authority to assign work.
- **Project Expediter** - Coordinates projects across the various functional units. The expediter has limited formal authority. This form is used when the project's cost and importance are relatively low.
- **Project Management Team** - The members of the project team who are directly involved in project management activities. On some smaller projects, the project management team may include virtually all of the project team members.
- **Project Manager** - The individual responsible for managing a project.
- **Project Team Members** - The people who report either directly or indirectly to the project manager.
- **Projectized Organization** - Any organizational structure in which the project manager has full authority to assign priorities and to direct the work of individuals assigned to the project.
- **Responsibility Assignment Matrix** (RAM) - A structure that relates the project organization structure to the WBS to help ensure that each element of the project's scope of work is assigned to a responsible individual. Also called an Accountability Matrix.
- **Team Development** - Developing individual and group competencies to enhance project performance.

The Project Human Resource Management section of the PMP® exam focuses heavily on organizational structures, roles and responsibilities of the project manager, team building, and conflict resolution.

In contrast to other areas of the PMBOK® Guide in which commonly known terms are used, much of the terminology developed for Project Human Resource Management seems peculiar to PMI®. In spite of the unfamiliarity of some terminology, most people do find the human resource questions to be difficult.

Project Human Resource Management involves all aspects of people management and personal interaction including leading, coaching, dealing with conflict, and more. Some of the project participants whom you'll get to practice these skills on include stakeholders, team members, and customers. Each requires the use of different communication styles, leadership skills, and team-building skills. A good project manager knows when to enact certain skills and communication styles based on the situation.

The PMP® exam is heavily weighted toward team development (that is, behavioral topics). In the past only a few questions have appeared on administrative issues, and they should be relatively easy to answer, given familiarity with general corporate—personnel policies governing your everyday work life.

The questions predominantly focus on forms of organization, project manager roles and responsibilities, types of power, project conflict, conflict management, and team building.

Forms of Organization

There are eight approaches to project organizational structure, and those are as follows:

1. **Functional** - In a functional organizational structure, a project is assigned to the functional department that is best equipped to implement the project or that is most capable of ensuring the project's success.

    When using the functional organizational form to complete a project, the tam comprises individuals from the functional department to which the project is assigned. This structure not only allows individuals to use their expertise and demonstrate special abilities, but also presents them opportunities for professional growth.

    A downside to this organizational structure is that no single person has full accountability for the project, which increases the likelihood that the project will fail. Since the project manager is not given much formal authority, the functional organizational structure placed the project manager in the weakest position of all the organizational structures.

2. **Project Expeditor** - This form of organization retains the functional specialization but adds a project expeditor who serves as a communication link and coordinator for the project across the various functional units. The expeditor cannot personally make or enforce decisions. The project expeditor acts as a staff assistant to the executive who has ultimate responsibility for the project. The workers remain in their functional organizations and provide assistance as needed. The project expeditor has little formal authority. The project expeditor's primary responsibility is to communicate information between the executive and the workers. Most useful in the traditional functional organization where the project's worth and costs are relatively low.

3. **Project Coordinator** - The project coordinator organization is similar to the project expeditor structure, except that the coordinator reports to a higher-level manager than do

functional managers. The project expediter is moved out of facilitator position into a staff position reporting to a much higher level in the hierarchy. The project coordinator has more authority and responsibility than a project expediter. The project coordinator has the authority to assign work to individuals within the functional organization. The functional manager is forced to share resources and authority with the project coordinator. The size of projects in terms of dollars is relatively small compared to the rest of the organization.

4. **Weak Matrix** - A matrix organizational structure is a combination of functional and purely project structures. In a weak matrix organizational structure, the project manager has a low level of authority. The project manager is in charge of making sure activities are completed but cannot do certain things such as reallocate resources or make changes to a project's schedule.

    Lack of authority to make project-related decisions puts the project manager at a disadvantage, so in order to ensure that project goals are met, the project manager must use technical and interpersonal skills to influence the direction of the project.

    In some instances, the project manager is given some authority, but must share that authority with a functional manager. Shared authority often results in power struggles that disrupt the project environment and can jeopardize the successful completion of a project.

5. **Strong Matrix** - A strong matrix organizational structure is similar to a purely project structure in that the project manager has full decision-making authority. However, unlike a purely project organization, a strong matrix does not separate a project from the parent organization.

    There is a general division of responsibility in the matrix organizational structure. For example, the project manager controls what the project team does and when they do it, while the functional manager controls who is assigned to the project and what technology is used.

    Despite this division of responsibility, a strong matrix does not eliminate role ambiguity between project and functional managers. To avoid conflicts, the project and functional managers must communicate, negotiate, and be flexible when deciding who is responsible for what activities. The project manager has medium to high formal authority.

6. **Balanced Matrix** - The balanced matrix is a structure that includes some weak matrix characteristics and some strong matrix characteristics. In this structure, the project manager's authority is considered to below to moderate given that only 15 to 60 percent of the organization's personnel are assigned to project work.

7. **Projectized** - In a projectized organization, a separate, vertical structure is established for each project. Personnel are assigned to particular projects on a full-time basis. The project manager has total authority over the project, which is subject only to the time, cost, and performance constraints specified in the project targets.

8. **Composite** - The composite organization shows that most modern organizations involve all the organizational structures at various levels. Even an organization that is structured as a classic functional organization may create a special project team to handle a critical project. This team may then have characteristics of a fully projectized structure and may use full-time staff members for the work.

All forms of organizations are pretty well described here, but you will want to know that there are functional organizations and project expeditors, which are little more than functionaries and help support the idea of project management, without really practicing the practice; the project coordinator is a step up from that. A weak matrix is where the project manager gets resources from functional organizations; a strong matrix is where the balance of power has shifted to the project manager. The way to determine if the balance of power has shifted is to note where the money and the reporting flow from. If all money and reports are generated by the project and are respected as being from the project, then it is a strong matrix. If the functional organizations are seen as generating revenue for the organization rather than the project organizations, then it is a weak matrix. And if it is a mix? It is a balanced matrix

PMI's ideal organization is one that is projectized; it's a place where the project has its own little home within the organization. You should know that a project manager is a professional in the eyes of PMI®.

Project Interfaces
PMI® discusses three types of interfaces that should be considered in organizational planning. You should be familiar with each one and with specific examples. These interfaces often occur simultaneously.
- **Organizational Interfaces** - deal with the types of reporting relationships that exist within an organization's structure, be they functional, matrix, or projectized.
- **Technical Interfaces** - deal with the reporting relationships that exist within the technical areas of an organization.
- **Interpersonal Interfaces** - deal with the relationships that exist among project team members and among other project participants.

Organizational Planning Constraints
Constraints are discussed in almost all of the project management knowledge areas. In human resource management, a number of constraints are mentioned. Human resources planning, in particular, is affected by constraints such as the following:
- **Organizational Structure of the Performing Organization** - Organizational structures can become a constraint. For example, a strong matrix structure provides the project manager with much more authority and power than the weak matrix structure.
- **Collective Bargaining Agreements** - Collective bargaining agreements with unions and contractual obligations with other organized employee associations may require specialized reporting relationships and are considered constraints.
- **Team Preferences** - Partiality of the project management team might be a constraint. Failure or success with a certain organizational structure in the past might lead team members to prefer one type of team or organizational structure over another type.
  Expected Staff Assignments - The organization of the project team should be influenced by the skills, experience and knowledge of the project team members who wills operate on the team. This constraint is called expected staff assignments.

Key Human Resource Planning Outputs
- **Role and Responsibility** - Project roles in this context refer to the project manager, project team member, and stakeholders. The roles and responsibilities for this process are tied to the project scope and the work breakdown structure. Many times a project manager will design

and use Responsibility Assignment Matrix (See PMBOK® Guide figure 9.5) to graphically display this information. Note the importance of linking these roles and responsibilities to scope definition, and know the purpose of and how to prepare a responsibility assignment matrix.

- **Staffing Management Plan** - This plan documents how and when people resources will be introduced to the project and then upon completion of the project how they will be released. Recognize that project managers may have responsibilities for human resource redeployment and release. Resource histograms often are part of this plan (see PMBOK® Guide figure 9.6).
- **Project Organization Chart** - This type of chart shows the reporting relationship of the project team members. Note that the organizational breakdown structure, discussed also in the scope definition section, is a type of organization chart that shows which organizational units are responsible for which work packages.

Acquire Project Team

The acquire project team process involves obtaining and assigning personnel to perform project activities. The project manager's goal during staff acquisition is to obtain personnel who have the skills that are outlined in the project's staff management plan.

It is important to understand that acquiring staff is a component of the human resource management variable and is also part of the planning step of the project management process. A key input to this process is the staffing pool description.

Before acquiring staff for a project, it is helpful to answer the following questions:
- What type of organizational structure will be used for the project?
- Who should be on the project team?
- What skills would each team member bring to the project?
- Will team members work well together?
- What can result when the project loses a key team member?

Because staff assignments must be negotiated on most projects, negotiating is a principal tool and technique. Negotiation is defined as the art of achieving what you want from a transaction, leaving all other parties involved content that the relationship has gone well. Negotiating for project personnel is not an easy task. The most critical element of successful negotiating is preparation. NEVER GO INTO A NEGOTIATION PROCESS UNLESS YOU ARE PREPARED.

Negotiating also relates to the project manager's ability to influence the organization to "get things done," so again, review the definitions for power and politics. PMI® explains that the team's influencing competencies and politics play an important role in negotiating staff assignments. For example, a functional manager may be rewarded based on staff utilization. This in turn creates an incentive for this manager to assign available staff who may not meet all the project's requirements.

Virtual Teams

A team is a small number of people with complementary skills who are committed to a common purpose, performance goals, and approach for which they hold themselves mutually accountable. Generally, teams have from two to twenty-five people. Teams need complementary skills or the right mix of skills to do the job assigned. A team's purpose and performance goals go together. Both must be clear or confusion will likely result. It is important that the team own and commit to the purpose and shape it if necessary. In addition, teams need to develop a common approach or method on how they will work together to accomplish their purpose. Finally, groups become teams when they hold themselves accountable for the outcome.

A virtual team is a group of people who primarily interact electronically and who may meet face-to-face occasionally. Examples of virtual teams include a team of people working at different geographic sites and a project team whose members telecommute.

Strategies for Virtual Teams
- Hold an initial face-to-face startup
- Have periodic face-to-face meetings, especially to resolve conflict and maintain team cohesiveness
- Establish a clear code of conduct or set of norms and protocols for behavior
- Recognize and reward performance
- Use visuals in communications
- Recognize that most communications will be non-verbal -- use caution in tone and language

Benefits of Virtual Teams
- People can work from anywhere at anytime.
- People can be recruited for their competencies, not just physical location.
- Many physical handicaps are not a problem.
- Expenses associated with travel, lodging, parking, and leasing or owning a building may be reduced and sometimes eliminated.

Functions of the Project Manager
- Planning, scheduling, and estimating
- Performance, cost, and trend analysis
- Progress reporting
- Maintaining client/consultant relations
- Logistics management
- Cost control
- Procedure writing and administration
- Interface management (identifying; documenting; scheduling; communicating; and monitoring personnel, organizational, and system interfaces relating to the project)
- Integration of the efforts of project subsystems
- PMI® considers planning, organizing, leading, and controlling the four most important functions of the project manager. Effective management of the dual reporting relationship—a situation in which team members are accountable to both a project manager and a functional manager—generally is the project manager's responsibility.

Roles of the Project Manager
- Integrator
- Communicator
- Team leader
- Decision maker
- Climate creator/builder

Qualifications of the Project Manager
- Works well with others
- Experienced in his or her area of expertise
- Supervisory experience

- Familiar with contract administration
- Able to accurately present the company's position
- A qualified negotiator
- Experience and Education Requirements of the Project Manager
- Formal college education desirable
- Continuing education in topics such as negotiation, conflict management, group dynamics, and leadership
- Experience as a functional manager, or preferably, a project management assistant

Types of Power

According to PMI®, the project manager can exert the following types of power:

- **Legitimate Power** - Legitimate power is derived from the person's formal position within the organization. The project manager's ability to use this power derives from his or her position in the organizational hierarchy and his or her degree of control over the project, as modified by the organizational climate. Use of this power should be in conjunction with expert and reward power whenever possible.
- **Coercive Power** - Coercive power is predicated on fear (for example, a subordinate fears being deprived of something for failing to do what the supervisor asks). The ability to use this power derives from the project manager's control over the project and project personnel.
- **Reward Power** - Reward power involves positive reinforcement and the ability to award people something of value in exchange for their cooperation. The project manager's ability to use this power derives from his or her position in the organizational hierarchy and degree of control over the project.
- **Expert Power** - Expert power can only be exercised by individuals who are held in particular esteem because of their special knowledge or skill. The project manager's ability to use this power derives from reputation, knowledge, and experience.
- **Referent Power** - Referent power is based on citing the authority of a more powerful person (for example, one's supervisor or someone's spouse is the CEO) as the basis for one's own authority. The project manager's ability to use this power derives from his or her position in the organizational hierarchy.

PMI® recommends that project managers rely on reward and expert power to the greatest extent possible, and that they avoid use of coercive power. Please be aware that in addition to the above list, other project management luminaries have also coined terms to describe forms of power or influence. These terms include:

- **Purse-string Power** - Denotes budget or spending authority held by the project manager
- **Bureaucratic Power** - The ability of the project manager to use the rules and procedures of the organization to maximize personal effectiveness.
- **Charismatic Power** - Power and influence derived from the project manager's personality and persona to encourage people to accomplish things they may not be inclined to do.
- **Penalty Power** - Involves negative reinforcement and the ability to withhold something of value as a response to lack of cooperation or poor performance.

What types of power do we have as a project manager? Legitimate, coercive, reward, expert and referent. The thing that is critical here is to recognize that reward and expert power are the best kinds of power that a project manager can exert. The worst kind, from PMI's perspective, is coercive power—power by virtue of threat.

Team Development

Team development is an important aspect of resource planning that is often overlooked. This is often viewed as an Execution Phase issue; however, if thought through early in the planning of the project, the issue can be dealt with during the Planning Phase.

Team development revolves around activities that are directed to enhance the cohesiveness of a team and get a better understanding of its strengths and weaknesses. Quite often the problem lies in team members seeing the work they do as functionally independent of other team members and therefore contributing very little, if anything, to the team itself.

The benefits of team development include improvement in project performance, improvements in agency skill areas, improvement in team interaction and behaviors, and a feeling of team satisfaction.

The following are examples of team development tools and techniques:
- **Team Building Activities** - Activities that provide interaction among team members and two-way communications are encouraged. These include events such as team-building activities in which the project team members spend time together doing work-related or non-work-related activities in order to build a sense of team unity. Team-building activities can be work related, such as meetings in which different people discuss their views on project issues, or they can be fun extracurricular activities.
- **Co-location** - In today's workplace with limited office space and functional specialties, it is sometimes difficult to co-locate project team members. If the option of having all of your team members sit together is available, however, take advantage of it. Co-location fosters increased communication and often quick problem solving.
- **Training** - The idea behind training is to increase and hone the skills of the project team to improve project performance. Training can be both formal (taking classes in particular skill areas) and informal (receiving feedback from managers and team members). Project team members benefit professionally from learning new skills, and that benefit is returned to the project in the form of increased productivity and better products. Training is an element that should be considered early based on the skill needs of the project team, and funds should be allocated for training purposes.

Team Building

Team building is a key tool and technique for team development. PMI® points out the difficulty of developing a team in a matrix organization structure in which team members must report to a project manager and a functional manager and in which development as a team is critical to the project's ability to meet its objectives. Team development serves to promote performance improvements both in terms of individual skills and in team behaviors. A mandatory prerequisite for team building is commitment from top management. PMI® recommends a concerted team-building effort at the start of every new project.

Goals and Results of Project Team Building
- Team members are interdependent
- There is a consensus on well-defined project goals and objectives
- Team members are committed to working together
- Team is accountable as a functioning unit within the larger organization
- There is a moderate level of competition and conflict

Benefits of Team Building
- Establishment of realistic, achievable, objectives for the team
- Commitment of team member support to make the team successful
- Understanding of team member's priorities to help address difficulties

Encouragement of Open Communications
- More effective problem solving due to broader base of expertise
- More meaningful performance feedback based on establishment of expectations
- Allows for more effective conflict resolution

- Maintenance of balance between group productivity and individual team members needs
- Encouragement of team members to test their abilities and ideas
- Conformation of individual behavior to meet team standards
- Creates a pool of effective team members for future projects

Symptoms of Poor Teamwork
- Frustration
- Conflict and unhealthy competition among team members
- Team meetings are unproductive and demoralizing
- Team members work independently and avoid needed cooperation
- Problem-solving activities like constructive conflict are avoided
- Lack of trust or confidence in the project manager
- Team members are unresponsive to the needs of the team or the project

Ground Rules for Project Team Building
- Start as soon as possible
- Continue team building throughout the life of the project
- Recruit the best possible people
- Make sure that everyone who will significantly contribute to the project, full- or part-time, is on the team
- Obtain team agreement on all major actions
- Recognize the existence of team politics but stay out of them
- Behave as a role model
- Use delegation as the best way to assure commitment
- Don't try to force or manipulate team members
- Regularly evaluate team effectiveness
- Plan and use a team-building process

The Team-building Process
Plan for team building
- Carefully define project roles and assignments
- Ensure project goals and members' personal goals coincide

Negotiate for team members
- Obtain the most promising personnel available
- Choose candidates with both technical expertise and potential to be effective team members

Organize the team
- Make specific assignments to specific people
- Prepare and circulate responsibility matrixes

Hold a kickoff meeting
- Set technical and procedural agendas
- Ensure sufficient time for members to get to know one another
- Establish working relationships and communications

Obtain team member commitments
- Time commitment
- Role commitment
- Project priority commitment
- Build communication links
- Conduct team-building exercises

Incorporate team-building activities into all project activities

- Meetings, planning sessions, and technical/schedule reviews
- Group and individual counseling sessions
- Recognition of outstanding performance

A project manager needs to realize that establishing trust should be the first step in generating positive team performance, when project team members are not collocated. Look down this list of issues associated with team building. What you want to remember are the things that make team building sound great, make it sound positive, and make it sound like something every project should strive for on a regular basis.

Characteristics of Effective Groups
- Clearly defined goals
- Open, goal-directed communication
- Equally shared power
- Flexible decision making
- Controversy considered healthy
- Diversity encouraged
- Evident interpersonal problem-solving

Characteristics of Ineffective Groups
- Goals vague or imposed without discussion
- Communication guarded
- Power with leader—not shared
- Decision making without consultation
- Controversy and conflict not tolerated
- Individual resources not utilized
- Undervalue of member contributions

Problems with Groups
- Splitting: clique and/or opposing groups
- Hidden Agendas: past baggage gets in the way of group goals and work
- Social Loafing: slacking off to let (force) other members complete majority of work
- Destructive Behavior: damaging to group and individuals; must be dealt with by leader

Role Functions of Members
- Maintenance: make others feel good
- Aggressor: attacks other members
- Blocker: rejects and argues to block the work of the others
- Joker: does not take work seriously
- Avoider: whispers, doodles, passive
- Self confessor: works on personal issues
- Recognition seeker: seeks to be the center of attention

Ground Rules

The purpose of ground rules is to help guide constructive behavior. Ground rules can also outline process procedures, such as how decisions are made and how information is shared. Typically, ground rules frame expectations about the way project tasks and activities should be completed by the project team. An effective way for a project manager to establish collaborative group behavior is to introduce a draft set of suggested ground rules at the first team or project meeting.

During the discussion of ground rules, the project manager needs to explain the purpose of the ground rules and encourages the project team to discuss them. To illustrate how this may occur, the project manager may say something like, "I drafted some suggested ground rules we could all follow for this project. Although they are only suggestions, let's go over the ground rules and see how people feel about following them."

Examples of "Suggested Ground Rules" include:
- Focus on interests and ideas, not positions or solutions to the problem.
- Listen to understand each idea and interest. Ask questions.
- Respect different viewpoints.
- All ideas count, even wild ones.
- Everybody participates.
- Everyone shares responsibility for following the ground rules.

Co-location

Co-location is an approach in which all team members are brought together in one location. It has proven to be beneficial for team development. PMI® states that collocation is effective in facilitating better communications and rapid team building. PMI® also notes that co-location may be impractical at times but should be considered when drastic steps are indicated because it effectively prevents dilution of the project effort by decreasing distractions and focusing the entire team on the same problems.

Maslow's Hierarchy of Needs

According to Maslow's Hierarchy of Needs, people have the following five kinds of needs:
- Physiological needs, of which the most important are the need for food and other things necessary for survival
- The need for safety—from danger, threat, and deprivation
- Social needs for association with one's fellows, for friendship, and love
- The need for self-respect, self-esteem, the respect of one's fellows, status
- The need for self-fulfillment through the development of powers and skills, and a chance to use creativity (self-actualization)

Maslow theorized that people are driven to satisfy survival needs first, followed by safety needs, and so on. Once these needs are fulfilled, the drive to fulfill them goes away until the needs arise again. The application to human resource management is that certain needs must be met in order for people to function at their peak physical and mental levels, enabling them to fulfill their project responsibilities.

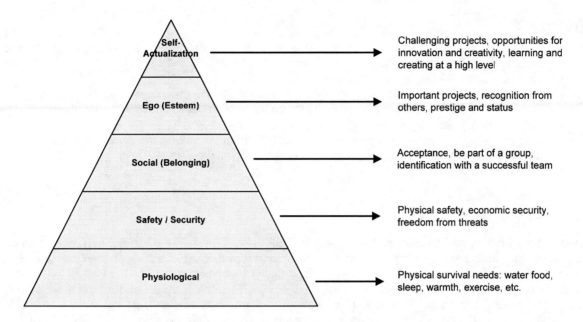

Figure 30 - Maslow's Hierarchy of Needs

Maslow's Hierarchy of Needs is shown above. The pyramid illustrates the five levels of human needs. The most basic are physiological and safety/security, shown at the base of the pyramid. As one moves to higher levels of the pyramid, the needs become more complex.

Douglas McGregor

According to Douglas McGregor's Theory X, the average person is lazy, avoiding work and responsibility whenever possible, needs constant supervision, and is motivated to work only when threatened. McGregor's Theory Y suggests that the average person is willing to work without constant supervision.

A project manager who agrees with Theory X is strict with team members, motivating them with undesirable consequences. This kind of project manager does not allow team members to participate in making project decisions.

A project manager who agrees with Theory Y motivates team members by allowing them to work with little supervision and encourages participation in making project decisions. Allowing team members to work somewhat independently can build confidence. Listening to their input before making decisions can strengthen team members' commitment to a project.

Theory X

With Theory X assumptions, management's role is to coerce and control employees.
- People have an inherent dislike for work and will avoid it whenever possible.
- People must be coerced, controlled, directed, or threatened with punishment in order to get them to achieve the organizational objectives.
- People prefer to be directed, do not want responsibility, and have little or no ambition.
- People seek security above all else.

Theory Y

With Theory Y assumptions, management's role is to develop the potential in employees and help them to release that potential toward common goals.
- Work is as natural as play and rest.
- People will exercise self-direction if they are committed to the objectives (they are not lazy).
- Commitment to objectives is a function of the rewards associated with their achievement.
- People learn to accept and seek responsibility.
- Creativity, ingenuity, and imagination are widely distributed among the population. People are capable of using these abilities to solve an organizational problem.
- People have potential.

Theory Z

Theory Z was developed by William Ouchi, in his 1982 book Theory Z: How American management can Meet the Japanese Challenge. Theory Z is often referred to as the "'Japanese" management style, which is essentially what it is. Theory Z essentially advocates a combination of all that's best about theory Y and modern Japanese management, which places a large amount of freedom and trust with workers, and assumes that workers have a strong loyalty and interest in team-working and the organization. Theory Z also places more reliance on the attitude and responsibilities of the workers, whereas McGregor's XY theory is mainly focused on management and motivation from the manager's and organization's perspective.

Herzberg's Theory of Motivation

Frederick Herzberg constructed a two-dimensional paradigm of factors affecting people's attitudes about work. He concluded that such factors as company policy, supervision, interpersonal relations, working conditions, and salary are hygiene factors rather than motivators. According to the theory, the absence of hygiene factors can create job dissatisfaction, but their presence does not motivate or create satisfaction.

In contrast, he determined from the data that the motivators were elements that enriched a person's job; he found five factors in particular that were strong determiners of job satisfaction: achievement, recognition, the work itself, responsibility, and advancement. These motivators (satisfiers) were associated with long-term positive effects in job performance while the hygiene factors (dissatisfiers) consistently produced only short-term changes in job attitudes and performance, which quickly fell back to its previous level.

In summary, satisfiers describe a person's relationship with what she or he does, many related to the tasks being performed. Dissatisfiers, on the other hand, have to do with a person's relationship to the context or environment in which she or he performs the job. The satisfiers relate to what a person does while the dissatisfiers relate to the situation in which the person does what he or she does.

Expectancy Theory

Expectancy theory holds that people will tend to be highly productive and motivated if the following two conditions are satisfied: (1) people believe that their efforts will likely lead to successful results and (2) those people also believe they will be rewarded for their success. Expectancy theory says two things. One, you get what you expect—self-fulfilling prophecy. The other is, if people think that their outcomes are going to be significant, if they think they are going to matter in terms of the organization, then they do better. People like to be involved in something where they think they are making a difference.

Reward and Recognition Systems

PMI® explains that people are motivated in direct proportion to the value they feel is being placed on them. Rewards demonstrate this value. Reward and recognition systems are formal ways of recognizing and promoting desirable behavior. To be effective, the link between project performance and reward must be clear, explicit, and achievable. In addition to rewarding individuals for outstanding work, team incentive rewards are effective motivators. If the organization does not have a reward system, or if that reward system is inappropriate for project-based work, then the project should have its own reward and recognition system. It is desirable for project staff to provide input to the appraisals of any project staff members with whom they interact in a significant way. PMI® suggests that a good rule for project managers is to give the team all the glory possible during the life cycle of the project because there may be little left at the end.

Personnel Issues

The project manager or project teams rarely have the responsibility of the administration of the human resource procedures. These matters are typically handled by the personnel department. However, you should be aware of any administrative requirements to ensure compliance. A variety of personnel issues may appear on the exam, such as the following:

- **Fringe Benefits** - Education, training, profit sharing, medical benefits, and the employer's matching of 401(k) contributions, and so on.
- **Perquisites** or "Perks" - A window office, a corner office, use of the executive dining room, special parking space, a company car, and so on.
- **Arbitration** - A technique for resolving conflict in which the parties agree to have a neutral third party hear the dispute and make a decision. The parties agree in advance to abide by this decision.
- **Productivity** - Measured as a ratio that divides some measure of output by the input required. For example, the number of items produced per hour of labor.
- **Human Resource Functions** - Aside from the traditional role of hiring, there are several other important functions often performed by human resource departments. These include training, career planning, and team building.

One big thing to remember out of this is knowing the difference between a fringe and a perk. A fringe benefit is something provided across the organization to anyone who is eligible for it. A perk is something given to an individual based on individual performance.

Conflict Management

Conflict is a natural disagreement resulting from individuals or groups that differ in attitudes, beliefs, values or needs. It can also originate from past rivalries and personality differences. Other causes of conflict include trying to negotiate before the timing is right or before needed information is available. PMI® considers dealing with conflict to be absolutely necessary to improving team behaviors.

Why Conflict is Unavoidable on Projects
- High-stress environment
- Ambiguous roles
- Multiple bosses
- Prevalence of advanced technology concerns

Seven Sources of Conflict in Project Environments
1. Project priorities
2. Administrative procedures
3. Technical opinions and performance trade-offs

4. Personnel resources
5. Cost
6. Schedules
7. Personalities

Among these sources, PMI® considers conflict over program priorities, personnel resources, technical issues, and scheduling problems to create the most tension in the project management environment.

Every project has conflicts and PMI® wants you to understand that. It also wants you to know why that happens and the sources for conflict. Make sure you know that PMI® considers conflict over program priorities, personnel resources, technical issues, and scheduling problems as being the ones that cause the most tension in the project environment.

Conflict and the Project Life Cycle

The highest-ranked sources of conflict evident in each phase of the life cycle are:
- Concept phase - Project priorities, administrative procedures, and schedules
- Development phase - Project priorities, schedules, and administrative procedures
- Implementation phase - Schedules, technical issues, and personnel resources
- Termination phase - Schedules, personality conflicts, and personnel resources

Whether conflict has a net positive or negative effect on a project and its parent organization depends on how the project manager handles it. PMI® recognizes these five methods for dealing with conflict:
- **Problem Solving** (or Confrontation) - With problem solving, the project manager addresses conflict directly in a problem-solving mode to get the parties working together to define the problem, collect information, develop and analyze alternatives, and select the most appropriate alternative. PMI® recommends problem solving as the conflict resolution method of choice.
- **Compromising** - Compromising consists of bargaining and searching for solutions that attempt to bring some degree of satisfaction to the conflicting parties. Neither party wins but each may get some degree of satisfaction. PMI® considers this the second-best conflict resolution mode, after problem solving/confrontation.
- **Smoothing** - Smoothing consists of de-emphasizing the opponents' differences and emphasizing their commonalties over the issues in question. Smoothing keeps the atmosphere friendly, but avoids solving the root causes of the conflict.
- **Withdrawal** - Withdrawal is defined as retreating from actual or potential disagreements and conflict situations. It is really a delaying tactic that fails to resolve the conflict but does cool down the situation temporarily.
- **Forcing** - Forcing consists of exerting one's viewpoint at the potential expense of another party, thus establishing a win-lose situation. PMI® recommends using forcing only as a last resort, because it can cause additional conflicts as antagonism builds.

As you look at the various ways that we can manage conflict, PMI's preferred approach is the very first one: problem solving/confrontation. PMI® will almost always in the PMP® exam recognize this as confrontation rather than problem solving. That makes it a little harder to recognize the most positive or the most optimistic way to approach a particular problem. Confrontation is always the PMI® approach.

One Party Conflict Management

This method relates more specifically to personal styles of the leaders handling conflict.

The five styles of handling conflict include:
1. **Win-Lose** - High concern for personal goals and low concern for relationships. Related to the forcing method above.
2. **Yield-Lose** - Low concern for personal goals and high concern for relationships. Related to the smoothing method above.
3. **Lose-Leave** - Low concern for personal goals and low concern for relationships. Related to the withdrawal method above.
4. **Compromise** - Moderate concern for personal goals and moderate concern for relationships. Related to the compromise method above.
5. **Integrative** - High concern for personal goals and high concern for relationships. Related to the problem solving method above.

Issue Log

The issue log is a vehicle used to register all project related issues requiring follow-up. It contains information regarding the issue or problem, likely impact, severity, planning assumptions, actions required and date of resolution.

Project Performance Appraisals

An appraisal is a formal evaluation of the extent to which the worker has achieved the objectives established in the performance plan. Managers typically conduct the appraisal within a month of the closing of the appraisal period (but not before the end). The appraisal is formally written, but presented in a face-to-face meeting with the worker (even workers who work at different locations than their managers).

An appraisal typically presents statements that describe how the worker performed on each objective, numerical assessments of the performance in each area, and a numerical assessment of overall performance evaluation. The numerical assessment usually indicates whether or not the employee met expectations. Most appraisal systems also indicate the extent to which the worker exceeded expectations (sometimes, usually, or always).

Appraisals also provide workers with feedback on their strengths and areas in which they should focus improvement efforts.

Upward appraisal occurs when employees give information on a manager's performance. 360 degree appraisal is a variant of upward appraisal, and extends the use of appraisers to include people from all around the manager, rather than just reporting staff. 360 is often used as a shorthand for any combination of upward, downward, peer, colleague, customer or supplier appraisal of an employee. Variations on this concept include 90 degree feedback, which is based on peer assessments from work associates, and 180 degree feedback - or upward review - based on feedback from multiple, direct reports.

Chapter Review

1. A document or tool which describes when and how human resources will be brought onto and taken off the project team is called a:
    A. Staffing Management Plan
    B. Responsibility Assignment Matrix (RAM)
    C. Organizational Breakdown Structure (OBS)
    D. Resource Assignment Chart

2. Which of the following organization types results in the project managers having the least authority
    A. Projectized
    B. Balanced Matrix
    C. Functional
    D. Strong Matrix

3. Management by projects:
    A. Is the same as program management
    B. Treats many aspects of ongoing operations as projects in order to apply project management techniques to them
    C. Refers specifically to the application of project reporting techniques
    D. Uses the OBS to assign specific responsibilities for projects to the different units within an organization

4. Which of the following is not a technique for team development?
    A. Collocation
    B. Reward and recognition systems
    C. Confronting
    D. Training

5. The belief that management's high levels of trust, confidence and commitment to workers leads to high levels of motivation and productivity on the part of workers is a part of which motivation theory?
    A. Theory Y
    B. Theory Z
    C. Theory X
    D. Contingency Theory

6. Legitimate power is:
    A. Power derived from a person's formal position in the organization.
    B. Power bestowed due to a person's personal qualities and abilities.
    C. Power earned based on a person's technical knowledge, skill, or expertise in a particular area.
    D. Power to distribute information as one sees fit.

7. A document or tool used to show which work elements have been assigned to which organizational units:
    A. Staffing Management Plan
    B. Responsibility Assignment Matrix
    C. Organizational Breakdown Structure
    D. Resource Assignment Chart

8. Which of the following statements describes the difference between a balanced matrix project organization and a strong matrix project organization?
    A. A strong matrix has a project manager and a balanced matrix does not have a project manager
    B. In a strong matrix organization, the project manager reports directly to the CEO, while in the balanced matrix, the project manager reports to a functional manager
    C. In a strong matrix organization, project coordination is performed by the project manager who resides in a department of project managers while in the balanced matrix; coordination is performed by a project manager who resides in a functional department with other staff members.
    D. There is no difference. A balanced matrix is another name for a strong matrix.

9. Which of the following is not true about the team development process?
    A. Team development includes enhancing the ability of stakeholders to contribute as individuals
    B. Team development occurs throughout the project life cycle
    C. Reward and recognition systems are important techniques for team development
    D. The primary output from team development is the identification of required training

10. Which of the following is not part of the definition of leadership?
    A. Leadership is concerned with consistently producing results expected by stakeholders
    B. Leadership is developing a vision of the future and the necessary strategies
    C. Leadership is aligning people through communication
    D. Leadership is helping people to energize themselves to overcome barriers to change

Answers

1. A, PMBOK® Guide 3rd Edition, page 208
2. C, PMBOK® Guide 3rd Edition, page 28
3. B, PMBOK® Guide 3rd Edition, page 8
4. C, PMBOK® Guide 3rd Edition, page 212
5. B, Verma's "Human Resource Skills for the Project Manager", pg. 71-73
6. A, See Adams, "Principles of Project Management", pg. 74 and Verma's, "Human Resource Skills for the Project Manager", pg. 233
7. C, PMBOK® Guide 3rd Edition, page 205
8. C, PMBOK® Guide 3rd Edition, page 28
9. D, PMBOK® Guide 3rd Edition, page 212
10. A, PMBOK® Guide 3rd Edition, page 15

Chapter 10

Project Communications Management

Reference Material to Study
- A Guide to the Project Management Body of Knowledge (PMBOK® Guide 3rd Edition), Chapter 10
- Human Resource Skills for the Project Manager, Verma, Vijay K., 1996, Chapter 1

What to Study
- The PMBOK® phases of Project Communications Management: Communications Planning, Information Distribution, Performance Reporting, and Administrative Closure (Be familiar with Inputs, Tools and Techniques, and Outputs for each phase)
- Know the difference between the general management skill of communicating and Project Communications Management. The general management skill of communicating is the broader subject and involves knowledge such as: sender-receiver models, choice of media, writing style, presentation techniques, and meeting management techniques.
- Be familiar with the goals of interpersonal communication.
- Understand how interpersonal communication works. (sender-receiver model)
- Know the different methods of communication. (written, verbal, and non-verbal including body language)
- Be familiar with the barriers to successful communication.
- Be familiar with communication channels and links. Know the formula for communications channels: $(N * (N - 1)) / 2$
- Be familiar with effective listening techniques.
- Be familiar with the barriers to effective listening and the guidelines for active listening.
- Know the four major communication styles: concrete-sequential, abstract-sequential, concrete-random, and abstract-random.
- Know the amount of time project managers spend communicating

Key Definitions
- **Active Listening** - Is engaged listening. It requires patience, self-control, empathy, and a willingness to understand the other person's perspective. Helps facilitate the development of mutual trust, respect, and good working relationships thus improving the overall performance of the team.
- **Communication Barriers** - Obstacles that impede communications. For example: limited communication channels, distance, noise, cultural differences, organizational climate, perceptions, limited information, withholding of information, terminology, number of communication links, manipulation (hidden agenda), etc.
- **Communications Requirements** - Communications requirements are the sum of the information requirements of the project stakeholders.

- **Communicator** - The originator of the message. The source of the communication. Also known as the Sender.
- **Effective Listening** - Is the ability to recognize the importance of verbal and nonverbal listening behaviors including body language. It's also the ability to utilize gestures and body language consciously (with consideration for cultural differences) to put people at ease and enhance communication.
- **Feedback** - Information on how well the message was received.
- **Filtering** - Occurs when a large portion of the message is lost from the sender to the receiver. Generally caused by problems of language, culture, semantics, knowledge base, etc. Filtering can be deliberate and positive as in the case of upward communications where the subordinate "filters" information that the superior does not need or want to know.
- **Noise** - Any interference or disturbance that confuses the message.
- **Receiver** (Recipient) - The person for whom the message is intended.
- **Tight Matrix** - Refers to bringing together all the project team members into one location or in close proximity.

The Project Communications Management questions on the PMP® exam are basic and are taken primarily from the PMBOK® Guide and other PMI® published materials. Common sense and your own expertise will play a large role in your ability to answer the questions on this topic.

PMI® considers management style to be an essential component of how a project manager communicates, and thinks of the kickoff meeting as one of the most effective mechanisms in Project Communications Management. The questions on the exam about this focus on formal and informal communication, verbal versus written communication, conflict resolution, and management styles.

The processes that make up the Project Communications Management knowledge area are as follows: Communications Planning, Information Distribution, Performance Reporting, and Manage Stakeholders.

The processes in the Project Communications knowledge area are related to general communication skills but aren't the same thing. Communication skills are considered general management skills that the project manager utilizes on a daily basis. The processes in the Communications knowledge area seek to ensure that all project information including project plans, risk assessments, meeting notes, and more is collected and documented. These processes also ensure information is distributed and shared with appropriate stakeholders and project members. At project closure, the information is archived and used as a reference for future projects. This is referred to as historical information in several project processes.

Communication Skills

The general management skill of communicating is related to, but not the same as, project communications management. Communicating is the broader subject and involves a substantial body of knowledge that is not unique to projects.

Communicating consists of using sender receiver models which includes both feedback loops and barriers to communication. Note that you will want to create internal and external feedback loops to help evaluate the effectiveness of communications. Feedback is considered either positive or negative based on the effect it has, not on its content. Research suggests that, amongst the many reasons why information fails to be communicated, the following are the main barriers:
- Different status of the sender and the receiver - (e.g. a senior manager sends a memo to a production supervisor - who is likely to pay close attention to the message. The same information, conveyed in the opposite direction might not get the attention it deserves).
- Use of jargon - employees who are "specialists" may fall for the trap of using specialist language for a non-specialist audience (e.g. the IT technician who cannot tries to explain how users should log onto a network, in language that sounds foreign to most users of the network).
- Selective reporting - where the reporter gives the recipient incorrect or incomplete information.
- Poor timing - information that is not immediately relevant (e.g. notice of some deadline that seems a long way off) is not always actioned straightaway.
- Conflict - where the communicator and recipient are in conflict; information tends to be ignored or distorted.
- Choice of Media - Choice of media is when to communicate in writing versus orally, when to write an informal memo versus a formal report, and when to communicate face-to-face, or via e-mail. The media chosen for communication activities will depend upon the situation.
- Writing Style - Writing style deals with grammar issues such as voice structure (active versus passive), sentence structure, and proper word selection.
- Presentation Techniques - This area includes both body language and presentation of material. It also includes such things as agenda preparation and dealing with conflict.

The Communications Model

According to PMI®, the communications model consists of four major parts, as indicated below:
- Sender - The originator of the message.
- Message - Thoughts, feelings, or ideas, reduced to "code" that are understandable by both sender and receiver.
- Medium - The vehicle or method used to convey the message. The choice of medium will color and influence the effect of the message. The most common media are visual, audio, and tactile.
- Receiver - The person for whom the message is intended. He or she must accept and understand the message before communication has taken place.

The receiver may filter the information, that is, selectively reduce its quantity or quality. If the receiver is actively listening, he or she is attentive and asks for clarification or repetition of ambiguous messages. The sender should request feedback to ensure the message has been received in its entirety.

Communication Channels

As the scope of a project grows, it is also natural in most cases for the size of the project team to grow. In fact, it is known that the number of possible communication channels among project team members is determined by the following formula: $(n^2 - n) \div 2$ where "n" represents the number of people on the team. Know this formula!

Using the formula above—$(n^2 - n) \div 2$—we could calculate the communication channel for the picture above. Based on the formula and information given $(5^2 - 5) \div 2 = (25 - 5) \div 2 = 20 \div 2 = 10$ different communication channels.

A sample exam question may be similar to this: If you have a communication team with five members and you add four more people to the team, how many additional communication channels were added?

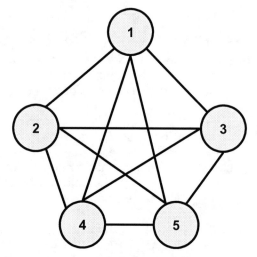

Figure 31 - Communication Channel

Such a mathematical relationship is known as a geometric series. In ordinary language this simply means that as team size grows, the number of potential communication channels grows at greater than a linear rate. Although not everyone on the team needs to communicate with everyone else on each type of communication, the potential exists to overwhelm the team with communication requirements. Accordingly, the larger a team grows the more important it is for the project manager to reorganize the team structure to enhance formal communications.

There is an easy way to handle this on the exam if you do not want to memorize the mathematical formula. When it comes to communications channels, think of it as a game of connecting the dots. All you need to do is draw a circle to represent each participant in the communications loop. Let's say there are four members in the communications loop. You draw the line from the first circle over to the other three, then from the second to the remaining two, and from the third to the remaining one. What you wind up with is a series of lines connecting them. That series of lines represents the number of communications channels that must exist, and is the same as the formula $(n^2 - n) \div 2$.

Communications Planning

The process of determining the information and communications needs of the project stakeholders:
- Who needs what information?
- When will they need it?
- How will it be given to them?
- Who will give it to them?

While all projects share the need to communicate project information, the needs and methods of distribution can vary. Identifying the informational needs of the stakeholders and determining a suitable means of meeting those needs is an important factor for project success. Communications planning is often tightly linked with organizational planning since the organizational structure will have a major effect on the project's communications requirements. The majority of communications planning is usually done in the early phases of the project; however, the process results should be regularly reviewed and revised as appropriate.

The project communications variable is broken down into the following components: communications planning, information distribution, performance reporting and managing stakeholders. Project communication is a project variable that consists of orchestrating timely, accurate, and concise distribution of project data and updates to the appropriate people. The goal of project communication is to make sure everyone involved in a project has the information they need to fulfill their responsibilities.

A project's success or failure depends largely on the quality of communication within the project team, within the project's parent organization, and outside the project, with contractors and vendors. The smallest breakdown in communication can result in project failure. Therefore, project communication should be a priority during project planning and throughout project execution.

Communications Requirements

Once you have identified a project's stakeholders, the next step is to determine what their information requirements are. When determining information requirements, it is helpful to answer the following questions:
- Who is responsible for which project activities?
- Where are the stakeholders located?
- When do stakeholders want information?
- How often do stakeholders want information?
- What kinds of information do stakeholders want?

Communications Technology

Once you have determined what information the project's stakeholders need, you must decide how to get them the necessary information. The means of communication depends on such things as proximity of stakeholders, their level of involvement in a project, and the type of information they both need and want. Factors that may affect the project include: frequency need of the information, available technology, expected project staffing, and length of the project.

For example, if project team members work in close proximity to each other, then hardcopy reports, e-mail messages, meetings and telephone calls are appropriate. If stakeholders want to see progress reports but are thousands of miles from the project site, then reports can be faxed or e-mailed to them.

Stakeholder Analysis

Conducting a stakeholder analysis enables you to identify all project stakeholders. It should consider methods and technologies suited to the project that will provide the information needed to ensure that resources are not wasted on unnecessary information or inappropriate technology. You must also consider information distribution when considering or defining stakeholders.

Communications Management Plan

The communications management plan outlines the roles and responsibilities of project participants in the review, approval and dissemination of information about key project processes, events, documents and milestones. The communications management plan is the output of the communications planning process and is a subsidiary component of the project plan.

The communications management plan should contain and provide the following information:
- What methods will be used for gathering and storing various information
- Who should receive the information and how will it be sent
- A description of the information to be distributed including formats and content
- Schedules showing when each type of communication will be produced
- A method for updating the communications plan

The Communications Management Plan is a subsidiary element of the overall project plan. It may be formal/informal, highly detailed or broadly framed depending on project needs.

A preliminary Communications Plan should be developed early in the project. The basic steps are as follows:
- Identify the project audience(s) - include internal and external stakeholder groups.
- Assess information needs - determine what groups need to know, want to know, and expect, taking into consideration frequency and length of involvement of each audience and organizational standards of practice. NOTE: Project resources should be expended only on communicating information that contributes to success or where a lack of communication can lead to failure.
- Identify information sources and assign responsibility for collecting information to be communicated.
- Identify the best media and methods available for use on the project, e.g. meetings, presentations, e-mail - remember people absorb information in different ways.
- Identify key messages, announcements, and/or marketing that needs to be delivered and can or should be included with routine or recurring communications.
- Define when and how communications will be provided.
- Document the approval process needed for any of the communications.
- Assign responsibilities for creating and delivering the various types of communications.
- Identify all triggers, such as key events/milestones/deliverable dates that will initiate communications.
- Define a process for handling ad hoc inquiries the project is likely to encounter.
- Develop a library of project information and assign responsibilities for its maintenance.
- Create internal and external feedback loops to help evaluate the effectiveness of communications as well as other project management processes.
- Schedule the work of communications and related triggers into the project schedule to ensure they are part of the overall plan.
- Define a process for updating/changing the Communications Plan.

Every project should go through all 14 steps at least one time. The steps should be revisited as a project progresses. Projects with long implementation timeframes should go through the steps multiple times, revising and updating the Communication Plan each time. Any significant change in a project should prompt a review of the Communications Plan. Communication is a key success factor for almost all projects.

Like other project management artifacts, the Communications Plan is scaleable. The plan for a very large or high risk project may be quite complex. More stakeholders will mean more information needs and that may mean more delivery mechanisms. There may be several individuals with responsibilities for the different types of communications required by a project. There may be many steps involved in the process of developing and approving communications on a large project in order to ensure communication is accurate, effective, and sensitive to the needs of the project. Highly visible projects may require separate public information or communications expertise.

Most projects will require some form of both internal and external communication on a regular basis to sustain momentum on the project and to fulfill organizational reporting requirements. For small projects that have only a handful of stakeholders who are intimately familiar with all project details, it may be sufficient to provide a standard status report to all stakeholders on a regular basis. Be sure to include an open invitation for feedback on even such small projects.

Information Distribution

Information distribution is the process of making needed information available to project stakeholders in a timely manner. It includes implementing the communications management plan, as well as responding to unexpected requests for information.

Communication Skills

Communication skills are used to exchange information. The sender is responsible for clarity, accuracy, completeness of information, and for ensuring that the message is understood. The receiver is responsible for ensuring the information is received in its entirety and correctly understood. The many dimensions of communication include:
- Written and oral, listening, and speaking
- Internal (within the project) and external (customer, the media, the public)
- Formal (reports, briefings) and informal (memos, ad hoc conversations)
- Vertical (up and down the organization) and horizontal (with peers).

Information Gathering and Retrieval Systems

Information can be obtained through various types of media including filing systems, databases and project management software. Methods for sharing information include:
- Manual filing systems
- Electronic databases
- Project management software
- Systems allowing access to technical documentation such as specifications, test plans, drawings, etc.

Information Distribution Systems

Information Distribution is the collection, sharing, and distribution of information/documents to project stakeholders in a satisfactorily and efficient manner. Methods for distributing project information include:
- Hard copy documents
- Shared access to networked, electronic databases
- Fax / Electronic mail
- Voice mail / Video-conferencing

Information distribution is vital to a project's success. People need information to fulfill their responsibilities to a project. If project team members do not have access to the information they need, then they cannot complete their activities effectively.

In addition, distributing information allows stakeholders to see what progress has been made on a project, as well as what changes have been, or should be, made.

It is important to understand that distributing information is not only a component of the communications variable, but also part of the third step of the project management process—executing.

There are a number of ways information is distributed during project execution. The following are some common means of information distribution:
- Written, which includes reports, memos, spreadsheets, business letters, faxes, and files.
- Oral, which includes presentations, meetings, and conference calls.
- Multimedia, which includes video conferencing.
- Internet or Intranet, which includes e-mail, Web sites, and online bulletin boards.

The form of communication you use depends on three factors:
- Who is the recipient?
- What is the information?
- When does the recipient need the information?

Suppose a client who lives far away, or who travels frequently wants an update on the project's status every Friday by noon. If the client has regular access to a computer, then the best way to communicate is through e-mail.

The information distribution process results in three outputs: project records, project reports, and project presentations.

Five Verbal Communication Skills
1. Speaking (encoding)
2. Writing (encoding)
3. Listening (decoding)
4. Reading (decoding)
5. Thought/Reasoning (encoding and decoding)

Barriers to Communication
PMI® recognizes the following barriers to effective project communications:
- Lack of clear communications channels
- Physical or temporal distance between the communicator and receiver
- Difficulties with technical language
- Distracting environmental factors (noise)
- Detrimental attitudes (hostility, disbelief)

The presence of communication barriers may lead to increased conflict! When it comes to communication barriers, make sure you know these five bullets listed above. Also note that noise is not just loud rumbling noises in the background, but that it can be visual or tactile. Make sure you are aware of the issues of distance, the issues of hostile attitudes, and particularly, when it comes to hostile attitudes, remember the term "communication blocker." That is what hostile attitudes lead to.

Communications Role of the Project Manager
According to PMI®, project managers spend about 90 percent of their time acquiring and communicating information. This includes about two hours a day in meetings and more than an hour a day in one-on-one coaching or interviewing sessions.

The project manager is the key to all project communications and must be skilled at communicating with the following:
- Top management
- The project team
- Competing project teams (peers)
- The customer

Notice the first sentence here. It has a statistic in it: 90 percent of our time is spent acquiring and communicating information. That statistic is important because you may run into a question on the exam that asks, what percentage of the project manager's time is spent acquiring and communicating information – 90 percent, 80 percent, 75 percent, 70 percent. Notice I didn't give you any wild low numbers. The number cluster will be kept together. You need to know that it is about 90 percent. Also, remember that communications go laterally, vertically, and diagonally through the organization.

The Project Manager and the Customer
- The project manager must keep both top management and the customer informed of project, technical, budget, and schedule status.
- He or she must also act as top management's representative to the customer and maintain open and friendly relations with the customer.
- The project manager serves as the focal point for ensuring real, two-way communication between the project team and the customer.

Building Effective Team Communication
PMI® advises that project managers undertake six actions to ensure effective project team communications:
1. Be an Effective Communicator - The project manager must recognize the importance of an interpersonal communications network among team members and encourage their informal communications. Project managers must also recognize that communication is a two-way street; they cannot simply issue orders, but instead must encourage feedback and consensus-building.

2. Be a Communication Expeditor - The project manager must bring people together; initiate relationships, which become communications links; and establish both formal (reporting and responsibility) and informal communications channels.
3. Avoid Communication Blockers - Communication blockers are negative responses that kill or inhibit innovative ideas. For example: "We can't make it work", "Don't waste your time, the boss won't like it" or "Let's be honest, we can't do it."
4. Use a "Tight Matrix" - The project manager should allocate all team members a single office space, rather than allowing them to work on the project from the offices of their functional departments. This prevents dilution of project effort, decreases outside distractions, and focuses the efforts of the entire team on the same problems. The term "tight matrix" is not to be confused with the terms "strong" matrix or "weak" matrix.
5. Have a Project "War Room" - The project manager should establish a single location where the project team or any portion of the project team can get together for any purpose. This room should be for the exclusive use of one project and should provide a repository for project artifacts, records, and up-to-date schedules and status reports. A war room is also called a "control room" or "project information room."
6. Conduct Effective Meetings - Meetings are essential for building teams, making group decisions, solving group problems, and achieving a group consensus. The project manager should adhere to the following guidelines for leading effective meetings that hold the attention and interest of all team members and stakeholders:
    - Start on time
    - Establish a meeting policy
    - Only call a meeting when there is a real need
    - Make the purpose of the meeting very clear
    - Encourage participation
    - Include a team-building element
    - Issue minutes
    - Follow-up on all task assignments and action items

In a PMI® survey of project managers, the respondents said they attended more than six meetings each week. In those meetings, an average of 25 percent of the time was spent on nonproductive items. The three most prevalent responses on why meetings are not effective were:
- Meeting was not properly planned
- Inept leadership
- Undisciplined participants

You need to know the difference between a tight matrix in contrast to the strong and weak matrix mentioned in the other sections of the exam. Specifically a tight matrix refers to physical proximity. Keeping team members close together. To that end, to keep a tight matrix you may want to use a project war room where everyone works together.

Management Styles

The Project Communications Management section of the exam may address the following management styles:
- **Authoritarian** - Lets individuals know what is expected of them; gives specific guidance; expects adherence to rules and standards.
- **Disruptive** - Tends to disrupt unity and cause disorder.
- **Ethical** - Honest and sincere; presses for fair solutions; goes "by the book".
- **Combative** - Eager to fight or be disagreeable over any situation.

- **Conciliatory** - Friendly and agreeable; attempts to unite players into a compatible working team.
- **Facilitating** - Does not interfere with day-to-day task, but is available for help and guidance when needed.
- **Intimidating** - Reprimands employees for the sake of a "tough guy" image.
- **Judicial** - Applies sound judgment.
- **Promotional** - Cultivates team spirit; rewards good work; encourages subordinates to realize their full potential.
- **Secretive** - Not open or outgoing in speech, activity, or purpose.

These are a few easy points to pick up on the exam, but they can also be a few easy points to lose. They sound rather self-evident; they sound like they explain what they are but look at authoritarian. It does not necessarily mean that you are passing down many edicts. It gives specific guidance, expects adherence to rules and standards, and lets individuals know what is expected of them. It does not sound like a mean individual. An authoritarian sounds like somebody who is providing some measure of authority. Go through these and make sure you understand the true meaning behind each.

Management Skills

The Project Management Context section of the PMBOK® Guide paragraph 1.5.5 focuses on the following interpersonal skills:
- **Leadership** - Establishing direction, aligning people, and motivating and inspiring.
- **Effective Communication** - The exchange of information, which has a variety of dimensions including written and oral, internal and external, formal and informal, as well as vertical and horizontal.
- **Negotiation and Conflict Management** - Conferring with others in order to come to terms or reach an agreement; may focus on any or all of the following: scope, cost, and schedule objectives; changes; contract terms and conditions; assignments; or resources.
- **Problem Solving** - A combination of problem definition and decision making.
- **Influencing the Organization** - The ability to get things done, based on an understanding of the formal and informal structures of the organization.
- **Motivation** - Motivation can be defined as a concept used to describe the factors within an individual which arouse, maintain and channel behavior towards a goal. Another way to say this is that motivation is goal-directed behavior.

Performance Reporting

Performance reporting is the process of collecting and disseminating performance information to provide stakeholders with knowledge of how resources are being used to achieve project objectives. When reporting periods do not coincide with project phases, it might be helpful to team members if the project manager includes dates for reporting periods on the project's schedule. Including reporting periods on the schedule helps team members know when they need to write performance reports.

Types of performance reporting include:
- Status reporting - where the project currently stands
- Progress reporting - what has been accomplished versus what is in process
- Forecasting - where the project is going.

It is important to understand that performance reporting is not only a component of the communications variable, but also part of the fourth step of the project management process: controlling.

Performance reporting can affect project costs when time for writing the reports is not allocated in a project's schedule. The time spent writing the reports should be included as part of a project's costs. If the time is not recorded, then the project's total cost will be inaccurate. The time between one performance report and the next is called a reporting period. A reporting period might coincide with the beginning and end of a project phase.

A variety of techniques are used for performance reporting. Earned value analysis is important to performance reporting because it can give the project manager and team members the most accurate measure of whether or not a project's activities are being completed as planned. The most commonly used measures are the cost variance and the schedule variance. These two values can be converted to efficiency factors to reflect the project's cost and schedule performance. The cost performance index is the most commonly used cost-efficiency indicator, and the cumulative CPI is widely used to forecast project costs at completion.

Status Review Meeting

A status review meeting is held regularly to determine progress against the project plan, from a cost, schedule, and quality perspective. It is preferable to collect status prior to the meeting so people can discuss issues intelligently.

Performance Reports

Performance reports provide the information as documented in the communications management plan. The performance reports present the analysis of information in organized, summarized, and leveled format. It is essential to arrange for some report to be made regularly on each feature of the performance standards so that the requirements will be measured. Regular and prompt reports should be made by the project manager for all stakeholders of items for which a performance standard has been established, measurable or not. Some of the reports will be by-products of other data processing functions; most of the information will come from the project team. Typical performance report format include:
- Bar chart
- S-curves
- Tables
- Earned value analysis

Earned value analysis is the most commonly used method of performance measurement in its various forms. It integrates scope, cost (or resource), and schedule to help the project management team assess project performance. Earned value (EV) involves calculating three key values for each activity:
- The Planned Value (PV) is that portion of the approved cost estimate planned to be spent on the activity during a given period.
- The Actual Cost (AC) is the total of costs incurred in accomplishing work on the activity during a given period.
- The Earned Value (EV) is the value of the work actually completed.
- The above three values are used in combination to provide measures of whether or not work is being accomplished as planned. These include the Cost Variance (CV=EV-AC) and the Schedule Variance (SV=EV-PV).
- The cost and schedule variances (CV and SV, respectively) can be converted to efficiency indicators to reflect the cost and schedule performance of any project.
- The most commonly used cost-efficiency indicator is the Cost Performance Index
- (CPI = EV/AC). The cumulative CPI (the sum of all individual EV budgets divided by the sum of all individual AC's) is widely used to forecast project costs at completion.

- **The Schedule Performance Index (SPI = EV/PV)** is sometimes used in conjunction with the CPI to forecast the project completion estimates.

The following are common classifications of performance reports:
- **Routine** – Routine or regular, performance reports are not necessarily scheduled, but might be distributed at intervals that coincide with project phases or milestones. The frequency of performance reports depends on how smoothly the project is functioning.
- **Exception** – Exception performance reports provide project team members with information they need to make decisions or notify them of a change that affects their work. Exception performance reports are also distributed to stakeholders to inform them that a decision has been made.
- **Special Analysis** – Special analysis performance reports contain information about the results of a special study. Special studies might be conducted as part of a project or to determine a solution to a problem encountered during a project. Special analysis reports are useful not only to a current project, but are valuable documentation of lessons learned for future projects.

Documentation

Good documentation is usually associated with successful projects. This is true regardless of the project's size. It is not acceptable to ignore documentation just because "the project is too small" to bother with it. Further, good documentation coupled with a disciplined change control process will go a long way toward reducing unauthorized changes in the scope of a project. PMI® states that all documentation is produced to record and analyze project performance, including documents that describe the project's product, must be available for review during administrative closure.

There are two types of project documentation that PMI® considers especially important in fostering good project communication:
- **Progress Reports** - One of the most important ongoing components of effective project communication
- **Project Management Plan** - The careful analysis required to document the project plan tends to reduce uncertainty on the project, and the distribution of the plan does a lot to keep appropriate people informed

Manage Stakeholders

Stakeholder management refers to managing project communications to satisfy the needs and wants of the project stakeholders. Managing stakeholder's increases the likelihood the project will not veer off schedule because of unanswered stakeholder questions or concerns, increases the ability of persons to work together as a team, and limits disruptions during the project. The project manager is usually the one who maintains and monitors stakeholder management.

Communications Management Plan

As stated previously the communications management plan outlines the roles and responsibilities of project participants in the review, approval and distribution of information about key project processes, events, documents and milestones. Stakeholder needs and wants and project expectations provide an understanding of stakeholder goals, objectives, and level of communication needed during the project. The needs, wants and expectations are identified, analyzed, and documented in the communications management plan.

Importance of Communication

By using communication skills, project managers help to plan, direct, control, and coordinate their operations throughout the project life cycle. Peter Drucker states that the communicating ability is essential for success and is perhaps the most important of all the skills an individual should possess. In project management, Sievert emphasizes the importance of communication by stating that a high percentage of the friction, frustrations and inefficiencies in working relationships are traceable to poor communication.

Interpersonal Communication

Interpersonal communication is used to ensure messages are received and understood, two-way communication is necessary. When communicating in a project environment, both the sender and receiver have a duty to understand and to be understood. This is accomplished through feedback. Interpersonal communication is the process of sharing information with others. Three basic elements of interpersonal communication:
- The sender (or encoder) of the message.
- The signal or the message.
- The receiver (or decoder) of the message.

Goals of interpersonal communication include:
- Understanding the exact meaning and intent of others.
- Being understood by others.
- Gaining acceptance for yourself and/or your ideas.
- Producing action or change.

Process of interpersonal communication: (Wilbur Schramm)
- Sender determines what information to share and with whom and encodes the message.
- Sender transmits the message as a signal to the receiver.
- The receiver receives the message.
- The receiver decodes the message to determine its meaning and then responds accordingly.
- Communication is successful if the decoded message is the same as the sender intended.
- Utilizing experience, the sender anticipates how the message will be decoded and encodes the message, accordingly.

Methods of Interpersonal Communication

Project managers must have the ability to think logically and communicate effectively. The three forms of communication are verbal, non-verbal and written communication.

Verbal
Advantages:
- Timely exchange of information
- Rapid feedback
- Immediate synthesis of message
- Timely closure

Disadvantages:
- Technical jargon especially in complex projects may make verbal communication difficult for non-technical people and other stakeholders.
- No paper trail.

Three stages of effective verbal communication and presentation:
- The introduction: Tell them what you're going to tell them.
- The explanation: Tell them.
- The summary: Tell them what you just told them.

Non-verbal
Encoding a message without using words. Includes gestures, vocal tones, facial expressions, environmental settings, manner of dress, and body language. Generally, a receiver's interpretation of a message is based not only on the words in the message, but also on the nonverbal behaviors of the sender. In an interpersonal communication situation in projects, nonverbal factors generally have more influence on the total impact of a message than verbal factors. Total Message Impact = Words (7%) + Vocal tones (38%) + Facial expressions (55%) (Albert Meharabian). Project managers may use nonverbal ingredients to complement verbal message ingredients whenever possible but must be careful that contradictory messages are not presented. Project managers should avoid sending ambiguous messages by "walking the talk" (mean what you say and say what you mean).

Written Communication

In a project environment, written communication includes reports, plans, proposals, standards, policies, procedures, letters, memoranda, legal documents, and other forms of information to be transmitted. The main aim of business writing is that it should be understood clearly when read quickly. The message should be well planned, simple, clear, and direct. Project managers and others can increase their personal power or influence by developing a "power" vocabulary when writing executive summaries, cover letters, bid proposals, project reports, marketing strategies, presentations, etc.

Major steps to writing:
- Establish the basic purpose of the message.
- Collect and organize material.
- Prepare draft.
- Check the overall structure.
- Send the message.

Determine when to put the message in writing. Written communication is effective in the following cases:
- When conveying complex information or data.
- When requiring future action from team members.
- When it is the receiver's preferred communication style.
- When communicating company policies or changes to policies.
- When conveying a message that could be misunderstood either accidentally or intentionally.

Macro-Barriers to Successful Communication

Macro-barriers are elements of the communication environment that hinder successful communication in a general sense. Such as the following:
- Lack of subject knowledge - Must have sufficient knowledge to send message. Must know level of understanding of receiver.
- Information overload - Keep messages simple and direct. Provide sufficient information - keep it simple and short.
- Cultural differences - Meanings and interpretations may vary among different cultures. Encourage team members to learn each other's cultures.
- Organizational climate - Minimize the differences associated with status and ego within the organization. Create an atmosphere of openness and trust by talking with people. Avoid talking down to people.
- Number of links - Reduce the number of transmission links. The more links, the more opportunity for distortion in the message. Be aware of entropy. 23-27% of message is lost in upward communication.

Micro-Barriers to Successful Communication

Micro-barriers are elements of the communication environment that obstruct successful communication in a specific sense and include the following:
- Perceptions - Sender's view of the receiver: senders communicate differently depending on how they perceive the receiver's level of knowledge and ability to understand the message. Senders should be careful not to imply any negative attitudes towards the receiver through communication behavior. Receiver's view of the sender: How the receiver personally feels about the sender may influence how carefully the receiver listens. If negative, these feelings may cause the receiver to ignore the message. If overly positive, these feelings may inhibit the receiver's judgment.
- Message competition - Communicate only when you have the total attention of the recipient. Try to minimize noise or other factors contributing to message interference.
- Project jargon and terminology - Define project terminology used in messages. Be aware of the use of project terminology and the intended audience.

Types of Project Communications
- **Interpersonal communication** - Listening, self-presentation, problem solving, decision making, negotiating, and conflict management. Necessary skills for interacting with the project team and with the client on a daily basis.
- **Communication with public and community** - Includes all public relations efforts necessary to encourage community involvement, enhance public understanding of the project, break down resistance, gain acceptance, and be a project spokesperson. May involve public speaking, making presentations, dealing with media representatives, and producing written publicity or PR materials.
- **Formal communication** - Is carried out through traditional responsibility and relationship channels. Includes strategic plans, project planning systems, standards, policies, procedures, proposals, letters, etc. Most effectively done in written form.
- **Informal communication** - Done through informal groups in which relationships are dependent upon common ties such as interests, hobbies, kinship, friendship, social status, etc. Project managers must identify the strengths and limitations of informal communications and explore strategies to increase overall project effectiveness through informal communications.

Managing Meetings Effectively

Meetings provide a means to exchange and share messages, ideas and information. Meetings require a great deal of time and effort and therefore should be called only when necessary. Meetings should not take the place of project managers resolving problems and issues by working individually with the team members via the telephone, personal discussion, or e-mail. Avoid calling a meeting just for the sake of calling a meeting. Meetings should be productive.

Guidelines for effective meetings:
- Before the meeting: Determine purpose, set ground rules for discussion, determine necessary attendees, notify participants in advance of location and agenda, start and end on time.
- During the meeting: Identify the specific objectives of the meeting, gather input from participants, stick to the agenda, use visual aids to illustrate points, periodically summarize the results of the discussion, assign action items as appropriate, and stick to the specified time limit.
- After the meeting: Follow up on individual action items, distribute concise minutes and use the minutes at the next meeting to measure results.

Communication Channels and Links

The project manager must recognize and understand the project's formal communication channels. Three basic channels of communication in the project environment:
- **Upward communication** (vertically or diagonally) - Information provided to upper management for their purposes of evaluating the overall performance of the projects for which they are responsible, or to refine organizational strategy. Project managers may use the "by exception" format for project status. This feedback helps top management assess priorities and make organizational modifications to effectively meet project goals and objectives and be more effective in the future.
- **Downward communication** (vertically or diagonally) - Provides direction and control for project team members and other employees. Contains job-related information focusing on scope and definition, quality, schedule, implementation, and evaluation and feedback. May include statements of organizational philosophy, policies, project objectives, schedules, budgets, and constraints, position descriptions and other written information relating to the importance, rationale and interrelationships and interactions of various departments projects, and jobs in an organization.
- **Lateral communication** (horizontally) - Information exchange between the project manager and his/her peers: functional managers, staff personnel, contractors, other project managers, etc. Involves negotiating resources, schedules, and budgets; coordinating activities between groups, as well as developing plans for future operating periods. Is vital to the success of a project and is also the most important factor for survival and growth in a highly competitive and turbulent environment. Requires diplomacy and experience. If managed properly, it creates a harmonious, cooperative environment based on trust and respect for one another. If poorly managed, it may lead to conflict, blame, and failure to meet project objectives.

High Performance Communication

A project manager's performance depends upon how well he/she works with the project team in planning, implementing, coordinating, interfacing, integrating, and controlling the project. Project managers must be aware of their own communication strengths and weaknesses. The project manager achieves project objectives by using effective communication to inspire high team performance.

Key requirements for achieving high team performance include:
- Openness in communication
- Development of trust (so that accuracy of communication is achieved)
- Continuous support and counseling

Effective Listening

Effective listening is one of the most important skills for a project manager to acquire and practice. It is essential for successful project management and improves communication and helps develop mutual respect, rapport, and trust among project participants.

Verbal Listening Behaviors

Verbal listening behaviors in such things as asking questions to clarify and gather more information. Questions should be probing and constructive. Summarizing at intervals what the speaker has said to confirm what you have understood. Asking the speaker for examples. Ascertaining the speaker's feelings and acknowledging them. ("You seem angry."). Directing the speaker to the most appropriate listener. ("George can best help you with that.") Or, just listen if the person needs to let off steam.

Non-Verbal Listening Behaviors

Actions that reinforce the message or undermine it. Includes:
- Making eye contact. (indicates honesty and openness)
- Being expressive and alert. (indicates interest - motivates speaker to be open)
- Moving closer to the speaker. (establishes friendly environment)
- Listening for the intention behind the speaker's communication. (sometimes the real message is not what's said, but how it is said)
- Facial expressions, touching, use of personal space, use of time.
- Body language (a subset of non-verbal) accounts for 55 percent of communication) It includes facial expressions, touching, and body positioning.

Barriers to Effective Listening

The mismatch between our speed of talking (100-400 words per minute) and our speed of thinking (approx. 600 words per minute) makes effective listening tough. Some of the personal and environmental barriers that influence the overall effectiveness of communication include:
- Poor listeners - people do not talk freely when they know the audience isn't listening. This inhibits effective communications.
- Resistance to the message - people don't like to listen to something that is contrary to their preconceived ideas. When they should be listening, they are concentrating on their response or defense, instead.
- Physical distractions - telephone calls, people coming in and out of office/meetings, etc. Also, environments that create feelings of inequality in status discourage effective listening.
- Perceptual differences - can influence the behavior of people which in turn can affect communications. For example, when perceptual differences occur, people tend to:
  - Jump to conclusions
  - Confuse facts with opinions
  - Make frozen evaluations (those that cannot be easily changed)

Project managers must be aware of these barriers to effective listening that might be caused by interpersonal conflict, distractions, management response to new ideas or the overall project climate.

Project managers should try to minimize barriers by nurturing better understanding and good working relationships necessary to effective communication among project participants. Use of "I" messages instead of "you" messages assists the speaker with delivery of a nonjudgmental, non-critical message while still conveying the speaker's points.

Checking perceptions and asking for clarification from speaker of intended message helps facilitate effective communications.

Guidelines for Active Listening (part of effective listening)

Effective listening requires paying attention to the task, relationship and environmental dimensions of communication. Effective listening requires being genuinely concerned for the individual as a person, practicing neutrality, and taking an objective approach. It requires patience, mutual trust and respect. Active listeners empathize with the speaker, ask questions to clarify the message, and provide frequent feedback so that the sender can evaluate the accuracy of his or her message. Active listeners are equally aware of the influence of vocal tones, facial expressions and other nonverbal components in addition to the verbal component of communications.

Some practical guidelines for active listening include:
- Stop talking!
- Show the speaker you are ready to listen:
- Silence: signals you are ready to listen.
- Few distractions: shut the door, put the phone on hold, refrain from impatient mannerisms, etc.
- A receptive attitude: empathize with the speaker's point of view. Listen for total meaning, not just for points of opposition.

Communication Styles

The project manager uses communication more than any other skill set to manage the project throughout its life cycle and to ensure that team members are working cohesively and resolving problems.

Two dimensions of thinking and action include:
- The thinking and decision-making approach which varies from logical (sequential) to intuitive (random)
- The action style which varies from hands-on (concrete) to research based (abstract)

When the two dimensions are combined, the results are four major communication styles all of which are applicable at various times in the project life cycle. The styles are:
- Concrete-sequential: (Mr./Ms. Fix-it)
- Person likes to focus on ideas and tasks, thinks systematically and predictably.
- Person wants to complete tasks and minimize change.

Abstract-sequential: (Organizer)
- Person who relies on logical analysis and systematic planning to solve problems.
- These communicators are people and task-oriented, which makes them effect team builders.
- These communicators prefer to have all information before making a decision, and they know how to control resources and information.

Concrete-random: (Explorer/entrepreneur)
- Person relies on people and technology, finds practical use for theories and models.
- These communicators make decisions after thorough analysis and evaluation and excel at facilitating planning sessions, discussions, and changes.

Abstract-random: (Intuitive free thinker)
- Person views experiences from different perspectives and sees the big picture and the long-term vision.
- These communicators make good brainstormers because they can listen actively and enjoy the process of generating new ideas.

How Project Managers Spend their Time

Approximately 75-90% of project manager's time is spent communicating. Of the PM's time spent communicating, approximately 45% is spent listening. Another 30% is spent speaking. Approximately 10% is spent reading; another 10% writing, and 5% other. Project managers spend 50% of their time in meetings.

Chapter Review

1. Referring to the process of interpersonal communication as defined by Wilbur Schramm which of the following statements is false?
    A. The process of encapsulating information into a message and then transmitting the message is called decoding.
    B. The destination decodes the message to determine its meaning and then responds accordingly.
    C. Communication is considered successful if the message decoded is the same as the sender intended.
    D. Perceptual differences can influence the way the message is decoded.

2. How much time does the typical project manager spend communicating both formally and informally?
    A. 40-60%
    B. 50-70%
    C. 60-80%
    D. 75-90%

3. In the general management skill of communicating, to assimilate through the mind or senses is the process of:
    A. Receiving
    B. Decoding
    C. Comprehending
    D. Understanding

4. The sending or conveying of information from one place to another is the process of:
    A. Networking
    B. Transmitting
    C. Encrypting
    D. Promoting

5. Which of the following types of body signals is generally associated with a person feeling uncertainty?
    A. Sighing
    B. Bending forward
    C. Concealing mouth with hands
    D. Crossed arms

6. In Albert Meharabian's interpersonal communication dynamics formula of Total Message Impact = Words + Vocal tones + Facial expressions, words make up what percentage of the total message impact?
    A. 20%
    B. 55%
    C. 7%
    D. 38%

7. All of the following are outputs from the Performance Reporting process EXCEPT:
    A. Trend analysis
    B. "S" curves, histograms, bar charts, and tables
    C. Performance reports
    D. Change Requests

8. All of the following aid in achieving consensus except:
   A. Maintaining a focus on the problem, not each other.
   B. Avoiding conflict.
   C. Seeking facts.
   D. Avoiding voting, trading, or averaging.

9. A person who is visionary and enjoys being a catalyst for organizational change, but prefers the conceptual phase over the implementing phase is most likely to have a preference for which communication style? (choose the best answer)
   A. Concrete-sequential
   B. Abstract-sequential
   C. Abstract-random
   D. Concrete-random

10. What are the four parts of the communications model?
    A. Sending, Receiving, Decoding, and Comprehending
    B. Sender, Message, Medium, Receiver
    C. Communicator, Message, Receiver, Decoder
    D. Communicating, Transmitting, Receiving, Comprehending

Answers

1. A, Verma's Human Resource Skills for the Project Manager, pgs. 17-18
2. D, PMI®
3. A, Decoding is deciphering a message once assimilated.
4. B, Verma's Human Resource Skills for the Project Manager, pgs. 17-18
5. C, Verma's Human Resource Skills for the Project Manager, pg. 43
6. C, Verma's Human Resource Skills for the Project Manager, pg. 19
7. A, The outputs are change requests and performance reports. Option B provides examples of the formats for performance reports. Trend analysis is a tool and technique of performance reporting.
8. B, In the modern view, conflict is inevitable and is a natural result of change. If managed properly, conflict is frequently beneficial. Withdrawal tends to minimize conflict but also fails to resolve the issue.
9. C, Reference Verma, "Human Resource Skills for the Project Manager", pg. 49 The abstract-random communicator is a brainstormer and visionary.
10. B, Reference Verma, "Human Resource Skills for the Project Manager", Chapter 1

Notes

Chapter 11

Project Risk Management

Reference Material to Study

- A Guide to the Project Management Body of Knowledge (PMBOK® Guide 3rd Edition), Chapter 11
- Project and Program Risk Management, A Guide to Managing Project Risks and Opportunities, PMI®, Edited by R. Max Wideman, 1992
- Project Management, A Managerial Approach, Meridith, Jack R. 1995, Chapter 2, 2.4

What to Study

- The PMBOK® phases of Project Risk Management: Risk Management Planning, Risk Identification, Qualitative Risk Analysis, Quantitative Risk Analysis, Risk Response Planning, and Risk Monitoring and Control (Be familiar with Inputs, Tools and Techniques, and Outputs for each phase)
- The means for determining the value of a risk event: $R = P * I$ where "R" is the calculated value of the risk event, "P" is the probability of the occurrence of the risk event, and "I" is the impact of the risk event should it occur. (A risk event is a discrete occurrence that could affect the project for better or worse.)
- The relationship of risk and the project life cycle: the amount of uncertainty and risk is highest at the start of the project and lowest at the end of the project
- Positive risk as defined by opportunities and negative risk as defined by threats
- The various means of classifying risk: business, pure (insurable), known, unknown
- Risk assessment using Decision Trees and Expected Monetary Value
- Monte Carlo Analysis, Delphi Technique, Cause-and-effect (also called Ishikawa or fishbone) diagrams
- The different types of scales used in risk analysis: ordinal and cardinal

Key Definitions

- **Assumptions** - Factors that for planning purposes are considered to be true, real, or certain. Assumptions affect all aspects of project planning and are part of the progressive elaboration of the project. Project teams frequently identify, document, and validate assumptions as part of their planning process. Assumptions generally involve a degree of risk.
- **Assumptions Analysis** - Explores the accuracy of the assumptions and identifies risks to the project from inaccuracy to incompleteness of assumptions.
- **Brainstorming** - A general creativity technique that can be used to identify risks using a group of team members or subject-matter experts. Typically, a brainstorming session is structured so that each participant's ideas are recorded for later analysis.
- **Checklist** - A comprehensive listing of many possible risks that might occur on a project. Several types of risk that have been encountered on previous projects are included.

- **Contingency Planning** - The development of a management plan that identifies alternative strategies to be used to ensure project success if specified risk events occur.
- **Contingency Reserve** - The amount of money or time needed above the estimate to reduce the risk of overruns of project objectives to a level acceptable to the organization.
- **Decision Tree Analysis** - A diagram that describes a decision under consideration and the implications of choosing one or another of the available alternatives. It incorporates probabilities or risks and the costs or rewards of each logical path of events and future decisions.
- **Deflection** - The act of transferring all or part of a risk to another party, usually by some form contract provision, insurance policy, or warranty. Also called risk transference.
- **Expected Monetary Value** - The product of an event's probability of occurrence and the gain or loss that will result. Expected Monetary Value = Money at Risk x probability. For example, if there is a 50% probability it will rain, and rain will result in a $100 loss, the expected monetary value of the rain event is $50 (.5 * $100).
- **Impact Analysis** - The mathematical examination of the nature of individual risks on the project, as well as potential arrangements of interdependent risks. It includes the quantification of their respective impact severity, probability, and sensitivity to changes in related project variables, including the project life cycle.
- **Management Reserve** - A separately planned quantity used to allow for future situations which are impossible to predict. Management reserves are intended to reduce the risk of missing cost or schedule objectives.
- **Mitigation** - Taking steps to lessen risk by lowering the probability of a risk event's occurrence or reducing its effect should it occur.
- **Monte Carlo Analysis** - A technique that performs a project simulation many times in order to calculate a distribution of likely results.
- **Probability** - The likelihood of occurrence.
- **Probability and Impact Matrix** - A common way to determine whether a risk is considered low, moderate, or high by combining the two dimensions of a risk: its probability of occurrence and its impact on objectives if it occurs.
- **Project Risk Management** - Includes the processes concerned with identifying, analyzing, and responding to project risk.
- **Reserve** - A provision in the project plan to mitigate cost and/or schedule risk. Often used with a modifier to provide further detail on what types of risk are meant to be mitigated.
- **Residual Risk** - A risk that remains after risk responses have been implemented.
- **Risk** - An uncertain event or condition that, if occurs, has a positive or negative effect on a project objective.
- **Risk Event** - A discrete occurrence that may affect the project for better or worse.
- **Risk Management Plan** - A subsidiary element of the overall project plan which documents the procedures that will be used to manage risk throughout the project.
- **Risk Response Plan** - A document detailing all identified risks, including description, cause, probability of occurrence, impacts on objectives, proposed responses, owners, and current status. Also known as the risk register.
- **Threats** - As related to risk, negative outcomes of risk.
- **Triggers** - Indications that a risk has either occurred or is about to occur. (Also referred to as risk symptoms or warning signs)
- **Uncertainty** - The possibility that events may occur which will impact the project either favorably or unfavorably. Uncertainty gives rise to both opportunity and risk.
- **Workaround** - A response to a negative risk event. Distinguished from contingency plan in that a workaround is not planned in advance of the occurrence of the risk event.

On past exams many people find the project risk management questions demanding because they address many concepts that some project managers have not been exposed to in their work or education. However, the questions correspond closely to the PMBOK® Guide material so you should not have much difficulty if you study the concepts and terminology found in the PMBOK® Guide. Although the questions included do not contain mathematically complex work problems, they do require you to know certain theories, such as expected monetary value (EMV) and decision-tree analysis. Additionally, you are likely to encounter questions related to levels of risk faced by both buyer and seller based on various types of contacts.

Project Risk Management contains six processes: Risk Management Planning, Risk Identification, Qualitative Risk Analysis, Quantitative Risk Analysis, Risk Response Planning, and Risk Monitoring and Control.

As the name of this knowledge area implies, these processes are concerned with identifying and planning for potential risks that may impact the project. Organizations will often combine several of these processes into one step. The important thing about this process is that you should strive to identify all the risks and develop responses for those with the greatest consequences to the project objectives.

In order to manage project risk, you must first understand what constitutes risk. First, risks are generally associated with uncertain outcomes or a lack of knowledge of future events. Second, risks are measured according to the probability of their occurrence and the consequences of not achieving project goals. Finally, project risk compares actual project and product results to the project's quality standards. Know the concept of risk versus reward.

A risk is any factor that may potentially interfere with successful completion of the project. A risk is not a problem—a problem has already occurred; a risk is the recognition that a problem or opportunity might occur. By recognizing potential problems, the project manager can attempt to avoid or minimize a problem through proper actions.

The procedure that the team will use to manage project risks is defined in the Planning Phase, documented in the Project Plan, and then executed throughout the Execution Phase of the project.

The Risk Management Plan, documents the parameters used to manage risk throughout the project. In addition to documenting the results of the risk identification and analysis steps, it must cover who is responsible for managing various areas of risk, how risks will be tracked throughout the project, how contingency plans will be implemented, and how project contingency reserves will be allocated to handle risk.

Project reserves are resources (people, dollars, and commodities) that are available to the project if needed. Reserves can come in two types -- contingency reserves (known unknowns) and management reserves (unknown unknowns). Contingency reserves are developed based on the results of risk planning, and are usually available for release at the project manager's discretion to address risks that materialize, and to ensure the project succeeds even if the risk occurs. Management reserves are developed at the discretion of management, and are put in place when the ability to obtain additional budget may compromise the success of the project. Management reserves are typically part of project budgeting, and not part of risk planning.

Project risks are identified, monitored and carefully managed throughout the life of the project. It is particularly important in the Planning Phase to document risks and identify contingency reserves that have been applied to the risks.

There are various areas that can affect a project's risk level:
- The technology used on the project
- The environment in which the project is executed
- The relationships between team members
- How well the project fits the business area or strategic objectives of the organization
- How great of a change will result from the project

Risks are documented so that contingency measures can be taken to mitigate their effects. Risks to both the internal and external aspects of the project should be tracked. Internal risks are those items that the project team can directly control (e.g., staffing), and external risks are those events that happen outside the direct influence of the project team.

As stated before, risk identification begins early in the Planning Phase of the project. A Risk Management Plan is started during the Planning Phase. Then, as scheduling, budgeting, and resource planning occur, the plan is updated to reflect further risks identified throughout the Planning Phase.

Just prior to the Project Execution Phase, the Risk Management Plan should be reviewed again, and any new risks should be added to it. As the project progresses, members of the team identify new risk areas that are added to the Risk Management Plan. Also, during the Project Control Phase (concurrently with the Project Planning and Project Execution Phases), risks identified earlier may be removed.

Types of Risk

Project risk includes both threats to the project's objectives and opportunities to improve on those objectives. A risk has a cause, and if it occurs, a consequence. There are two broad categories of risk:
- Known Risks - situations that the project team is certain will occur and can manage.
- Unknown Risks - situations that cannot be anticipated, or managed and controlled directly.

There are two main types of risk:
1. Business Risks: Normal risks of doing business that carries opportunities for both gain and loss.
2. Pure or Insurable Risks: Those risks that present only an opportunity for loss. They are divided into four categories:
    - Direct property damage (including automobile—related risks)
    - Indirect consequential loss (business interruptions)
    - Legal liability
    - Personnel

The assumption is that you need not actively manage pure risk if you can insure against it; insurance is a type of risk transfer. You, therefore, focus your efforts on the business risk that may affect the organization.

Risk Factors

Risk factors are characterized as follows:
- Risk event: precisely what might happen to the detriment of the project
- Risk probability: how likely the event is to occur
- Amount at stake: the extent of loss or gain that could result

As you read through this area, pay special attention to the questions:
- What is risk management?
- What are the types of risk?

Know the difference between a pure and a business risk. Using the analogy of an auto accident, the risk for you, as the driver, is generally a pure risk; you only have the opportunity for loss. However, the risk for your insurance company is a business risk. It is part of that company's opportunity for gain or loss whenever they do business.

PMI® argues that you do not really have to deal with pure risks; you can insure those away on your project. You may say, "I cannot afford to insure them." It does not matter. For the PMP® exam, you need to know that you generally do not worry about managing the pure risks.

You need to know the factors of risk. Every risk consists of an event, a probability, and an amount at stake. You need to ask yourself: What bad things can happen during this event? What are the odds that this bad thing is going to happen? In addition, how much is it going to cost me if it does happen?

Finally, for this section, you need to know process identification, quantification, risk response development, and risk response control.

Risk Processes

The remainder of the review focuses on the key points of PMI's approach to risk management, which include the six major risk processes (PMBOK® Guide figure 11.1):
- Risk management planning
- Risk identification
- Qualitative risk analysis
- Quantitative risk analysis
- Risk response planning
- Risk monitoring and control

Risk Management Planning

Risk management planning must be done during the whole life of the project. In the beginning of the conceptual stage of the project, risks are identified almost without effort as the different aspects of the project. It is important that when these risks are thought of, they are recorded and placed in a risk management file or folder so that they can be dealt with later in the project.

As time goes by and progress is made on the project, the risks need to be reviewed, and the identification process must be repeated for the discovery of new risks. This must be an ongoing, continuous process. Risks that are identified early in the project may change as time goes by. As the project advances, some risks will disappear and other risks that were not thought of earlier will be discovered. As the possibility of the risk approaches, the risk needs to be reevaluated to be sure that the assessment of the risk made earlier is still valid.

The output of this process is the project's risk management plan, which is prepared with the assistance of the project manager, project team leaders, and other key stakeholders as needed.

The risk management plans includes:
- **Risk Management Methodology** - defines the approaches, tools, and data sources used to perform risk management on this project. Different types of assessments may be appropriate,

depending upon the project stage, amount of information available, and flexibility remaining in risk management.
- **Roles and Responsibilities of Team Members** - Defines the lead, support, and risk management team membership for each type of action in the Risk Management Plan. Risk management teams organized outside of the project office may be able to perform more independent, unbiased risk analyses of project than those from the sponsoring project team.
- **Detailed Qualitative and Quantitative Analyses** - This area includes identified project risk probabilities and impacts. The process of assessing the impact and likelihood of identified risks. This includes results from qualitative and quantitative analyses.
- **Schedule of Risk Management Activities** - Defines the frequency and duration of the risk management process, and when it will be performed throughout the project life cycle. Results should be developed early enough to affect decisions. The decisions should be revisited periodically during project execution.
- **Risk Threshold Criteria** - the threshold criteria for risks that will be acted upon, by whom, and in what manner. The project manager, customer, and sponsor may have a different risk threshold.
- **Risk Documentation Procedures** - Documents how all facets of risk activities will be recorded for the benefit of the current project, future needs, and lessons learned. Documents if and how risk processes will be audited.
- **Risk Ranking/Scoring Techniques** - The ranking/scoring methods appropriate for the type and timing of the qualitative and quantitative risk analysis being performed. Methods and scoring of the various risk components must be determined in advance to ensure consistency.

Risk Identification

Risk identification is the responsibility of all members of the project team. The project manager is responsible for tracking risks and for developing contingency plans that address the risks identified by the team. Sometimes a risk identification brainstorming session can help in the initial identification process. Such meetings help team members understand various perspectives and can help the team better understand the big picture.

Risk identification involves determining which risks might affect the project and documenting their characteristics. Participants in risk identification generally include as many of the following as possible: project team, risk management team, subject matter experts from other parts of the organization, customers, end users, other project managers, stakeholders, and outside experts. Risk identification is an iterative process. The first iteration may be performed by a part of the project team, or by the risk management team.

The entire project team and primary stakeholders may make a second iteration. To achieve an unbiased analysis, persons who are not involved in the project may perform the final iteration. Often, simple and effective risk responses can be developed and even implemented as soon as the risk is identified.

Risk identification is a recurring event; it is not performed once and then set aside. The risk identification process begins in the Project Initiation Phase, when initial risk areas are identified. During the Planning Phase, risks and mitigation measures are identified and documented. During the resource allocation, scheduling, and budgeting processes, associated risk planning is also documented.

Risk identification, management, and mitigation continues after the Project Initiation Phase throughout the life of the project. New risks develop as the project matures and external and internal situations change. When the probability of a risk event increases or when a risk becomes a reality and the project manager must deal with a real problem, re-planning occurs. At this point, the project manager and project team develop strategies that assess the impact of the risk event. This re-planning results in budget, schedule, or resource changes for completion of the project.

Risk identification involves recognizing and classifying all of the areas of potential risk related to a project. The attention to detail used when performing risk identification determines how effectively project risks can be managed. This process involves identifying three related factors:
1. Potential sources of risk
2. Possible risk events
3. Risk symptoms.

The timing of risk identification is also important. PMI® advocated that risk identification should first be accomplished at the outset of the project and then updated regularly throughout the project life cycle. It is an iterative process.

Information Gathering Techniques

- **Brainstorming** - This is probably the most used technique in the risk identification process. Its goal is to obtain a comprehensive list of potential risks that can be addressed later in the risk process. Brainstorming is useful in generating any kind of list by pulling out the ideas and thoughts of the participants. After the brainstorming process, risks are categorized by type, and their definitions are sharpened.
- **Delphi Technique** - This method relies on gathering expert opinions through the following process. A group of experts are asked to provide answers to a list of questions. The experts work individually and are often not even physically present in the same location. The answers from all the experts are combined and summarized, and the information is provided to everyone. The process is repeated until some reasonable consensus emerges from the group. Historical experience has shown that some degree of consensus usually emerges after about three rounds.
- **Interviewing** - The person responsible for risk identification identifies the appropriate individuals, briefs them on the project, and provides background information such as the WBS and any assumptions. Interviewees then identify risks based on their experience, project information, and other sources they may find useful.
- **Root Cause Identification** - Helps identify what, how and why something happened, thus preventing recurrence. Root causes are underlying, are reasonably identifiable and can be controlled by management.
- **Strengths, Weaknesses, Opportunities, and Threats (SWOT) Analysis** - A strengths, weaknesses, opportunities, and threats (SWOT) analysis also may be conducted to increase the breadth of risks considered. SWOT analysis is a simple framework for generating strategic alternatives from a situation analysis. It accomplishes this by assessing an organizations strengths (what an organization can do) and weaknesses (what an organization cannot do) in addition to opportunities (potential favorable conditions for an organization) and threats (potential unfavorable conditions for an organization). SWOT analysis is an important step in planning and its value is often underestimated despite the simplicity in creation. The role of SWOT analysis is to take the information from the environmental analysis and separate it into internal issues (strengths and weaknesses) and external issues (opportunities and threats). Once this is completed, SWOT analysis determines if the information indicates something that will assist the firm in accomplishing its objectives (a strength or opportunity), or if it indicates an obstacle that must be overcome or minimized to achieve desired results (weakness or threat).

Other Risk Identification Tools and Techniques

- **Checklists** - These can be developed based on historical information and knowledge from previous projects. Be aware of the advantages of checklists (quick and simple) and

disadvantages (it is impossible to ensure all risks are covered in the checklist and it may limit its users). Take care to explore items on the checklist before using it to make sure the checklist is relevant for the specific project. Also note that if checklists are used, they should be reviewed and updated as appropriate during the closing stages of the project.
- **Assumption Analysis** - Explores the validity of the assumptions on which the project is based.
- **Diagramming Techniques** - Cause-and-effect or fishbone diagrams and system or process flowcharts were discussed in Chapter 6. Influence diagrams that show graphically causal influences, time ordering of events, or other relationships among variables and outcomes also can be used.

Risk Identification Output

The risk register is the output of this process. The assessment and management of risk are (respectively) recorded and monitored using a risk register. The Risk Register records identified risks according to probability of risk, likely impact. The Risk Register should contain the following information as a minimum:
- Risk Reference - this should be a unique reference code for the risk. This will be essential to ensure that no risks are missed and will act as a key where risks are escalated
- Description - should describe the nature of the risk and how the risk will impact on the project. When identifying and describing risk you should think in terms of the following, or similar phrases to express the risk in terms of threat and impact (or cause and effect) - i.e.
  'There is a risk of/that........ which may result in ......'; or,
  'There is a threat of .... which may result in ....';
- Owner - This is the person who carries the responsibility for ensuring that the risk is monitored and, where appropriate, effectively managed. They might not be the person who has to do the necessary tasks, but they must be continuously aware of the risk status;
- Proximity - Timing of the threat of the risk. Is the threat strongest at a particular point in time? (i.e. certain period, date etc?) Does the threat disappear sometime in the future? Or does the probability or impact change over time?
- Risk Responses - Risk response measures should be represented on the relevant project plan as they require activity and consume resource – as above risk should be re-assessed to see if either probability or impact has been reduced by the identified/deployed counter-measure and assessed residual risk should be recorded/shown on the risk register;
- Target Date or Trigger - Timing by which risk responses needs to be started (or completed) based on what it is and how it will address the risk - e.g. contingency actions will identify the trigger that would warrant the plan being invoked. Other actions may need to be undertaken at a specific point in time.

Here is a trick that may help you. PMI® argues that risk identification should first be accomplished at the outset of the project. So you may run into a question that asks, when should we first do risk identification? The answer is, throughout the entire project. Good project managers do risk identification constantly. However if the question is phrased as, when should we first do risk identification? The answer is, at the concept phase, at the very beginning of the project.

Qualitative Risk Analysis

The qualitative risk analysis process prioritizes risks according to their potential effect on project objectives. Qualitative risk analysis is one way to determine the importance of addressing specific risks and guiding risk responses. The time criticality of risk-related actions may magnify the importance of a risk.

Qualitative risk analysis requires that the probability and consequences of the risks be evaluated using established qualitative analysis methods and tools. Qualitative risk analysis should be revisited during the project's life cycle to stay current with changes in the project risks. This process can lead to further analysis in quantitative risk analysis or directly to the risk response planning step.

Inputs to qualitative risk analysis include the risk management planning information developed in step 1, which includes project complexity and technology maturity, data precision techniques, measurement scales, organizational risk factors, and risk assumptions. The potential project risks identified in step 2 and any other pertinent information that would help in the qualitative risk analysis process are also inputs.

Tools and techniques for performing qualitative risk analysis include a probability/impact matrix – which is a matrix that assigns risk ratings (very low, low, moderate, high, and very high) to risks or conditions based on combining probability and impact scales. Risks with high probability and high impact are likely to require further analysis, including quantification, and aggressive risk management. The risk rating is accomplished using a matrix and risk scales for each risk.

PMI® suggests that a probability and impact matrix be constructed to assign a risk rating such as very low, low, moderate, high, and very high to risks and risk conditions based on combining probability and impact scales. A risk's probability scale falls between 0.0 or no probability to 1.0 or certainty. The impact scale reflects the impact of the risk on the project objectives. The intent is to assign a relative value to the impact on the project objectives if the risk occurs. The probability and impact matrix is a common way to combine two dimensions to determine whether a risk is considered very low, low, moderate, or high. The risk score or risk exposure helps put the risk into a category that will guide risk response actions.

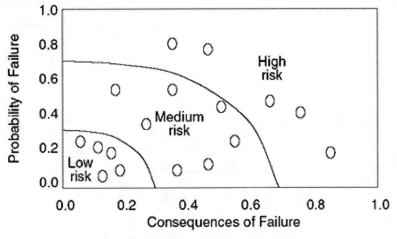

Figure 32 - Risk Probability Scale

Risk probability assessment may be difficult because of dependence on expert judgment. It should be noted that risk impact assessment can be done using ordinal scales (very high to very low) or cardinal scales (either linear or non-linear).

Risk rating matrix can be prepared by combining the probability and impact scales. Risks with high probability and high impact require either further analysis by quantification or aggressive risk management.

Qualitative risk analysis can produce the following results:
- An overall risk ranking for the project. Risk ranking may indicate the overall risk position of a project relative to other projects by comparing the risk scores. This rating can be used to assign personnel or other resources to projects with different risk rankings, to make a cost-

benefit analysis decision about the project, or to support a recommendation for project initiation, continuation, or cancellation.
- Prioritized risks. Risks and conditions can be prioritized by a number of criteria. These include rank (very low, low, moderate, high, and very high) or work breakdown structure level, such as Phase, Activity, and Task. Risks may also be grouped by those risks that require immediate attention and those that can be handled in a later part of the project.

Quantitative Risk Analysis

The quantitative risk analysis process aims to analyze numerically the probability of each risk and its consequence on project objectives. Quantitative risk analysis should be performed after qualitative risk analysis. Quantitative risk analysis should be performed for identified risks that require precise probability and impact measures; risks where the quantitative data is readily available; risks associated with large scale projects requiring such data, or for risks identified on projects that are predetermined to be of high risk.

Quantitative risk analysis uses techniques such as Monte Carlo simulation and decision analysis to:
- Determine the probability of achieving a specific project objective
- Quantify the risk exposure for the project, and determine the size of cost and schedule contingency reserves that may be needed
- Identify risks requiring the most attention by quantifying their relative contribution to project risk, via a risk rating
- Identify realistic and achievable cost, schedule, or scope targets

In order to quantify risks, a quantitative value must be assigned to each weighting factor. One such scale may use the following:
- Very low = 10 percent (.1)
- Low = 30 percent (.3)
- Moderate = 50 percent (.5)
- High = 70 percent (.7)
- Very high = 90 percent (.9)

Examples of software development risk factors

Project Size:
- Low = less than 10,000 lines of source code
- Medium = 10,000 to 100,000 lines of source code
- High = more than 100,000 lines of source code

Project Effort:
- Low = less than 1 person year
- Medium = 1 to 10 person years
- High = more than 10 person years

Project Cost:
- Low = less than $100,000
- Medium = $100,000 to $1,000,000
- High = more than $1,000,000

You will be heavily tested on the common tools used for quantifying risk. You do not have to perform any complex calculations; however, you must be familiar with the concepts as presented in the PMBOK® Guide and in the following review.

Interviewing

Interviewing techniques are used to help quantify the probability and consequences of risks on project objectives. An interview with project stakeholders and subject matter experts may be the first step in quantifying risks. The information needed depends upon the type of probability distributions that will be used.

Documenting the justification of the risk ranges is an important component of the risk analysis because it can lead to effective strategies for risk response in the risk response planning process.

Sensitivity Analysis

Sensitivity analysis helps to determine which risks have the most potential impact on the project. Sensitivity analysis examines the extent to which the uncertainty of each project element affects the objective being examined when all other uncertain elements are held at their baseline values.

Statistical Independence

The concept of statistical independence is a necessary condition for the use of tools such as expected value and decision-tree analysis. A practical definition of statistical independence is that two events are said to be independent if the occurrence of one is not related to the occurrence of the other.

If events are occurring at random, they are independent; if events are not occurring at random, they are not independent. A set or group of possible events are said to be mutually exclusive and collectively exhaustive if they are all independent, and the sum of their probabilities of occurrence is 1.0. This is the basic notion behind expected value.

Expected Monetary Value (EMV)

Expected monetary value (EMV) is a mathematical formula that can help make comparisons between a range of uncertain outcomes.
  EMV = P x O
  P = Probability and O = Outcome
  For example a risk has a 75% chance of occurring and may cost $1,000
  The EMV of the risk is: 0.75 x $1,000 so EMV = $750

Decision-Tree Analysis

A decision analysis is usually represented in the form of a decision tree. The decision tree is a diagram that describes a decision under consideration and the implications of choosing one of the available alternatives. It incorporates probabilities of risks and the costs or rewards of each logical path of events and future decisions. Solving the decision tree indicates which decision yields the greatest expected value to the decision maker when all the uncertain implications, costs, rewards, and subsequent decisions are quantified.

The following image depicts a decision tree. In order to make this decision correctly, one must determine whether it is more important to arrive on time or to travel economically. In this example, the decision to fly results in an expected value of $410 (-$300 + (.85 X $800) + (.15 X $200), while the decision to drive results in an expected value of $500 (-$150 + (.75 X $800) + (.25 X $200). In this case, the decision to drive would be made, baring other factors.

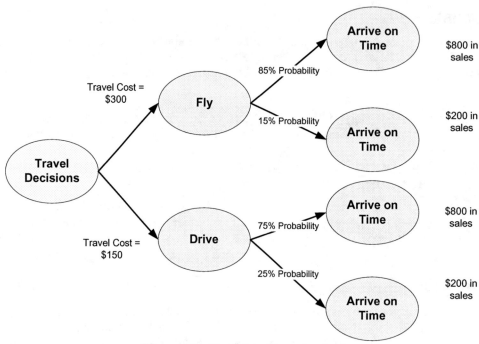

Figure 33 - Decision-Tree Analysis

Decision-Tree Analysis Guidelines
- A box represents a decision; circles represent events with multiple possible outcomes.
- The primary decision (root decision) you are evaluating is placed at the left side of the decision tree, and the tree is drawn from that root.
- Find the most advantageous path at each decision node (box). What makes a path advantageous—lowest cost, greatest return, and so on depends on the specific situation.
- Draw all possible paths for the scenario.
- Place dollar values on each path segment if appropriate.
- Place probabilities on the path segments leading from events. Decision nodes have no probabilities associated with their alternatives.
- Determine the risk values for each path segment by multiplying all probabilities to the left of the segment (including any probability for the segment itself) by each other and then by the dollar value of the segment (if any).
- For each decision node, determine the most advantageous path by adding the risk values for the alternatives. You must work from right to left. Determine the paths for the rightmost decision nodes, and then work
- Your way to the left. The reason for choosing one path is that the paths are mutually exclusive; you can only choose one path.
- For event nodes, consider each path and add the results. The reason for including all paths is that they are mutually inclusive; that is, together they form the entire universe of possible outcomes.
- Continue working to the left until you can determine the most advantageous path for your root decision.

Simulation
A project simulation is a technique to emulate a process. Simulation is usually conducted a number of times to understand the process better and to measure its outcomes under different situations. Project simulations are typically performed using the Monte Carlo technique.

Monte Carlo Analysis

The concept of simulation, typically using Monte Carlo analysis, is also tested. A project simulation uses a model that translates the uncertainties specified at a detailed level into their potential impact on objectives that are expressed at the total project level. One crucial point is that Monte Carlo analysis is considered a superior approach to analyzing the schedule when compared to CPM. This is true because CPM fails to account for path convergence and, as a result, tends to underestimate project durations. Another important point is that the choice of statistical distribution used in the Monte Carlo routine can have important effects on the results of the simulation. For a cost risk analysis, a simulation may use the traditional project WBS as its model.

When it comes to risk quantification, you are going to deal with the idea of statistical independence. That is, what risks do not relate to each other? Their probabilities do not change based on the occurrence of other risks. With statistical dependence one risk leads to another. That is when risks are statistically dependent.

For expected value understand that it is the probability multiplied by the impact. That is the basics of expected value. For example, there is a 10 percent probability that your car will be in an accident costing $10,000. Ten percent of $10,000 is $1,000. That is the expected monetary value of that accident.

Monte Carlo analysis and path convergence: Path convergence goes back to the issue of statistical dependence and independence. You have all three paths. All three paths in the network are critical. Draw three lines going into a single point. It could be the finish node of your project. You have three lines. The first line is a first path, and it has a probability of on-time completion of 40 percent. The second has path has probability of on-time completion of 40 percent. The third has a probability of on-time completion of 20 percent. What are the odds that you are going to complete those three paths, which are all critical, in time to bring in the project on time?

To do that you need to recognize that they are statistically dependent. All three have to be done on time for the project to be done on time. Thus, you multiply the probabilities: 40 percent times 40 percent is 16 percent and 20 percent of 16 percent is 0.032 or 3.2 percent. That means there is only a 3.2 percent probability that all three paths are going to get completed on time. That is the idea of path convergence, and it is generally applied when you do multiple simulations of a project.

Utility Theory

Utility theory is an attempt to infer subjective value, or utility, from choices. Utility theory can be used in both decision making under risk (where the probabilities are explicitly given) and in decision making under uncertainty (where the probabilities are not explicitly given). Extensions of utility theory include subjective probability as well as distortions of probability. There are three traditions in utility theory. One attempts to describe people's utility functions and is called the descriptive approach. Another attempts to use utility in the construction of a rational model of decision making and is called the normative approach. The third attempts to bridge the descriptive and normative approaches by considering the limitations people have with the normative goal they would like to reach; this is called the prescriptive approach.

Risk Response Planning

Risk response planning is the process of developing options and determining actions to reduce threats to the project's objectives. Risk Response Planning includes the further identification and assignment of individuals or teams to take responsibility for each agreed upon risk response.

Risk response planning must be appropriate to the severity of the risk, cost effective in meeting the challenge, timely, realistic within the project context, agreed upon by all parties involved, and owned by a responsible person. Selecting the best risk response from several options is often required.

Strategies for dealing with negative risks or threats
- **Risk Avoidance** - is changing the project plan to eliminate the threat of a specific risk event. Although the project team can never eliminate all risk events, some specific risks may be avoided. Creativity is often required in order to come up with proper risk avoidance strategies.
- **Risk Transference/Deflection** - is seeking to shift the consequence of a risk to a third party via a contract provision with a third party, through an insurance policy, or a vendor warranty. This third party also takes ownership of the risk response. It is important to note that transferring the risk to another party does not eliminate it.
- **Risk Mitigation** - is reducing the probability and/or the consequences of an adverse risk event to an acceptable threshold. It is commonly known that taking early action to reduce the probability of a risk occurring or its impact on the project is more effective than trying to repair the consequences after it has occurred. Mitigation costs should be appropriate, given the likely probability of the risk and its potential consequences.
- **Risk Acceptance** - this is a risk response strategy that prepares for, and deals with, the consequences of a risk event – either actively (developing a contingency plan) or passively (accepting the consequences). There is no plan on the part of the team to take action on this risk.

Contingency Planning

Contingency plans are developed as a result of a risk being identified. Contingency plans are predefined action plans that can be implemented if identified risks actually occur. If a risk event actually occurs, the contingency plan may need to be implemented and contingency reserves allocated, depending on the risk's impact.

As a guideline, contingency plans may initially be developed for the top five risks associated with a project, but don't forget to monitor the remaining identified risks further into the project. For large projects, the top five risks of each major subsystem may be actively tracked. To properly implement a contingency plan, a contingency reserve is usually required where dollars and/or time are held by the project manager to apply to the execution of a contingency plan. Without maintaining a contingency reserve, the project manager is forced to go back for additional time or dollars for every risk as it becomes a problem. It is far more desirable to maintain a level of contingency reserve where problems can be dealt with from within the original budget and schedule of the project.

There are some situations where nothing can realistically be done to prevent or deal with a risk. In this case, the project must be managed in such a way that the probability of the event occurring is minimized. If the event does occur, the project manager must re-plan the project and include the effect of the risk event.

Strategies for Positive Risks or Opportunities

The following options are intended to deal with potentially positive impacts on project objectives:
- **Exploit** - This type of strategy may be selected for risks with positive impacts where the organization wishes to ensure the opportunity is realized. This strategy seeks to remove the confusion associated with a particular upside risk by making the opportunity definitely happen.
- **Share** - Sharing a positive risk involves allocating ownership to a third party who is best able to capture the opportunity for the benefit of the project.
- **Enhance** - This strategy changes the "size" of an opportunity by increasing probability and/or positive impacts, and by identifying and maximizing key drivers of these positive-impact risks.

Risk Monitoring and Control

Risk monitoring and control is the process of keeping track of all the identified risks and identifying new risks as their presence becomes known and residual risks that occur when the risk management plans are implemented on individual risks. The effectiveness of the risk management plan is evaluated on an ongoing basis throughout the project.

When a risk is apparently going to take place, the contingency plan is brought into place. If there is no contingency plan, then the risk is worked on an ad hoc basis using what is termed a workaround. A workaround is an unplanned response to a negative risk event.

The concern of the project manager and the project team is that the risk responses have been brought to bear on the risk as planned, that the risk response has been effective. Additional risks may develop, and additional responses may be necessary.

Risk management is a continuous process that takes place during the entire project from beginning to end. As the project progresses, the risks that have been identified are monitored and reassessed as the time that they can take place approaches. Early warning indicators are monitored to reassess the probability and impact of the risk. As the risk approaches, the risk strategies are reviewed for appropriateness, and additional responses are planned.

As each risk occurs and is dealt with, or is avoided, these changes must be documented. Good documentation ensures that risks of this type will be dealt with in a more effective way than before and that the next project manager will benefit from "lessons learned."

Chapter Review

1. Which of the following processes is not part of Project Risk Management?
    A. Qualitative Risk Analysis
    B. Risk Identification
    C. Risk Analysis Planning
    D. Risk Response Planning

2. Using the PMBOK® Guide definition of contingency reserve, which of the following statements about contingency reserves is false?
    A. A contingency reserve is a separately planned quantity of money or time that has been set aside to allow for future situations which may be planned for only in part.
    B. Contingency reserves are used to reduce the risks of overruns of project objectives to a level acceptable to the organization.
    C. Contingency reserves may be set aside for known risks.
    D. Contingency reserves can be included in the project's cost and schedule estimates without any identifying documentation.

3. Which of the following is not a tool or technique used during the Quantitative Risk Analysis process?
    A. Earned value analysis
    B. Interviewing
    C. Decision Trees
    D. Sensitivity Analysis

4. Which of the following statements regarding pure risk is false?
    A. The risk can be deflected or transferred to another party through a contract or
    B. insurance policy. Also referred to as insurable risk.
    C. Pure risks involve the chance of both a profit and a loss.
    D. No opportunities are associated with pure risk, only threats.
    E. Pure risk could be classified as a known-unknown risk.

5. A contingency plan is:
    A. A planned response that defines the steps to be taken if an identified risk event should occur.
    B. A workaround
    C. A comprehensive listing of many possible risks that might occur on a project.
    D. a and b

6. The inherent chances for both profit or loss associated with a particular endeavor is called:
    A. Favorable risk
    B. Opportunity risk
    C. Pure risk
    D. Business risk

7. A risk response which involves eliminating a threat is called:
    A. Mitigation
    B. Deflection
    C. Avoidance
    D. Transfer

8. Deflection or transfer of a risk to another party is part of which of the following risk response categories?
    A. Mitigation
    B. Acceptance
    C. Avoidance
    D. Transference

9. When should risk identification be performed? (select best answer)
    A. During Concept Phase
    B. During Development Phase
    C. During Implementation Phase
    D. Risk identification should be performed on a regular basis throughout the project.

10. A risk probability or impact scale that uses rank-ordered values such as very low, low, moderate, high, and very high is called:
    A. An ordinal scale
    B. A cardinal scale
    C. A nonlinear scale
    D. All of the above

Answers

1. C, PMBOK® Guide 3rd Edition, page 237
2. D, PMBOK® Guide 3rd Edition, page 355
3. A, PMBOK® Guide 3rd Edition, page 254
4. B, Project & Program Risk Management by R. Max Wideman, Editor
5. A, A workaround is an unplanned response to a negative risk event. Option C is the definition of a checklist.
6. D, Project & Program Risk Management by R. Max Wideman, Editor. glossary
7. C, PMBOK® Guide 3rd Edition, page 261
8. D, PMBOK® Guide 3rd Edition, page 262
9. D, PMBOK® Guide 3rd Edition, page 246
10. A, PMBOK® Guide 3rd Edition, page 245

Chapter 12

Project Procurement Management

Reference Material to Study
- A Guide to the Project Management Body of Knowledge (PMBOK® Guide 3rd Edition), Chapter 12
- Principles of Project Management, John Adams, pgs. 213-280
- The New Project Management, Frame, J. Davidson, Chapter 10

What to Study
- The PMBOK® phases of Project Procurement Management: Procurement Planning, Solicitation Planning, Solicitation, Source Selection, Contract Administration, and Contract Close-out (Be familiar with Inputs, Tools and Techniques, and Outputs for each phase)
- Understand the viewpoint of the PMBOK®. Project Procurement Management is discussed from the perspective of the buyer in the buyer-seller relationship. The buyer is the organization seeking the service or product. The seller is the provider of the service or contract and is referred to as the vendor, the supplier, or the contractor.
- Understand the definitions and terms. (buyer, seller, express and implied warranties, "fitness for a particular use", invitation to bid, request for proposal, etc.)
- Understand the viewpoint of the reading material. Is procurement management discussed from the viewpoint of the buyer (the organization or person seeking to outsource) or the seller (the person or organization selling their services/products)?
- Understand the different types of contracts: fixed price, cost plus percentage, cost plus fixed fee, cost plus incentive fee, and fixed price plus incentive fee. Know who assumes the most risk (buyer or seller) in each type of contract. Study examples of each type of contract so that you are comfortable with the different types and can adequately distinguish between each type of contract (especially the various shades of cost plus contracts!).
- Know the elements of a legally enforceable contract: Mutual assent, consideration must be provided to both parties (sufficient cause to contract), signing parties must have legal right to contract, the contract must have a legal purpose, and the contract must not violate public policy.
- Be familiar with the reasons for contracting and subcontracting and the risks associated with procurement.

Key Definitions
- **Bidders Conference** - A meeting hosted by the buyer contracting organization to assist prospective bidders in understanding the Request for Proposal.
- **Bidders List** - A list of companies judged capable by the procuring organization from which bids, proposals, or quotations may be solicited.

- **Contract** - A legal document of purchase or sale which is binding on both parties. When entering into a contract, the people involved must have legal capacity to do so. (the definition of legal capacity varies from state to state). Consideration must be provided to both parties (in other words, there must be sufficient cause to contract). There must be mutual assent.
- **Cost Reimbursable Contracts** - This category of contract involves payment (reimbursement) to the contractor for its actual costs. Costs are usually classified as direct costs (costs incurred directly by the project such as salaries of project staff) and indirect costs (costs allocated to the project by the performing organization as a cost of doing business such as salaries for corporate executives). Indirect costs are usually calculated as a percentage of direct costs. Cost reimbursable contracts often include incentives for meeting or exceeding selected project objectives such as schedule targets or total cost.
- **Fixed Price or Lump Sum Contracts** - This category of contract involves a fixed total price for a well-defined product. Fixed price contracts may also include incentives for meeting or exceeding selected project objectives such as schedule targets.
- **Make-or-Buy Decisions** - A process in which it is determined whether to manufacture internally, or buy from external sources some component, article or item of equipment.
- **Performance Bond** - A bond that secures performance and fulfillment of the contractor's obligations under the contract.
- **Privity of Contract** - The legal relationship that exist between the parties to a contract that allows either party to enforce contractual rights against the other party and seek remedy directly from the other party.
- **Request for Proposal** (RFP) - A type of bid document used to solicit proposals from prospective sellers of products or services. In some application areas, it may have a more specific meaning.
- **Request for Quotation** (RFQ) - PMBOK® does not distinguish between RFQ and RFP. PMBOK® does recognize that some application areas have a more specific meaning for RFQ (appropriate for low dollar items such as supplies.
- **Seller** - The organization under contract to a buyer.
- **Statement of Work** (SOW) - Describes the portion of the product to be contracted. In general, this is different from the product description (which tends to be broader). Under the circumstance where the seller is producing the entire product, the distinction between SOW and the product description becomes moot.

The Project Procurement Management questions on the PMP® exam tend to be more process oriented than legally focused. The exam requires you to know the differences between the two categories of contracts (fixed-price and cost-reimbursement) and the risks inherent in each category for both the buyer and seller. Several questions will also test your knowledge of the various types of contracts within each category.

The processes in the Project Procurement Management knowledge area are as follows: Plan Purchases and Acquisitions, Plan Contracting, Request Seller Responses, Select Sellers, Contract Administration, and Contract Closure.

Project procurement management is the process required to acquire the goods and services necessary to attain project scope. Goods and services typically are referred to as a product and are obtained from outside the performing organization.

PMI® discusses Project Procurement Management from the perspective of the buyer in the buyer-seller relationship but notes that the buyer-seller relationship can exist at many levels on one project. On the exam the seller may be called a subcontractor, vendor, or supplier. The seller generally manages work as a project in and of itself. The buyer may also be referred to as the customer. The terms and conditions of the contract are a major input to the seller's processes. The terms and conditions may actually contain the input as it may describe key milestones, deliverables, or objectives, or they may serve as a constraint since they may limit the project team's options (for example, requiring buyer approval of staffing decisions or staffing changes).

PMI® further discusses project procurement management from the perspective of the seller being external to the organization but notes that the discussion is also applicable to formal agreements entered into with other units in the performing organization. If informal agreements are used, then processes in Human Resource Management and Communications Management are more likely to apply. Apply extra caution when answering questions in this area: make sure you know whom the question refers to when you see the words buyer and seller. In most cases, the buyer is the project manager.

Procurement planning is the process in which the project manager identifies those needs of the project that can be met by purchasing products or services from outside the organization.

Procurement planning deals with the following:
- What to procure
- When to procure
- How to procure
- How much to procure

It is very uncommon for an organization to be able to create or supply all the products necessary to complete a project internally. In those circumstances where it is necessary to go outside the organization, the response is to purchase the product or service from an external source or enter into a contract with an outside vendor to perform a service or develop the product for the organization. Whatever choice is made, there is definitely a considerable amount of forethought and planning that needs to go into such a decision.

Plan Purchases and Acquisitions

Plan purchases and acquisitions is a process of identifying what goods or services you are going to purchase from outside of the organization. Part of what you will accomplish in this process is determining whether you should purchase the goods or services at all, and if so, how much and when.

During this step, the project manager is responsible for describing the subcontract procurement need in terms of specification. Specification is a precise description of a physical item, procedure, service, or result for the purpose of purchase and/or implementation of an item or service.

In addition to remembering the above definition of project procurement, you should also know who on the project team is primarily responsible for creating the project specification. The project manager is responsible for ensuring that the job gets done but must rely on the technical people to do the work. In identifying the need, the project manager also determines whether it is more advantageous to make or buy the needed item or service.

Contract Categories and Risks

PMI® places a great deal of emphasis on types of contracts and the assignment of risk between buyer and seller. Contract type selection is a tool and technique in plan purchases and acquisitions. The buyer's objective is to place maximum performance risk on the seller while maintaining incentive for economical and efficient performance. The seller's objective is to minimize risk while maximizing profit potential.

PMI® recognizes three broad categories of contracts: fixed-price or lump-sum contracts, costs-reimbursement contracts, and time-and-materials (T&M) contracts. They are defined as follows:

- Fixed-price or Lump-sum - These contracts set a specific, firm price for the goods and/or services rendered. The buyer and seller agree on a well-defined deliverable for a set price. In this kind of contract, the biggest risk is borne by the seller. Fixed price contracts are usually used for projects that will take a long time to complete and have a high value to the company. This is the most common contract type, because it is best suited for situations with reasonably definite specifications and relatively certain costs.
- Cost-reimbursement - These types of contracts are as the name implies. The costs associated with producing the goods or services are charged to the buyer. All of the costs the seller takes on during the project are charged back to the buyer, thus the seller is reimbursed. Cost reimbursable contracts carry the highest risk to the buyer, as the total costs are uncertain. Three common types of cost-reimbursable contracts are cost-plus-percentage of cost (CPPC) also known as a cost-plus-fee (CPF) contract, cost-plus-fixed Fee (CPFF), and cost-plus-incentive Fee (CPIF).
- Cost-plus-percentage-of-cost (CPPC) - A CPPC contract provides for the reimbursement of allowable costs of services performed plus an agreed-upon percentage of the estimated cost as profit. The seller is only obligated to make its best effort to fulfill the contract within the estimated amount; the buyer funds all overruns. This contract type is prohibited in U.S. federal contracting and is only rarely used in the commercial sector.
- Cost-plus-fixed Fee (CPFF) - A CPFF contract provides for the reimbursement of allowable costs plus a fixed fee paid proportionately as the contract progresses. Although there is a ceiling on the seller's profit, there is no motivation to control costs. Therefore, most risk remains with the buyer. This contract type is used predominantly for research and development projects in which the effort required remains uncertain until the project is well under way.
- Cost-plus-incentive Fee (CPIF) - A CPIF contract provides for the reimbursement of allowable costs plus a predetermined fee as a bonus for superior performance. If the actual cost is less than the expected cost, the buyer and seller share the savings, based on a predetermined formula. This contract type is used predominantly for projects with long performance periods and substantial hardware development and test requirements.
- Time-and-materials (T&M) - Time and materials contracts are a cross between the fixed price and cost reimbursable contract. The full amount of the material costs is not known at the time the contract is awarded. This resembles a cost reimbursable contract, as the cost will continue to grow during the contract's life. The buyer assumes most of the risk in time and material contracts.

Contract Examples
CPPC:
Estimated cost: $1,000K   Percentage: 10% ($100K)
Estimated total price: $1,100K (Estimated cost + 10%*Estimated cost)
If cost increases to $1,100K the total price would be $1,100K plus 10% of the actual costs = $1,210K.

CPFF:
Estimated cost: $1,000K   Percentage: 10% ($100K)
Estimated total price: $1,100K (Estimated cost + 10%*Estimated cost)
If cost increases to $1,100K the total price would be $1,100K plus 10% of the original estimated costs = $1,200K.

CPIF:
Estimated cost: $1,000K   predetermined fee: $100K
Sharing formula: 85/15 (buyer absorbs 85% of the uncertainty and the seller absorbs 15% of the risk)
Actual cost: $800K Savings: $200K
Seller gets: $800K + $100K + $30K = $930K (Actual cost + Fee + 15%*Savings)
Buyer saves: $170K

FFP: (Lump Sum)
Price: $1,000K
Example A: Actual cost: $700K
Seller makes a profit of $300K (Price - Actual Cost)
Example B: Final cost $1,100K
Seller loses $100K on contract

For the test know the following:
CPPC, CPFF, CPIF, FPI, FFP --- seller's risk moves from low to high
FFP, FPI, CPIF, CPFF, CPPC --- buyer's risk moves from low to high

Contract Origination

To determine the type of procurement documents to develop, the contracting specialists survey potential sellers and originate either a unilateral or a bilateral contract. A contract, as defined by PMI®, is a mutually binding agreement that obligates the seller to provide a specific product and obligates the buyer to pay for it. A contract is a legal relationship subject to remedy in the courts.

A unilateral contract takes the form of a purchase order—a standardized form listing routine items at standard (for example, vendor catalog) prices. The seller usually accepts the purchase order automatically. Unilateral contracts issued in this way normally do not involve any negotiation and contain relatively low monetary amounts.

A bilateral contract is initiated through a request for quotations, request for proposals, or an invitation for bid. The choice of which bilateral method to use is guided by the following factors:
- An invitation for bid is usually appropriate for routine items when the primary objective is to find the best price. You must be able to clearly and accurately describe the items to be purchased. There are normally no negotiations and, although not an absolute requirement, the lowest bid usually wins.
- A request for quotations is used for relatively low monetary purchases of commodity items.
- A request for proposals is used for complex or nonstandard items of relatively high monetary value.

Contract Incentives

Incentives in a contract provide a "carrot" for the contractor in an attempt to bring the objectives and interests of the contractor in line with those of the buyer. Experience has shown that contract incentives are indeed usually cost effective. Incentives can be structured in a variety of ways and are flexible in that they can be used in conjunction with any of the types of contracts identified by PMI®.

As you read through this information, make sure you recognize what role the project manager has in the process. When it comes to procurement planning, the project manager has a very large role. They are responsible for creating the project specification with our project team. Also be familiar with the make-or-buy analysis—should we actually do this ourselves or should we subcontract the work out?

Another key component of this is trying to determine what the appropriate contract type is for any given project. There are different weights on who is responsible and who is taking the risk associated with each type of contract. The seller takes the greatest risk in firm-fixed-price contracts. By contrast, the buyer is taking the lowest risk in a firm-fixed-price contract.

At the high end of the spectrum, the buyer takes the greatest risk in a cost-plus-percentage-of-cost contract. The lowest risk to the seller occurs in a cost-plus-percentage-of-cost contract. Those contracts are so advantageous to the seller that they are illegal in certain environments, including the United States Federal Government.

You should know the range of risk that goes between the contract types. It goes firm-fixed-price at the lowest; fixed-price-incentive fee is next, then cost-plus-incentive fee, cost-plus-fixed fee, and then finally, cost-plus-percentage-of-cost. That is the range from low risk to high risk for the buyer. By contrast that is the range from high risk to low risk for the seller, and you need to be aware of that dichotomy.

Make-or-Buy Analysis

This is a simple method to determine the cost-effectiveness of creating a product in-house as compared to the cost of buying the product or having it produced outside the organization. All costs, both direct and indirect, should be considered when performing a make or buy analysis. The costs should then be compared with each other with consideration given to any compelling argument on either side by the project team. Consideration should also be given to the potential of leasing versus purchasing items. This could save money for the organization if cost is applied correctly against the useful life of the product or service supplied. Many of the decisions will be based on the length of need for the item or service as well as the overall cost.

Make-or-buy analysis is accomplished during the plan purchases and acquisitions phase (the first phase) in PMI's six-phase approach to procurement management. The purpose is to determine what to procure from outside the project team and when the procurement should occur. You should also be aware of the following key points:
- Make-or-buy analysis should consider both the direct as well as the indirect costs of a prospective procurement. In this context, PMI® considers the indirect costs of buying an item from the outside to include the cost of managing and monitoring the purchasing process. Direct costs such as salaries of full-time project staff are incurred for the exclusive benefit of the project, whereas indirect costs or overhead costs such as executive salaries, insurance, and benefits are allocated to the project by the performing organization as a cost of doing business.
- Make-or-buy analysis should reflect the perspective of the performing organization as well as the project's immediate needs. For example, purchasing a capital item rather than renting or leasing it may not be cost effective. But if the performing organization has an ongoing need

for the item, then the portion of the purchase cost allocated to the project may be less than the cost of the rental.

There are several possible decisions that might result from the make-or-buy analysis:
- Procure all or virtually all of the goods and services from a single supplier or from multiple suppliers
- Procure a significant portion of the goods and services from a single supplier or from multiple suppliers
- Procure a relatively minor portion of the goods and services from outside sources (single or multiple suppliers)
- Make everything in house; procure nothing from the outside

Expert Judgment

This process uses the expertise of people from within and outside the organization that have knowledge or training in the area in question to determine what steps should be taken. These people review the needs and the costs and deliver their opinion for consideration in the procurement decision.

Key deliverables (outputs) produced include a procurement management plan and the contract statement of work (SOW). The procurement management plan is a subsidiary element of the project plan and includes such information as follows:
- The type of contract to be used
- The need for independent estimates
- The roles and responsibilities of the organization's procurement department and the project management team
- Where standardized procurement documents are located
- Multiple-vendor management techniques
- How procurement will be integrated into the project life cycle

The SOW describes the procurement item in sufficient detail so that prospective sellers can determine whether they are capable of providing the item. It is a narrative description of the products or services to be supplied under contract.

If the procurement item is presented as a problem to be solved, the SOW may be called a statement of objectives (SOO). Although the SOW is prepared during procurement planning, it may be revised and refined as it moves through the procurement process. Each individual procurement item requires a separate statement of work, but multiple products or services may be grouped as one procurement item in a single SOW. It is important that the SOW be as clear, complete, and concise as possible.

Plan Contracting

Plan contracting begins once a project manager has gone through the plan purchases and acquisitions process and decided that resources are needed from outside the project's parent company.

A list of prospective contractors is a good starting point when deciding from which companies you want to procure project resources. Some companies keep lists of contractors they have used in the past. This list generally includes information about the contractors, such as what resources they provide, which contracts they have used and how successfully they fulfilled those contracts. This documentation is collectively called the "procurement documents," which are used to seek proposals from prospective sellers. Procurement documents should be structured to facilitate accurate and complete responses from prospective sellers.

The following should always be included with your procurement documents:
- Statement of Work
- A description of the desired form of response
- Required contractual provisions such as a copy of a model contract or nondisclosure provisions

Procurement Management Plan

The procurement management plan identifies what products and/or services to purchase in support of the statement of work. The plan will define how the relationship between the contracting organization and the contracted vendor will be managed; outline the types of contracts to be used; the evaluation criteria, and the timeframe in which to procure the goods and/or services; ensure that a valid, approved contract is in place before work begins; and defines the acceptance criteria of the goods and/or services to be rendered.

Contract Statement of Work

The statement of work (SOW) is the document which describes in clear understandable term what products and services are to be delivered or services to be performed by the contractor. Preparation of an effective SOW requires an understanding of both the products and services that are needed to satisfy a particular requirement. A SOW prepared in explicit terms will facilitate effective contractor evaluation after contract award. The SOW becomes the standard for measuring contractor performance. Therefore, the SOW must clearly define the work to be performed. In preparing the SOW for a system acquisition, the use of a standardized work breakdown structure as a template for constructing the SOW will help streamline the process. Use of the work breakdown structure will also provide the framework and facilitate a logical arrangement of the SOW elements, provide a convenient checklist to ensure all necessary elements of the program are addressed, and direct the contractor to meet specific contract reporting needs.

Evaluation Criteria

An evaluation criterion refers to the method your organization will use to choose a vendor from the proposals you receive from the solicitation process. Scoring models might be used along with a rating model or system. Sometimes, the evaluation criteria are made public in the procurement process so that vendors know exactly what you are looking for. They may be objective, such as "a supplier needs to be ISO certified," or subjective, such as "the proposed supplier must have documented previous experience with similar projects." When price is not the primary determinant of award, sellers may be evaluated by the following evaluation criteria:
- Understanding of product/project needs
- Technical proficiency

Request Seller Responses

This process involves obtaining responses, such as bids and proposals from prospective sellers/vendors in response to a request for proposal (RFP) and similar documents prepared during the plan contracting process. The term often used to describe this process is source qualification, which is described as follows:

> Working from internal files, qualified seller lists, trade journals, supplier catalogs, and industry contacts, contracting specialists develop a list of potential sellers. They then collect information on each potential seller's technical, manufacturing, financial, and managerial

abilities to fulfill the potential contract. Conferences with prospective sellers are often held to ensure that they have a clear, common understanding of the procurement. Responses to questions must be incorporated into the procurement documents as amendments so all prospective sellers remain on equal standing. Advertising also is used to expand existing lists of potential sellers where appropriate. The project manager working with the contracting staff performs this function.

Proposals are the main output from the request seller responses process. Proposals are prepared by prospective sellers and describe the seller's ability and willingness to provide the required product or service. Proposals may be supplemented with an oral presentation.

Bidder Conference

To select the contractor for your project, you can organize bidder conferences. Bidder conferences are meetings with all the prospective contractors. You establish bidder conferences to ensure that all prospective sellers have a clear and common understanding of the requirements of the process. The requirements that are involved in the process are:
- Technical - the technical requirements refer to technical aspects that the project has to accomplish - for example, how to construct a two-meter-high wall.
- Contractual - the contractual requirements of any project refer to the agreement between buyer and seller stipulating what is expected from both parties. Contractual requirement specifications regarding a project usually include how long the project will take to complete, how much it will cost, and so on.

The outcome of bidder conferences helps you to make changes to the procurement documents. The discussion may reveal various issues that need to be addressed and factors that need to be taken into consideration. Suppose you stipulated a specific building process in the initial procurement document without realizing the high risk involved in such a process. And at the bidder conference this gets pointed out to you by one of the contractors. This gives you the opportunity to alter the requirements or to think of other ways to resolve the issue. To broaden the base of your potential contractors, you may want to advertise. This you can do by placing an advertisement in a newspaper or a professional publication.

Qualified Seller List

A qualified seller list maintains information files on firms that have done work for the company previously. The list should include information about the product and the delivery history of the supplier. It is a good idea to keep a qualified seller list if you make use of outside contractors regularly. This means that you don't waste time by having to find suitable contractors every time you have a project.

Select Sellers

This process involves the receipt of bids or proposals and choosing a vendor to perform the work or supply the goods or services. The following questions can be helpful when evaluating proposals during solicitation and selection:
- Does the contractor understand the project's needs?
- Is the contractor capable of providing the required resources?
- What is the contractor's reputation?
- What is the price of the resource?

Based on the answers to those questions you may be able to compile a short list of qualified sellers.

Evaluating Prospective Sellers

Various techniques are used for evaluating and selecting prospective sellers and they are not mutually exclusive. Many factors aside from cost and price may need to be evaluated. Price may be the primary determinant for an off-the-shelf item, but PMI® notes that the lowest proposed price may not be the lowest cost if the seller proves unable to deliver the product in a timely manner. Proposals also often are separated into technical and price sections, and each may be evaluated separately. Evaluation criteria may include samples of the supplier's previously produced products or services to provide a way to evaluate its capabilities and the quality of its products. Suppliers may also include a review of past performance if they have worked with the contracting organization before. Several tools and techniques commonly used include:

- Contract Negotiation - Contract negotiation is an important part of the contract selection. During this process, the project manager bargains with a contractor to obtain project resources at a reasonable price. Once they reach an agreement, they negotiate the type of contract that will bind the agreement.
- Weighting System - A weighting system is an objective way to evaluate proposals and choose a contractor. When using a typical weighting system, a project manager assigns a numerical value to each evaluative criterion. Then, as the project manager reads the proposals, he can keep track of which proposals meet the criterion.
- Screening System - A screening system is another means of evaluating proposals and choosing a contractor. When using a screening system, a project manager sets minimum requirements for each evaluative criterion. If a proposal does not meet the minimum requirements, the project manager should reject the proposal.
- Independent Estimates - The procurement department might conduct an independent estimate of the costs of the proposal and use this to compare to the vendor prices. If there are large differences between the independent estimate and the proposed vendor cost, one of two things is happening: 1) The statement of work, or the terms of the contract were not accurate enough to allow the vendor to come up with an accurate cost; or 2) the vendor failed to respond to all the requirements that were stated in the contract or in the statement of work.
- Seller Rating System - Seller rating systems are usually databases kept by organizations and include such valuable information such as the seller's past performance, quality ratings, delivery schedule, and compliance issues.
- Expert Judgment - Expert judgment is any group or individual with specialized knowledge applicable to the procurement process. This would include representatives from the legal department, administrative department and even the sales department. What you're trying to develop is a multi-disciplinary committee of experts in order to evaluate the seller's proposals.
- Proposal Evaluation Techniques - When using a proposal evaluation technique you will normally use some kind of weighted scoring system, where the project manager will assign a numerical value to each evaluative each option. In addition we will have to involve some sort expert judgment to assist us in our evaluation.

For the exam, know that using the PMP® certification is an example of a screening system.

It is generally considered a good practice to ensure competition among a group of prospective sellers if possible. There is considerable literature documenting the benefits of competition. Why should we use a sole source?

- When a seller truly has a unique qualification that cannot be found or matched elsewhere.
- When other mechanisms exist to ensure that the price you are paying is reasonable. For example, you might have the in-house expertise to properly evaluate the seller's bid for reasonableness and accuracy.
- When your project is under extreme schedule pressure. Competitive contract selection almost always takes longer than noncompetitive contract selection because you must allow time for preparing a solicitation document, for sending and receiving the solicitation, for the prospective sellers to prepare and submit a proposal, and for you to evaluate the proposals and make a selection.

Contract Negotiation Stages and Tactics
According to PMI®, contract negotiation consists of five stages:
1. Protocol - Introductions are made and the atmosphere is set.
2. Probing - Negotiators identify issues of concern, as well as the strengths and weaknesses of the other party.
3. Scratch Bargaining - The actual bargaining occurs and concessions are made.
4. Closure - Positions are summed up and final concessions are made.
5. Agreement - The final agreement is documented.

In Negotiating and Contracting for Project Management PMI® identifies the following negotiation tactics:
- Deadline - Imposing a deadline for reaching an agreement.
- Surprise - Taking the other party by surprise with new information.
- Strategic Delay - Requesting a recess to divert attention from the present discussion or to regroup.
- Reasoning Together - Collaborating to resolve problems for everyone's benefit.
- Withdrawal - Making a false attack on an issue and then retreating (to divert attention from a weakness).
- Limited Authority - Claiming inability to finalize the agreement just reached (a stalling tactic).
- Missing Man - Claiming that the person with final authority is absent.
- Fair and Reasonable - Offering comparisons to other situations, for example, to show that the price offered is reasonable.
- Unreasonable - Making the other party's request appear unreasonable.
- Suggesting Arbitration - Attempting to scare the other party into agreement.
- Fait accompli - Claiming that a topic of dispute has already been decided or accomplished and cannot be changed.

The project manager's negotiation objectives are to:
- Obtain a fair and reasonable price, while still getting the contract performed within certain time and performance limitations.
- Develop a good relationship with the seller. This objective cannot be overemphasized, because the buyer will pursue the relationship throughout the contract period.

The output from the source selection process is the contract. Contracts may be called an agreement, a subcontract, a purchase order, or a memorandum of understanding. Most organizations have documented policies and procedures that define who can sign such agreements on behalf of the organization, typically called a delegation of procurement authority.

Also, when it comes down to contract negotiation; make sure you know the five stages and what they mean. Protocol is rapport-setting; it is the handshake that goes on at the beginning of a contract negotiation. Probing is when you go out and try to investigate what is going on at the other side. Scratch bargaining is also known as hard-core bargaining, and you may see either term on the exam. Closure is when you come to an end, and agreement is when there are actual signatures on a piece of paper.

Also, be aware of the negotiation tactics of deadline and surprise. One that shows up more often than any other on the exam is fait accompli, which means claiming it is a done deal, claiming that it has already been agreed to.

Contract Administration
Contract administration is the formal verification that the contractor has fulfilled his contractual obligations. As part of contract administration, the project manager must make sure all project team members are aware of their responsibilities with regard to a contract.

During this step, the project manager—with help from the contracting specialists—monitors the seller's performance against the contract's specifications, performance standards, and terms and conditions. PMI® emphasizes that the legal nature of the contractual arrangement makes it imperative that the project team be aware of the legal implications of actions taken during contract administration.

Contract Document

At a minimum, the following items are usually documented in the contract:
- Delivery schedule
- Payment schedule - method for determining the price
- Handling of changes
- Warranties, insurance, inspections
- Delays termination
- Subcontracts, performance bonds

Contracts may have specific terms or conditions for completion and closeout. You should be aware of these terms or conditions so that project closure is not held up because you overlooked an important detail. If you are not administering the contract yourself, ask your contracts/procurement department if there are any special conditions that you should know about.

Standard Clauses

The use of standard clauses is encouraged where possible because they are legally sufficient for most contractual situations and because they cost less (customized contract language takes time and can sometimes be expensive to develop).

The following is a brief description of clauses specifically addressed in PMI's Contract Administration for the Project Manager.

Changes
- Changes to project scope constitute one of the major areas of cost growth
- Control of change
- Who initiates a change request
- How change is funded
- Final approval authority
- Configuration control
- Do not price changes on a cost-plus basis; use lump-sum

Warranties
- Establish a level of quality
- Express warranty: Contract explicitly states what the level of quality is
- Implied warranty: Contract describes "merchantability" or "fitness of use"

Doctrine of Waiver: the relinquishing of one party's contract rights because of a lack of enforcement of those rights

Delays
- Who caused it
- Nature of the interruption
- Impact

Bonds
- ♦ Performance bond: Secures for the buyer the performance and fulfillment of the contract
- ♦ Payment bond: Guaranteed payment to subcontractors and laborers by the prime or the guarantor

Breach
- ♦ Failure to perform a contractual obligation
- ♦ Measure for damage is the amount of loss sustained by an injured party
- ♦ Material breach: More serious than a contract breach

Nonfaulted party discharged from any further obligations: for example, when a contract stipulates that time is of the essence, failure to perform within the allotted time constitutes material breach and the project manager will not be required to accept late performance.

Elements of a Legally Enforceable Contract: Finally, you should be familiar with the elements of a legally valid (enforceable) contract:
- ♦ The agreement must be voluntary (there must be both an offer and an acceptance).
- ♦ The people signing must have the legal capacity to do so
- ♦ There must be sufficient cause to contract—"consideration" must be provided to both parties
- ♦ The contract must be for a legal purpose and must not violate public policy

Changes and Change Control

All contracts should define the process by which any changes to the contract (project) can be accommodated and should include the paperwork, tracking systems, and approvals necessary for authorizing changes. The system should cover who initiates a change request, how it is processed and funded, and who has the final approval authority. Changes made, whether they are approved or unapproved, must be reflected in the appropriate project documents.

Undefined Work

Undefined work becomes an issue when "time is of the essence." The parties would like to proceed with the project, but the price and other important terms and conditions of the contract have not been specified or agreed to.

This situation can arise either at the outset of a contractual relationship or as a result of significant changes to an ongoing contract. At the outset of a contract, a contractor will often proceed on the basis of a "letter contract," with the details to be worked out later. Obviously, a certain amount of trust exists in such a circumstance. When undefined work arises as a result of changes, contractors often proceed without a formal change order authorizing them to do so.

Contract Closure

Contract closure is the formal verification that contractors have completely and successfully fulfilled their obligations to a project. During contract closeout, all paperwork and electronic files used during the project must be updated and filed in a database for future reference. Most often, the contract will specify how the contract and project should be closed.
Contract records are very important and include the contract itself and other relevant documentation such as progress reports, financial records, invoices, and payment records. These are often kept in a contract file, which should be part of the complete project file. The contract file is a complete set of index records.

Contract documentation is also important should a procurement audit be initiated. Such an audit is a structured review of the procurement process from procurement planning through contract administration. The purpose of the audit is to identify success and failures that warrant transfer to other procurement items on the current project or future projects.

The person or organization responsible for contract administration should provide the seller with formal written notice when the contract has been completed. The contract should define the requirements for formal acceptance.

Organizing for Contract Management

According to PMI® a company can assign project contracting responsibility in a centralized or decentralized manner.

Centralized Contracting

With centralized contracting, a single function within the company is responsible for the entire contracting process for all projects. Contracting procedures typically are stringent and standardized. This form works best in functionally organized companies.

Advantages
- More economical.
- Easier to control overall contracting efforts.
- Higher degree of contracting specialization.
- Orders can be consolidated across several projects.

Disadvantages
- The contracting office can become a bottleneck if several projects have heavy needs at once.
- Less attention is given to the special needs of individual projects.

Decentralized Contracting

With decentralized contracting, each project manager controls the contracting process for his or her project. This form works best if companies follow the projectized organization

Advantages
- Project manager has more control
- Contracting personnel are more familiar with project needs
- More flexible and adaptable to project needs

Disadvantages
- Duplication of contracting efforts across projects
- Higher costs
- No standard contracting policies

Force Majeure

Force Majeure literally means "greater force." These clauses excuse a party from liability if some unforeseen event beyond the control of that party prevents it from performing its obligations under the contract. Typically, force majeure clauses cover natural disasters or other "Acts of God," war, or the failure of third parties—such as suppliers and subcontractors—to perform their obligations to the contracting party. It is important to remember that force majeure clauses are intended to excuse a party only if the failure to perform could not be avoided by the exercise of due care by that party.

When negotiating force majeure clauses, make sure that the clause applies equally to all parties to the agreement—not just the licensor. Also, it is helpful if the clause sets forth some specific examples of acts that will excuse performance under the clause, such as wars, natural disasters, and other major events that are clearly outside a party's control. Inclusion of examples will help to make clear the parties' intent that such clauses are not intended to apply to excuse failures to perform for reasons within the control of the parties.

Privity of Contract

Privity of contract is a legal term that recognizes that the contractual relationship exists between a buyer and its prime contractor. No contract exists between the buyer and the subcontractors, and it is legally improper for a buyer to bypass a contractor and deal directly with a subcontractor(s).

Beyond the legal issue, there are other reasons for a buyer to be cautious about dealing with subcontractors. In doing so, the buyer may inadvertently relieve the prime contractor of certain responsibilities. For example, if a buyer informs a subcontractor that things might work better if the subcontractor would "try the following approach . . ." and the subcontractor runs into trouble, the prime contractor may rightfully claim that the buyer's interference caused the problems.

Chapter Review

1. A cost-plus-percentage-cost (CPPC) contract has an estimated cost of $120,000 with an agreed profit of 10% of the costs. The actual cost of the project is $130,000. What is the total reimbursement to the seller?
   - A. $143,000
   - B. $142,000
   - C. $140,000
   - D. $132,000

2. A cost-plus-incentive-fee (CPIF) contract has an estimated cost of $150,000 with a predetermined fee of $15,000 and a share ratio of 80/20. The actual costs of the project is $130,000. How much profit does the seller make?
   - A. $31,000
   - B. $19,000
   - C. $15,000
   - D. none of the above

3. A fixed-price-plus-incentive-fee (FPI) contract has a target cost of $130,000, a target profit of $15,000, a target price of $145,000, a ceiling price of $160,000, and a share ratio of 80/20. The actual cost of the project was $150,000. How much profit does the seller make?
   - A. $10,000
   - B. $15,000
   - C. $0
   - D. $5,000

4. Contract administration is the process of:
   - A. Product verification and administrative close-out
   - B. Obtaining information from prospective sellers
   - C. Clarification and mutual agreement on the structure and requirements of the contract
   - D. Monitoring contract performance, making payments, and awarding contract modifications

5. Which of the following is considered during the Procurement Planning Process?
   - A. Whether to procure
   - B. How to procure and how much to procure
   - C. What and when to procure
   - D. All of the above

6. From a buyer's standpoint, which of the following is true?
   - A. Procurement planning should include consideration of potential subcontracts
   - B. Procurement planning does not include consideration of potential subcontracts since this is the duty of the contractor.
   - C. Subcontractors are first considered during the Solicitation Process
   - D. None of the above

7. Which of the following processes involves obtaining information (bids and proposals) from prospective sellers?
    A. Plan Contracting
    B. Request Seller Response
    C. Select Sellers
    D. Plan Purchases and Acquisitions

8. Which of the following are examples of indirect costs?
    A. Salaries of corporate executives
    B. Salaries of full-time project staff
    C. Overhead costs
    D. a and c

9. Which of the following contract types places the greatest risk on the seller?
    A. Cost-plus-fixed-fee contract
    B. Cost plus-incentive-fee contract
    C. Firm-fixed-price contract
    D. Fixed-price-incentive contract

10. In which of the following contract types is the seller's profit limited?
    A. Cost-plus-percentage-cost contract
    B. Cost-plus-fixed-fee contract
    C. Fixed-price-plus-incentive
    D. b and c

Answers

1. A, PMBOK® Guide 3rd Edition, page 278
2. B, PMBOK® Guide 3rd Edition, page 278
3. A, PMBOK® Guide 3rd Edition, page 277
4. D, PMBOK® Guide 3rd Edition, page 290
5. D, PMBOK® Guide 3rd Edition, page 269
6. A, PMBOK® Guide 3rd Edition, page 269
7. B, PMBOK® Guide 3rd Edition, page 284
8. D, PMBOK® Guide 3rd Edition, page 277
9. C, PMBOK® Guide 3rd Edition, page 278
10. D, PMBOK® Guide 3rd Edition, page 277

Chapter 13

Professional Responsibility

Professional Responsibility will focus on the following tasks:
- Ensuring integrity and professionalism
- Contributing to the project management knowledge base
- Enhancing individual competence
- Balancing stakeholders' interests
- Interacting with team and stakeholders in a professional and cooperative manner
- Specific knowledge areas and skills have been identified in the Role Delineation Study for each of these tasks.

These questions will be based on situations or scenarios that require an understanding of the Project Management Professional Code of Conduct and the importance of professional ethics, awareness of legal issues, cultural sensitivity, and managing conflict of interest.

Example of Professional Responsibility Topics
The project manager's job is to ensure individual integrity and professionalism. This task requires knowledge of legal requirements, ethical standards, and understanding community and stakeholder values. It also requires skill in exercising appropriate judgment.

Each of these items can be related to specific knowledge areas of the PMBOK® Guide. For example, legal requirements can be related to the area of Project Procurement Management.

Ethical standards and stakeholder values can be associated with Human Resource Management and Communications Management.

The key is in understanding the relationship between the tasks identified in the Professional Responsibility Domain with the nine knowledge areas and the processes described in the PMBOK® Guide.

Ensure Integrity and Professionalism

As a project manager, your primary professional responsibility is to ensure integrity of the project management process that is outlined in the PMBOK® Guide. This applies not only to the project and product, but also in your own conduct.

A project has integrity if its product is sound and can be used by the stakeholders. If you follow the PMBOK® Guide and practice the proper project management processes you will help ensure that both the project and product will have integrity.

Personal integrity means adhering to the ethical code set forth by PMI® and that you will adhere to the PMP® Code of Professional Conduct. You should clearly understand this code because once you submit your application to PMI® you are agreeing to adhere to this code. The Code of Conduct is as follows:

As a PMI® Project Management Professional (PMP®), I agree to support and adhere to the responsibilities described in the PMI® PMP® Code of Professional Conduct.

I. Responsibilities to the Profession
  A. Compliance with all organizational rules and policies
    1. Responsibility to provide accurate and truthful representations concerning all information directly or indirectly related to all aspects of the PMI® Certification Program, including but not limited to the following: examination applications, test item banks, examinations, answer sheets, candidate information and PMI® Continuing Certification Requirements Program reporting forms.
    2. Upon a reasonable and clear factual basis, responsibility to report possible violations of the PMP® Code of Professional Conduct by individuals in the field of project management.
    3. Responsibility to cooperate with PMI® concerning ethics violations and the collection of related information.
    4. Responsibility to disclose to clients, customers, owners or contractors, significant circumstances that could be construed as a conflict of interest or an appearance of impropriety.
  B. Candidate/Certificant Professional Practice
    1. Responsibility to provide accurate, truthful advertising and representations concerning qualifications, experience and performance of services.
    2. Responsibility to comply with laws, regulations and ethical standards governing professional practice in the state/province and/or country when providing project management services.
  C. Advancement of the Profession
    1. Responsibility to recognize and respect intellectual property developed or owned by others, and to otherwise act in an accurate, truthful and complete manner, including all activities related to professional work and research.
    2. Responsibility to support and disseminate the PMP® Code of Professional Conduct to other PMI® certificants.
II. Responsibilities to the Customers and the Public
  A. Qualifications, experience and performance of professional services
    1. Responsibility to provide accurate and truthful representations to the public in advertising, public statements and in the preparation of estimates concerning costs, services and expected results.
    2. Responsibility to maintain and satisfy the scope and objectives of professional services, unless otherwise directed by the customer.
    3. Responsibility to maintain and respect the confidentiality of sensitive information obtained in the course of professional activities or otherwise where a clear obligation exists.
  B. Conflict of interest situations and other prohibited professional conduct
    1. Responsibility to ensure that a conflict of interest does not compromise legitimate interests of a client or customer, or influence/interfere with professional judgments.
    2. Responsibility to refrain from offering or accepting inappropriate payments, gifts or other forms of compensation for personal gain, unless in conformity with applicable laws or customs of the country where project management services are being provided.

Another important area discussed in the Professional Code of Professional Conduct is conflict of interest. A conflict of interest is when your personal interests are put above the interest of the project or your stakeholders. Although not always easy or clearly definable, you must put the interest of the project over your own interest. If a conflict of interest should arise from such things as membership association, vendor gifts, or undue stakeholder influence you must inform the project sponsor at once of the conflict, failure to do so could result in legal action from the stakeholder and loss of your PMP® certification.

Contribute to Knowledge Base

Contributing to the knowledge base is taking any opportunity available and helping educate or train others in the field about correct project management skills, techniques, and current project management practices. This includes not only team members, but also management and current stakeholders. Learn how to communicate and transfer knowledge effectively, as a coach and mentor, and to use available research strategies.

Part of your commitment to PMI® is that you will stay current on project management practices, theories, and techniques. To do this effectively you should set up a network of other project management professionals in your area. The first place you may wish to visit is the local PMI® Chapter in your state. (To find out more about this subject matter, please visit, http://www.pmi.org/info/GMC_ChaptersOverview.asp).

Balance Stakeholders Interest

As you are aware, projects are undertaken at the request of a stakeholder. Most often, these stakeholders will have different needs and interests, and your job as the project manager is to try to balance the needs of the stakeholders with the projects. To do this you will need to understand the various competing stakeholders' interests and needs. Not all stakeholders have the same knowledge or work in the same department; because of this, your stakeholders will have competing needs. An example is that one stakeholder may want a software application that is easy to install, while another wants a word processing program that has an expandable dictionary. As project manager, it is your job to balance the two.

You will need to comprehend certain conflict resolution techniques in order to handle differing objectives. You need to remember to be fair in resolving conflicts during this period; the idea is to come up with a solution that is win-win for all parties involved.

Interact with Team and Stakeholders

As the project manager you are the so-called "ring leader" and must learn to interact with the team members and stakeholders in a professional and cooperative manner. You need to also understand cultural diversity and make sure that your team members also understand this diversity. You must be able to show flexibility toward diversity, tolerance, and self-control.

More and more projects and project managers are working in a global situation. It is important to understand and respect that cultural differences do exist and not to impose your beliefs onto others. Realize that when you or your team members are working overseas that culture shock does occur. This can be true if you or your team goes overseas or if you have overseas visitors working in your office. Training and education are both good ways to provide information on cultural differences. It is extremely important to take the time to build solid relationships with others. Once a feeling of trust is established, the project planning process will go much smoother.

Defining Culture and Its Norms

We define culture in as general terms as possible because culture is so broad and encompassing. It is simply everything human that a group shares among its members. It includes thought processes, belief systems, rules for behavior, rules governing families and marriage, and how one should set priorities—me first or the group first. It can make a project very successful or doom it despite all other reasons for success.

Every culture faces the same common problems. It is how cultures approach and solve these problems (food, shelter, marriage, communication, government, trade) that make them different from each other. Many of the outward actions that we see are based on internal values we do not see, but are part of the psyche of the person we are communicating with across a cultural divide. We can see and experience a foreign language, music, costumes, and folk stories. The values that underlie these require much greater study and where the majority of friction often exists in international projects.

Study of culture is possible because every culture must be learned by its members. Everything from language to etiquette to beliefs and values are learned from childhood. Cultures are not static—they constantly react to changes around them and are impacted, in both good and bad ways, by this change. Even within single countries we find multiple cultures that vary from the stereotype that foreigners expect to find upon arrival.

Culture must be learned and we can therefore learn multiple cultures if we apply ourselves to that endeavor. But why bother? The reason is simply economics. The global network is already upon us and the successful projects will involve those who can adjust and make things happen globally.

A first step to understanding other cultures is to understand your own. You must understand your own background and realize your own biases to be able to overcome them. The second step is to realize there are no good or bad cultures—only different ones. In fact, cultures are constantly learning and borrowing from each other ideas created in foreign cultures. Due to international exposure, your project will, most likely, find solutions to problems that can be adopted for all future projects.

Consider when you got up this morning

Shaving first (a practice created in India and considered by other cultures as a very strange masochistic act), you then dress choosing a shirt made from Egyptian cotton that is one of your favorites. Your shoes and belt were made in Mexico. Maybe you probably had coffee, from Latin America, or chose tea, from China, while you watched for reports on traffic on a television made outside the United States.

Later, you heard news reports broadcasting live from around the world—something that your parents would have considered science fiction only decades earlier. You may have many friends living abroad that you have met, either physically or virtually on the 'Net, so news in those locations peaks your interest. You don't realize that you know many more people outside your town than in your own neighborhood.

Then you probably drove to work—most likely in a car manufactured by a foreign manufacturer or comprised of foreign parts (at least you know your tires were made in Japan). Or maybe you took a train that was manufactured in Germany or Austria. You pass billboards advertising new products by company names you might have problems pronouncing, but you understand the products and think about buying them regardless. The Czech crystal looks especially nice with Christmas, a celebration of a religion originating in the Middle East, is just around the corner. As you pass the airport, an aircraft manufactured in France, flown by a foreign airline, and arriving from a Canadian airport lands right on schedule.

While at work, you spend the morning reading emails from foreign offices that are now closed. With these updates you talk long distance to foreign suppliers about a change predicted and an existing order that will need adjusting. During lunch, you choose to eat at a restaurant that specialized in Italian food that you love and have adopted as a regular practice. In the afternoon, you update your project files and send out new tasks to your team in India and Singapore, knowing that they will receive and complete them later while you are sleeping.

After work, you pick up your children at school and go straight to their soccer practice, a fairly recent cultural adoption of a traditionally European sport. Your children's heroes are soccer stars from foreign countries, while you still follow tennis. Every year, you watch the big matches such as Wimbledon in England. On the way home, you pick up some take-out from a Chinese restaurant. You opt for chopsticks and show your kids how to use them successfully during dinner at home.

You spend the evening watching a travel show about the best beaches in the world that gets you thinking about a vacation with your wife reminding you she wants to vacation someplace where she can get a tan. She has a professional conference coming up soon in Acapulco or maybe another trip to the Caribbean. You explore the currency exchange rates on the Internet to come with some ideas. Then you check a Web site about international trade conferences that coming up soon. Comments from different sides' debate the impacts of new deals speculated. You make a couple of notes of things to look into tomorrow at work—the possibility of impacts on your domestic operations and on your exports.

Then you help with homework over math (using Arabic numerals we take for granted) and history lessons about wars where cultures came into conflict in centuries past. Some issues seem to be the same as today; the problems were never solved. Later, you read your youngest child a bedtime story from an old fairy tale that originated in Germany.

Before going to bed, you brush your teeth with a toothbrush made in China, wash your face with soap made in France, and put on silk pajamas you bought a few years ago when on business in Japan.

Face it, this is not the same world that your parents grew up in—and it won't be the same world next year.

Cultural Values

A culture develops values based upon common factors of:
- Environment - defeat nature or surrender to nature as a supreme force
- Time - focused on task accomplishments or on relationships
- Action - rapid decisions and action or contemplation forecasting all impacts carefully before proceeding
- Communication - direct or indirect, formal or informal, low content (just the facts!) or high content that requires emotion and personal contact to deliver the message as intended
- Space (personal versus public) - how physically close people are
- Power - shared or focused
- Individualism - collective or individual emphasis
- Competitiveness - highly competitive or not
- Structure - very structured and organized, or loose and very flexible
- Thinking - linear or circular logic, or long-term or short-term goals

Verbal Communication

Communication between cultures is basically the same as within a culture. It is the degree of understanding and the impacts of common misunderstandings that create a greater risk to international projects that are less dramatic with domestic projects. All communication consists of both verbal and nonverbal cues to transmit encoded messages to a receiver who must interpret the message through their own cultural biases to understand that message.

Verbal communication, of course, is a language. Language is the first thing that is often realized as a barrier between cultures. Every culture has its own language even if it is a modification of another language through slang, technical terms, or other adaptations. For example, there are many confusing meanings between Americans and the British over the same words, each using a common language. In some cases, though, there may not be a common language.

In addition, many languages contain multiple forms that can lead to problems if not understood and applied in the proper fashion. Social stature is often measured by the formality and titles used in the very first words spoken or written in a project proposal. Mistakes here can insult the receiver and terminate a project immediately. In some cultures there are words that are used when addressing a man and other words for addressing a woman or a child. Misusing these words can create a range of responses from humor to disgust—all at your expense to your credibility as a project manager.

So the first challenge to the project manager is to decide on a common language to create the project documentation. Ideally the project manager will be able to converse in whatever foreign language is required for better communication. Many nations are much further ahead of the United States when it comes to being multilingual. For example, business managers in Denmark are generally fluent in at least six different languages! As you can imagine, interpreters are becoming more important in the business sector. The translation of many terms and even common phrases must be run through a quality-control process.

Nonverbal Communication

Nonverbal communication takes on an important role in many cultures outside of the American culture. In fact, nonverbal communication is believed to consist of more than 60 percent of any intended message; it is also the most misunderstood part of communication, leading to great project problems. Nonverbal communication is also called metacommunications, paralinguistics, second-order messages, the silent language, and, very appropriately, the hidden dimension of language.

Again, every culture places different emphasis on different things. In the Orient, silence following a presentation, rather than applause, is actually a sign of respect for the ideas and wisdom of the speaker as the audience contemplates the information. Likewise, an American will become impatient with prolonged silence and will attempt to get everyone talking again, which is insulting to Asians.

Nonverbal communication is the best way to communicate emotions, underscoring key points, and controlling the information presented. It takes many forms, but a few common ones include:
- Facial expressions
- Stature
- Gestures
- Eye contact
- Proximity distance between people and things (for example, the way furniture is arranged in an office ... is it welcoming, or not?)

Many authors have written extensively about how to interpret nonverbal cues. Caution must be taken to read the cues in the context of the culture, remembering that cultures are constantly changing so generalizations may no longer match the author's interpretation.

Cultural Noise in the Communications Channel

Many problems within the communication channel come from
- Ethnocentrism - believing one's culture is superior
- False attributes - inserting your cultural interpretations of situations (especially nonverbal) while in a foreign context.

- Stereotyping
- Decorum - nonverbal behavior, proper time and place for certain subjects, taboo subjects never discussed, and protocol.

Overcoming the barriers requires action through
- thorough preparation (studying, anticipation, contingency planning)
- study your feedback (absence is also feedback in itself)
- active listening in multicultural setting
- putting data into environmental and cultural contexts
- remaining polite but not ingratiating
- focusing on building relationships and trust for this and future projects

Negotiation Cross Cultures

The key to success in negotiation is through personal relationships and persuasion using common values and goals. When conflict arises, it is important to study the situation and determine the real source of the conflict. Understanding the values of the other culture in order to know better what they are feeling is one of the most important factors in a conflict. Select a location for the meeting and establish acceptable agendas and ground rules in advance.

During negotiations, listen and speak carefully while looking for all the cues. Use everyone on your negotiation team to watch from different angles, miss nothing, and confer frequently during breaks to discuss what is really being transmitted for your choice of action.

Negotiation techniques
- Paradigm shift where you consciously flip your way of thinking to look at all angles and possibilities
- Brainstorming options and comparing to come up with an optimal and mutually acceptable solution.
- Fuzzy logic techniques to look into the gray areas to find better solutions and overcome obstacles.

Conflict Resolution
- Confrontation = Win / Lose
- Smoothing = Agree to disagree
- Avoiding = Withdraw from conflict
- Bargaining = Splitting the difference or meeting halfway
- Problem solving = Facing issues together for a solution

Common Negotiation Tactics
- Personal attack
- Ultimatums
- Good cop / bad cop
- Walk-out threat
- Piling on = last-minute "add-on items".
- Playing dumb (effort to gain more time)
- Bluff
- Information dump (hide bad news in details)

Ethics and Legalities

Ethics are the commonly shared organizational values that define correct behavior and determine to control incorrect behavior. Every culture has its own ethics and every corporation, as its own culture, has its own ethical code. Today, in dealing with a variety of cultural values, laws, and ethical codes the international project has a much more difficult problem determining the right course for project decisions.

Acceptable behavior norms are understood by all in every culture for:
- Self-interest versus organization
- Financial gains
- Efficiency
- Relationships
- Society responsibility
- Morality and belief systems
- Laws

The Project Management Institute has created a professional code of ethics for project management professionals (PMP®), and failure to follow this international professional code can lead to dismissal.

The key points of the PMP® Code are:
- Truthful representations of yourself and your work to PMI® and to your customers.
- Reporting any violations witnessed to PMI®.
- Maintaining customer confidentiality (unless unlawful) and focusing on customer objectives in work.
- Avoiding conflicts of interest.
- Promoting professional ethics including support to any investigation.

Today, some corporations accept a social responsibility to do the right thing regardless of cost, while others may see a more important obligation to prevent financial losses as for their shareholders' best interests.

A project manager can receive sources of ethical behavior from many directions: her own cultural bias, the foreign culture where the project resides, laws of different countries, the PMI®, and her own corporate policies. Is there a way to make international decisions easier?

Legality

The legal systems of different countries vary extensively and this area should not be taken for granted by any project manager. Foreign laws may be much stricter and carry extreme penalties; in other situations, the laws may be without teeth.

The United States realized the problems and created the Foreign Corrupt Practices Act in 1977 to police US companies dealing in unethical practices in foreign countries—primarily in the payment of bribes to foreign officials. The Securities and Exchange Commission (SEC) is responsible for enforcement, and violations carry stiff penalties—$2 million fine to corporation, and each individual faces $200,000 fine and up to five years imprisonment. Still, critics cite that the law leaves a great deal of interpretation as to what constitutes a bribe and what is commonly accepted business practice with foreign governments. It does require standard corporate accounting practices, reports submitted to the SEC, and audits for all assets in a foreign country to identify irregularities in assets that may be transferred as bribes.

Global Project Manager Competency

There are several forces that drive organizations to develop competency for international project management:
- Markets - global branding, smarter global customers focusing on better and tailored products

- Competition - domestic markets shrinking and international competition easily enter to compete with every company
- Technology - improved communications make many international operations possible and more profitable than ever before
- Cost Savings - production and presence overseas can provide lower costs to local foreign customers through avoidance of tariffs and reduced unit costs using local supply chains and production facilities
- Government - some governments reward local presence that induce corporations to establish partnerships or establish presence in foreign companies
- Relationship Management - corporations must establish and encourage positive relationships with customers, suppliers, partners, and operations on a worldwide scale upon entry into the international market place.

Corporations are usually at one stage of international exposure and development:
- Domestic company - focused on domestic market with strong domestic knowledge, possible export/import involvement, focus on cross-functional teams, and international strategy for market changes is entry or withdraw from foreign markets
- International (Multinational) Company - domestic home market and international markets on a parity, moves toward global company to build international customer relationships, focus is upon cross-cultural teams, and international strategy for market changes is reprioritizing resources between foreign operational units
- Global Company - focus is on serving one worldwide market, customizing products to fit local cultural norms, and management focusing upon international branding, and international strategy for market changes is a central strategic center supporting nearly autonomous foreign business unit operations through a free-flowing information network.

The future competitive advantage for corporations dealing in international endeavors or working with a foreign partnership focuses squarely on the management skills dealing across multiple cultures by project or program managers. The goal is a professional integrator that can transcend corporate and cultural boundaries to solve problems efficiently, and to keep projects on track. Key skills to develop and emphasize in training are:
- Communications skills - including foreign language, cultural interpretations, and nonverbal
- Personality - adaptable, analytical, open minded, empathetic
- Motivation - corporation must make foreign assignments and training a boost for career
- Family - personal support and adaptive to live in foreign assignments when required
- General skills - maintaining broad outlooks, juggle contradictions, experience "hands-on" in international teams and assignments, emotionally stable, can implement risk management

Specific skills for international projects:
- Leadership in chaos situations - ability to "think outside the box" and operating in uncertainty
- Ability to adapt "best practices" to fit a cultural situation by understanding the various contexts and completing detailed analysis of the culture
- Understanding of the historical perspectives from all angles that is often a critical basis in decision making in many cultures and can be used to sell new methods if affiliated with a historical link
- Developing subordinates into leaders and sharing power especially to present a diverse leadership perspective to all shareholders
- Focus on performance measurement for success versus relying on traditional management rules or procedures from domestic experience for success

Chapter Review

1. During project implementation the client interprets a clause in the contract to mean that he is entitled to a substantial refund for work recently completed. You review the clause and disagree with the client's conclusion. As the project manager which of the following actions should be taken?
   A. Disregard the customer's conclusion and continue to process invoices regardless of interpretations and disputes.
   B. Advise the customer that ambiguous information in contracts is always interpreted in favor of the contractor.
   C. Immediately correct the clause to remove any possible misinterpretation by the customer.
   D. Document the dispute and refer to the provisions of the contract that address.

2. Before reporting a perceived violation of an established rule or policy, the project manager should:
   A. Determine the risks associated with the violation
   B. Ignore the violation until it actually affects the project results
   C. Convene a committee to review the violation and determine the appropriate response
   D. Ensure there is a reasonably clear and factual basis for reporting the violation

3. You are ready to enter a negotiating session with a group that is from Russia. The Russians have been known to be aggressive and assertive people who like to talk much more than they like to listen. To earn your bonus, you must not be at a disadvantage in your negotiations with them. Therefore, you must concentrate on:
   A. Active listening
   B. Earning the trust on the other side of the negotiating table
   C. Seating arrangements in the negotiating room
   D. Setting and following strict time limits at each step of the negotiating process

4. A person's negotiating skills and temperament certainly are influenced by his/her culture. However, other factors, such as education and experience are, also at work and over time, an individual who is living in a culture that is different from his or her own may take on characteristics of the new culture. This person may behave from a new frame of reference. With respect to negotiation, this illustrates the importance of
   A. Always looking at those with whom you are negotiating as members of a particular cultural group
   B. Becoming overly dependent on cultural knowledge as the cornerstone for all negotiations
   C. Recognizing that cultural stereotyping should be used as a starting point for all international negotiations
   D. Moving beyond cultural stereotyping and seeing people as individuals with unique personality traits and experiences

5. You are the project manager and responsible for quality audits. You have been accused of being a fanatic because of your practice of conducting not one, but multiple, quality audits on a project. Which one of the following types of audits is not an example of a quality audit?
   A. Internal
   B. System
   C. Baseline
   D. Scope

6. You are managing the development of a highly controversial project. Today you called a team meeting and explained the project objectives to the team and several members stood up and left citing philosophical objections to the project. You chased them down the hall trying to convince them to work on the project and explained that you would use the best quality management plan available for this work. One of the team members stopped abruptly and demanded to know what the purpose of such a plan would be. You explained that the objective of any quality management plan is to
    A. Create some regulations to govern the project
    B. Ensure that process adjustments are made in a timely fashion
    C. Improve quality in every aspect of project performance
    D. Ensure that the scope management plan is followed

7. As a project manager, you know that the most important activity to ensure stakeholder satisfaction is
    A. Documenting the requirements
    B. Communication reports
    C. Maintaining a proper work breakdown structure
    D. Ensuring the staff is happy

8. As a project manager you are responsible for maintaining and ensuring integrity for all of the following except?
    A. Personal integrity
    B. Project integrity
    C. Product integrity
    D. Integrity of others

Answers

1. D - PMI® PMP® Code of Professional Conduct.
2. D - PMI® PMP® Code of Professional Conduct.
3. A - PMI® PMP® Code of Professional Conduct.
4. D - PMI® PMP® Code of Professional Conduct.
5. D - PMI® PMP® Code of Professional Conduct.
6. C - PMI® PMP® Code of Professional Conduct.
7. A - PMI® PMP® Code of Professional Conduct.
8. D - PMI® PMP® Code of Professional Conduct.